ANATOMY *of a* SECRET

First published 2024 by
FREMANTLE PRESS

Fremantle Press Inc. trading as Fremantle Press
PO Box 158, North Fremantle, Western Australia, 6159
fremantlepress.com.au

Cover photograph by Sonia Bonet, Adobe Stock
Designed by Nada Backovic, nadabackovic.com
Printed by Shanghai KS Printing Co. Ltd. Shanghai, China

NATIONAL LIBRARY OF AUSTRALIA
A catalogue record for this book is available from the National Library of Australia

ISBN 9781760992668 (paperback)
ISBN 9781760992675 (ebook)

GOVERNMENT OF WESTERN AUSTRALIA
Department of **Local Government, Sport and Cultural Industries**
lotterywest

Fremantle Press is supported by the State Government through the Department of Local Government, Sport and Cultural Industries.

Fremantle Press respectfully acknowledges the Whadjuk people of the Noongar nation as the Traditional Owners and Custodians of the land where we work in Walyalup.

FSC www.fsc.org
MIX
From well-managed forests
FSC® C133407

GERARD McCANN

ANATOMY *of a* SECRET

ONE MAN'S SEARCH *for* JUSTICE

FREMANTLE PRESS

WARNING: This book contains explicit and sensitive content, including references to child sex abuse.

The content within these pages deals with themes of child sex abuse, which may be distressing and triggering for some readers, and it is recommended to approach this material with care and consideration.

Beyond Blue 1300 22 4636
Lifeline 13 11 14
R U OK? ruok.org.au
Sexual Assault Resource Centre (SARC) 1800 199 888

To those who have not survived; to their brothers, sisters, parents and partners who have grieved, sometimes not knowing why.

To those who have survived; and their families, past, present and future, who all suffer from those wounds that continue to bleed.

Contents

PART ONE

Prologue

Staring out at the featureless landscape of tufted, white clouds far below, the 'Kyrie and Gloria' by the Italian Renaissance composer Lassus on my iPod had taken me into a dreamlike, separate-from-the-world state. A pressure started building in my chest, a balloon being inflated around my heart. Music sometimes makes me cry, especially religious choral music. But this was different, not joyous. Tears began to trickle down my cheeks. Embarrassed, I pretended to blow my nose. The crying quickly turned to sobbing. I tried coughing to mask it. The deep, racking sobs began pulsing up from my belly with such startling and increasing ferocity it was as though, with my whole body shaking, I was being drawn down into their dark depths. I could not stifle them. I turned to the window to hide my face. It's difficult concealing convulsive sobbing in a cramped plane. My wife, Louise, gently touched my arm.

'What is it?' she whispered.

I shook my head. The wrenching, bottomless sobs finally overtook my whole body. Tears streamed down my cheeks, dripping off my chin, saturating my shirt and jeans. I let go of trying to hide them and, in despair, surrendered. I pressed my forehead against the window, covered my face and unashamedly let myself sob. Minutes passed in tortured bewilderment. When it subsided, and the tears finally dried, there was nothing left. I felt emptied of all substance. Salt residue crackled as it dried on my cheeks.

I had no idea what had just happened.

It was 2004. I was fifty-two. I had endured years of sudden and terrifying rages from an unknowable, volcanic source and, every few months, awoke exhausted from the same unresolvable nightmare:

'There is a terrible war all around me. It has apparently been raging unabated for years. I'm on my own, being hunted and shot at. The shooting is incessant. Whatever side it is I'm on is in a state of perpetual defeat. I scramble terrified across fields devastated by the fighting, hiding behind mounds of earth, diving down into bomb craters, crawling along behind shattered brick walls. It's all I can do to avoid being hit by the sprays of bullets whistling past. I can't see anyone else on my side. I'm on my own. Neither can I see who's doing the shooting. This unseen enemy pursues me relentlessly across these ravaged landscapes. I'm mute. I can't shout or call for help.'

After a lifetime of skirting the repercussions of sexual abuse, of raging against everyone except the perpetrator and the Catholic Church, of blaming everyone and everything but him, a new, rising tide surged into my life. It was pervasive, unpredictable and overwhelming: the realisation that I was not okay.

I

The Sacristy

March 1961

Early morning sunlight streamed through the tall, stained-glass windows, flooding the sanctuary and seeping through the low-down, corner doorway into the medieval gloom of the sacristy. A dim light glowed yellow. Mass was finished. The priest and I bowed to the crucifix above the vestments cabinet. I picked up the snuffer and went back out to the altar to extinguish the candles. Wooden kneelers banged, echoing in the cavernous church, as the few weekday parishioners, mostly elderly women, shuffled along the front pews, genuflected and left. I bowed as I crossed in front of the tabernacle high up on the altar. I collected the cruets of water and wine, the water jug, the bowl and the finger towel, and carried them back into the sacristy. I paused in front of Father Leunig as he took the leftover wine and drank it. He stared at me as he dabbed his lips with the towel, handing it back to me in a careless sweep of his hand.

My tasks done, I crossed to the altar boys' sacristy on the other side of the sanctuary. I took off my white lace surplice and black soutane and arranged them on a wooden hanger, squeezing them back among the motley collection of altar boys' robes clustered in the dirt-brown cupboard in that musty room. As I crossed the sanctuary again, the hollow, grinding roar of the early morning traffic climbing up the hill on the highway outside echoed in the deserted church. I went through the panelled doorway into the priests' sacristy. The door to the car park was on the opposite side. It was the only way out.

Father Leunig's finger curled up, beckoning.

'Come here.'

His black cassock, its cotton-covered buttons from high at his priest's white collar to the swinging skirt at his feet, twisted and strained around his bulging belly. His beady eyes, deep-set in pudgy cheeks, peered intently over his turned-up nose. He took me by the shoulders, turned me around so I faced outwards, and pulled me against his chest. He leaned back against the wooden cabinet with the wide shallow drawers where he'd already packed away the vestments. I resisted the pull as his hands slid down across my chest and clamped around my stomach, his arms heavy on my shoulders. In affectionate moments, my father had held me like that, but Leunig was the new curate, and I didn't know him. He wasn't friendly. He didn't talk.

***

Everything in my family was centred around Catholicism with a capital 'C', even our playtimes. My older brother, Joe, and I often acted out the Mass in our spare room. Joe was always the priest, standing on a fruit crate, his head above the stained mahogany chest of drawers that was our altar. Years of watching from the pews at Mass had taught me the rules and the Latin responses, so I was his altar boy.

Joe had been an altar boy for two years already when I was finally initiated into the priestly caste, to be immersed in the mystery of the Holy Mass, the transubstantiation of water and wine into the blood of Christ, the host into His body. 'Do this in remembrance of Me,' Christ had instructed. The priest, we were told, was Christ's servant and I was now his altar boy.

Our family church was St Mary, Star of the Sea in Cottesloe, a coastal suburb of Perth. Altar boys were rostered into groups of three or four, with brothers always allocated to the same group. Joe and I would walk down the hill to the church on our own for the seven o'clock morning Mass on our designated weekday. In summer, it was often already sunny and hot. In winter, on freezing cold, dark mornings, we dressed in the kitchen, the sides of the toaster opened out to warm us. Busy with my siblings, neither of our parents came to Mass during the week. I soon began to think of Joe as less spiritual than me because he started making excuses to get out of serving at our weekday rostered Mass. Those days I had to serve on my own. This was my first day alone with the new curate.

***

Leunig pulled me harder against his stomach, the pressure on my chest now too forceful. I was trapped. Panic coursed through every fibre of my body as he started rubbing his belly across my back. My shoulders slid sideways across the smooth, shiny surface of his cassock. Across and back, across and back. The scorched smell of over-ironed cotton mixed with the fatherly, male smell of his shaving soap. All priests smelled like this, the familiar scent of the sacred. My Catholic senses swam in it.

One hand held me while the other slid down my stomach, behind the elastic of my shorts, feeling around until he found my penis, gently rubbing and caressing it. In my family, we called it 'little man', its privacy already imbued with shame and taboo.

I jerked my head around. The door out into the sanctuary was wide open. Someone would surely come into the sacristy and see him holding my 'little man'. And I was letting him. The panic morphed into a blinding terror.

His hand was huge inside my pants, encircling and stroking as his belly slid sideways behind me. My terrified stare oscillated around the sacristy – from the sanctuary door to the wooden cross on the wall, the carved oak chair in the corner, the panelled door, the handle, the way out. Then back to the sanctuary door.

He stopped, pulled his hands up, slid them onto my shoulders, pulled me tighter against his belly as though in emphasis.

'This is special. Just between us. Don't tell your mum or dad. Understand?' He was calm and direct.

Leunig turned me around so I faced him. He lifted his head up, thrust his chin forward, the tilt and nod asserting his authority, and fixed his eyes on me. I looked away toward a tall cabinet to the right, self-conscious in the lure and language of his face. But I knew, as the priest, he was the gatekeeper to Heaven.

'Now don't tell anyone. This is just between us,' he repeated. The secret.

He shoved me towards the door. I only understood this gesture much later; the contempt, the push that said 'Get out of my sight. Go!'

I scuttled outside and down the side of the church, hugging close to the rough-hewn limestone walls, touching their prickly sharp surface, grateful the church yard was deserted. I don't remember the next hours; the walk up the hill to home, going inside and past my parents, eating breakfast, running to catch the bus to school. I said nothing.

***

The nuns at school in my early years had pounded my imagination with the threat of evil and the nearly impossible road to salvation. The Devil was poised in every guise, tempting at every turn with whispers from Hell. He already had his claws in, thanks to Original Sin. I had to work hard to save my soul or be damned for eternity. Heaven, my reward for conquering evil, was not guaranteed and every waking moment had the sinister, lurking possibility of sin and guilt.

But something had just happened that was so shameful and wrong, I could not process it with the template I had been given of good and evil, of right and wrong. I hadn't done it. It had been done to me. And by the priest, God's servant. And I'd had to submit to him obediently. It was the guilt that I'd let him do it and the shame that he'd fondled my penis. I now had to hide it from my parents. The nuns had also hammered in two key commandments: 'Thou shalt not bear false witness' and 'Honour thy father and thy mother'. Yet I was being commanded by the priest not to tell the truth and not to honour my parents. I was nine.

I have often reflected on this dilemma. I was an obedient boy, mostly gentle and kind, not one to disrupt the peace. Being silenced, unable to share my fear, was to be set adrift in a chaotic, moral wilderness, an immediate effect being to obliterate my sense of my parents and our home life. From that day until three years later, when this first wave of abuse stopped, my memories are fragmented. Apart from Leunig abusing me, I clearly recall only injustices at school, my achievements in the cricket team, visiting my school mate Marty's parents' farm, and being with my cousins in Goomalling in country WA, where for a week or two on holiday each year I could live an imaginative life.

At home, any expression of negativity, criticism, blame or whingeing drew a sharp rebuke from my parents, the reminder that these were little sins, evidence that the Devil was lurking. There was another agenda, however, which I would observe being played out in time. We were a happy Catholic family, and nothing could be said or done that might pervert that myth.

The safety of family life was presumed, growing up in Cottesloe in the 1950s and 1960s where, on the surface, families like ours seemed well fed, well clothed, with basic cars, serviceable houses and token gardens. It was not a culture whereby sexual abuse might be discreetly discussed, or even inferred with euphemisms. Thanks to Adam and Eve, our naked bodies were inherently shameful. So, even if I could have overridden the pact of secrecy and reported my abuse, I could never have told my father. His prudish nature had reinforced the penis taboo in our household of mostly males. Being a kind man with very deep feelings but with no framework or language for their expression, his life journey had delivered him into marriage unprepared emotionally and physically. So, when he did have to show parental authority or guidance, it was in an inflexible, simplistic way, his rules rigid and moral. There were no opportunities for a child with a troublesome issue to engage with him. There were simply no words for this story.

My trust lay with my mother. With her I might have tried to talk about an injustice or a hurt and the story might then have been teased out. But the terms of the secret had set like concrete around the abuse, and she was outside it, rendered unavailable. My home was no longer a safe haven. And there was no precedent or mechanism in our Catholic family to navigate the disruption.

In 1989, twenty-eight years later, a psychiatrist convinced me it was imperative I finally tell my parents. My mother responded in a distressed wail. 'I knew! I knew! I knew something happened because you changed! You changed! You changed!' she howled.

In 1961 though, noticing my withdrawal from her, she did not follow her intuition and pursue me for the reason behind it. I had become stranded in the catastrophe of the abuse and its attendant secret. In therapy as a sixty-year-old, I came to understand this mechanism and its ramifications; the annulment of identity and personal authority, the freezing of feelings, and the dissembling of imagination. The family prohibition of negativity would have compounded the silencing, but whatever the components, my mother and I had become unavailable to each other.

Our separation never healed. The abuse and its aftermath were akin to the expulsion of my mother from my Eden, and me from hers. The ripples from these ruptures would radiate out, and on, until forty-three years later when I was swamped by the eruption of the trauma on the plane journey home to Perth from Sydney.

2

Childhood

1951–1961

My first breath, in December 1951, was in the hands of the Catholic Church. I'd been delivered by a midwife nun at the St John of God Hospital in Northam, a large country town north-east of Perth. I was wiped clean, swaddled and put in the cot where, two years earlier, Joe had been delivered by the same nun. 'This one is different from the first,' she'd told my mother.

We lived in Goomalling, thirty miles north-east of Northam, where my father had grown up and had returned as a married man to be the postmaster. Our home was half a house attached to the back of the post office. My childhood there had the imprint of life in a quiet country town, stencilled with the familiar images of open skies and ranging gum trees, the silence at night, and then in the morning the smells of the dew, of kerosene splashed on the woodchips in the Metters stove, of fresh bread wrapped in butcher's paper. I stood on a chair at the kitchen sink and watched out the window as the milkman pulled up in his horse and chariot, ladling milk from a churn into a billy can, the chariot bucking as he leaped off. The horse turned its head and watched him as he ran to the window and poured the milk into a cream-and-green enamelled saucepan perched on the sill. 'Morning, champ,' he said. The milk frothed in the saucepan and my mother put it on the stove to heat it.

In the afternoons, Joe and I sat on top of the mail bags as the postal clerk wheeled the mail cart to the station. The afternoon sun flashed through the dangling branches of the pepper trees in front of the railway cottages, the bitter-smelling pink peppercorns crackling as they were squashed under the rubber tyres of the cart.

A door from our half-house opened into the telephone exchange inside the post office. I often stood in the doorway breathing in those post-office smells: waxed linoleum, canvas mail bags, string, ink and teleprinter oil. Jean, the telephonist, worked the switchboard, snapping the cables out and clicking them into the rows of holes. She'd once let me sit on her knee, but her wool skirt itched my legs.

There was a wide gate in the gravel driveway beside the post office where the telephone linesmen drove through in their old truck. The driveway dipped in the middle so there was a gap under the gate, and where Joe began making his escapes. Slithering along the gravel, he'd cross the main street to the railway station where there was a hive of activity to engage him. Once, aged six, he was found sitting on a tractor on the back of an open wagon. Another time, the guard found him in a carriage as the train was leaving the station. Enticed to follow him once, I got stuck midway under the gate. A swarm of ants crawled across my face and I screamed for my mother.

Joe's adventures have been told and retold, how he challenged our parents with what they called his wilfulness. His highly inquisitive mind meant he was forever outpacing their authoritarian, but novice, attempts to curb his imaginative adventures.

There were some, though, who reveled in his spirit. Uncle Paddy and Aunty Grace were Irish immigrants who had settled in Goomalling. My father arranged for them to buy his parents' old cottage on the edge of town, his parents having moved to the city in their old age. Paddy and Grace became a natural extension of our family and their six children our surrogate cousins. Uncle Paddy's solid Irish smile and laughing, twinkling, blue-eyed winks tempered our father's frustrations. Aunty Grace's earthy wisdom and motherly fussing, as well as her cakes and scones, eased our mother's anxieties. They were the warmest, wisest people on earth, and they celebrated Joe's spirit.

I was an observer, and watched and marvelled at this world around; perhaps because Joe's energy consumed everyone's attention, I was labelled the quiet, compliant one. This difference in our natures, foreshadowed by the midwife nun, played out throughout our childhoods and into adulthood.

Another brother, Terry, was born in 1954. I remember him standing in the safe-cot in the corner of our bedroom. Joe, notoriously, had managed to escape from it, but Terry was just standing quietly, his fingers pressed against the repaired flywire.

In 1956, we moved to Perth when my father arranged a transfer as postmaster to Mosman Park. My mother's parents were elderly, and she wanted to live closer to them as they needed care. As well, our parents wanted us to have access to a good education without being consigned to a boarding school. On my birthday in December that year, the doorbell rang at my mother's parents' house where we were staying, and I was handed a telegram. Uncle Paddy and Aunty Grace's birthday wishes were my first memory of being celebrated for myself, acknowledged separately from big brother Joe.

We soon moved to a rented house, not far away on Stirling Highway, two hundred yards up the hill from the Catholic church. It was to be our home for the next eight years. Joe and I started school at the Church primary school that occupied two rooms at the back of the hall adjacent to the church. The school was run by the Sisters of the Presentation of the Blessed Virgin Mary – fierce apparitions in voluminous black habits tied off with oversized rosary beads that dangled down the folds of their habits. Stiff white bibs, pushed up under their chins, white wimples, and heavy black veils pinched and framed the stern portholes of their faces. They may have been gentle souls, but their appearance emanated the direst of devilish warnings. Their teaching followed suit. I was so afraid of going to Hell that after one particular day of fearful finger-waving, I couldn't cross the highway alone after school in case I was knocked over and killed. I stood opposite our house and waved frantically for my mother to rescue me.

After a three-year gap in her child-bearing, two more brothers were born in quick succession. Paddy and Dom became known as the 'little ones'. In one scene, I am standing on a chair at the kitchen sink, counting out half-moons of Lactogen with a spoon, arranging the soft white domes in a pattern on a large white plate so our mother could check their number. Warm water was measured in a glass jug, into which she tipped the plate of half-moons and stirred until it frothed. She filled the babies' bottles, sprinkling the liquid onto her wrist to check the temperature.

I do not remember my father being part of these rituals. Mum ran the household – shopping, cooking, cleaning, sewing our clothes, managing the finances and reading our bedtime stories. I would cuddle up to her, lost in faraway European Catholic lands, listening to the lyrical tales of the heroic and noble saints, like St Francis of Assisi and his friends the animals, or St Teresa the 'Little Flower', or the children at Lourdes. Catching a cold had some benefits. She would tuck me into her double bed, warm up camphorated oil and rub it in gentle circles on my back and chest to ease the congestion. I drifted off to sleep following the geometric patterns of light travelling across the walls of the room, as the headlights of cars on the highway outside shone through the cut-glass leadlight windows.

We were not poor, but neither were we well off. Mum kept meticulous account of every penny, entering the family finances in a large ledger, the numbered columns written in beautiful copperplate. The need to scrimp and save week to week was a constant in family conversations, as was the need to look after what we already had.

'If you boys don't stop rocking on these chairs, don't think they'll be replaced. You'll be sitting on packing cases!' Dad never let up. I suppose we never did either.

His realm was outside. He generously played sport with us when he got home from work. The wide verge, glossy green with Guildford grass, was a football oval in winter. In summer, we played cricket and he bowled to us for hours, chastising us for using cross-bats, miming the correct stroke as he growled his kindly growl. He had been a good sportsman in his youth, but as a parent and a husband, he mostly seemed to have an eye for mistakes. Good shots were met with silence. But he was there, outside with us, every day. And we loved it.

He built a sandpit from old railway sleepers dragged up from the side of the railway line at the bottom of the hill. We drove to the nearby beach and filled our rubbish bin with beach sand and, with it balanced precariously in the boot of our FJ Holden, brought it back to fill the sandpit. In this new world, my brothers and I built towns and villages out of twigs and cardboard, then demolished them to make way for the high-rise buildings we saw springing up in the city.

There were few rules and few constraints outside the house. Joe was the creator and director of all our play. We all willingly fell under his spell and travelled with him in his imagination. He cobbled together fruit boxes and packing crates from the nearby telephone exchange to make yachts in which we circumnavigated the globe. On Boxing Day, we competed in the Sydney to Hobart yacht race. Old sheets, purloined from the linen cupboard, were hoisted onto broom handles and held tightly against the Roaring Forties with nappy pins. We always went to see Bullens or Wirths circus when they came to Perth. Afterwards, Joe rigged up tents on the verge, the same old sheets stretched over broom handles again, and toy animals paraded at the entrance. Mr Church, our elderly, widowed neighbour, was so impressed with Joe's reconstruction, he painted a 'WIRTHS' sign to fix to the big top. I was disappointed he chose Wirths because I preferred Bullens. Their tent was bigger, and they had more lions.

During the Rome Olympics in 1960, he co-opted all the neighbourhood kids and organised our own Games. There were high jumps, long jumps and sprints on the wide street verge, the hundred yards marked with chalk on the footpath. We threw large rocks in the shot-put and pie tins in the discus. But the main event was the javelin throw and as it turned out, a swift culmination of the Games.

Joe had fashioned a javelin from a three-foot length of metal rod, meticulously filing its tip toothpick-fine. It needed testing. Running across the verge and in through the side gate, he swept past the swarm of expectant kids and hurled the lethal dart towards the red corrugated iron water tank. We all gasped as it disappeared, leaving only a short shank protruding at right angles through the corrugations. No-one breathed. Nothing happened. The javelin had formed a perfect seal. Rather unwisely, he quickly removed the evidence. A jet of water three yards long chased him back up the pathway. Everyone ran. It pissed for hours until the water level reached the hole. Every time it rained, water trickled out until one day, when Uncle Paddy came to visit, he wound a rag around a dolly peg and rammed it in the hole. For years, water dribbled down the corrugations, a slimy, green, mossy delta.

Play in the holidays was a privilege granted after household jobs were done. As well as being a practical help, there was a moral tone to these duties. Making your bed was mandatory, but it came with a codicil: Air it first! Hospital corners! Turn the pillow! Then there was a choice: vacuuming, dusting or the dishes. I chose a job that was independent of anyone else having to finish an earlier task. Joe took forever, his head already in the next adventure, procrastinating until desperation delivered a half-hearted job. Avoid following him. Terry drifted along in his own, sweet universe. Avoid following him.

Summer holiday mornings were spent lazing and swimming at Cottesloe beach, orbiting around our pink-and-white umbrella under which our mother sat and read. In the afternoons, we had an enforced rest, lying on our beds reading comics until it was cool enough to venture outside again. We then roamed the neighbourhood unchecked until we heard Mum's 'come-home-now-for-dinner' whistle at five-thirty. She could really whistle. One of the other mothers blew an umpire's whistle, leaning out her dining room window at five o'clock on the dot. I felt sorry for those kids, not only that they had to go home early, but also that their mother couldn't whistle with her lips like ours did.

We mucked around in neighbours' gardens and shade houses or had treasure islands in unkempt vacant lots. Miss Briggs's ancient loquat tree was a good climb, and we winced eating the sour fruit just to get to the slimy pips for pip-spitting contests. Mr Redding's backyard was next to the Seventh-day Adventist church further down our street. If you crouched in the straw in his chook pen and peeped through the gaps in the picket fence, you could catch a glimpse of the back of their church. That was the nearest we dared go. There was a reason.

Sister Petra in the Year One and Two classroom had taught us that unless you were a baptised Catholic, and in a State of Grace, you couldn't get into Heaven. We were the lucky ones, belonging to the one true Church, and although we were told we were the only ones who *could* get into Heaven, there still seemed to be a hierarchy of other religions jostling for no good reason. There were Anglicans, Baptists, Congregationalists, Presbyterians and Methodists. The list was long and, when they were talked about, it was in hushed tones, as though the mere utterance of their names might taint our purity.

At the very bottom of the religious hierarchy, in my assessment, were the Seventh-day Adventists. They worshipped on Saturdays. You couldn't possibly be a real religion unless you went to church on Sundays like everyone else. Their church building, which looked more like a hall than a Gothic stone church, cemented the rationale for my disdain. They were so different they became the embodiment of 'other', the hook on which we could hang our fears, and Mr Redding's chook pen was the last frontier.

Despite the 'official line' on other religions, we still played with kids in the street no matter what religion they belonged to. I noticed that there were no paintings of Jesus and His Sacred Heart on the walls of the Methodist children's house three doors down, no holy pictures or statues of the Blessed Virgin Mary like in our lounge room. Though there was a black-and-white photo of their mother assembled with a group of men in suits. She was dressed in a neat, tightly buttoned, coarse fabric dress-suit. The inscription under the photograph read, 'Moderators of the Methodist Church'. I had unquestioningly absorbed the patriarchal structure of our Catholic Church, so I struggled with this conundrum: she was a generous, caring and loving mother like ours, but also a leader in her Church, a brand that lacked legitimacy. When their family left for church on Sunday mornings, I saw she wore a solid brown woollen skirt and matching jacket. I was sure it was the one in the photograph. The colour brown thus came to represent Methodism. In country towns, Methodist churches were always brown-painted, weatherboard buildings, not the grand, brick-and-stone edifices of *our* churches. As well, brown seemed a joyless sort of colour, certainly not one that could get you into Heaven. Somehow this justified the Methodists being close to the bottom of the list.

***

On Sunday afternoons, Dad always took my brothers and me for a drive, leaving Mum in peace. Squashing into the FJ, we set off across the city, sometimes to visit aunts and uncles, and sometimes to watch the marching-girl parades in East Perth. The brightly coloured uniforms of the girls swirled and flapped as they precision marched under the watchful eyes of usually older men. Very occasionally we visited the Presentation Sisters in their convent, up on the hill in Mosman Park. The convent – ominous, heavy-doored, dark-timbered and solemn – was at the top of a long drive. Inside, unknowable, black-cloaked sisters glided in and out of doorways and corridors, their rosary beads clacking softly against their habits. My father would have tea with Sister This or Sister That. They offered each of us a Mills and Ware cream biscuit off a plate with a silver bow handle. We knew to take just one.

Mostly though, these Sunday drives took us somewhere we could adventure. The inactivity in the harbour at Fremantle on Sundays meant we could play unhindered on the bitumen-coated, timber-planked wharves. We pushed little cargo trolleys around, coupling them together to make trains, giving each other rides, backwards and forwards between the bollards and the timber goods sheds. Above us, high-sided, black-painted ships, their hulls stitched with rivets and rust, leaned in and out with the swells, the ratguards straddling the hawsers easing up and down with the sagging and tightening of the ropes, creaking in rhythm with the sea. Names and ports of registration named far-off countries where we had sailed in our packing-case boats.

Impassive, foreign seamen fished silently off the sterns, cigarettes dangling from their lips, their lines disappearing into the bottomless, green water wobbling below.

When television came to Perth in 1959, Dad took us older boys down to the shopping centre after dinner to watch television in the window of the electrical goods store. Kids sat in their pyjamas on the footpath, their parents huddling behind in a motley arc. The latest television – a Healing or a Kriesler or an HMV with thin, tapered legs – straddled the toasters and kettles and radios in the window. Faraway voices from the screen echoed down from a tinny speaker hung with wire on the underside of the awning.

Joe, the relentless innovator and trendsetter, made a television set out of a Watsonia butter box, about the right size and shape for a small HMV. He copied the Channel Seven black-and-white test pattern and sticky-taped it behind an oval hole he'd cut in the base of the box. Buttons became knobs, stuck in a row under the screen. He made a television aerial with two broomsticks and rows of dowels nailed at right angles to form the bars. He painted it silver with stove paint and, climbing up onto the roof, wired it to the chimney as was the fashion. He ran a length of string down the chimney, across the lounge room floor and into the back of the butter box. We were the first in our street to get a TV! The neighbourhood kids came and sat on the sofa and the floor, and we all stared at the test pattern. The next morning, I saw people in the buses crawling up the hill past our house pointing at our aerial and laughing. The humiliation!

Sunday afternoon drives then became a hunt to count television aerials. 'Drive to Dalkeith,' we shouted, 'where all the rich people live.' We kept a tally, noting the steadily increasing numbers week to week, then rushing inside when we got home to be the first to tell Mum this week's score.

At Christmastime, preparations were a collaborative joy. Decorations packed away in a cardboard box were retrieved and spilled out onto the floor, the familiar red Chinese lanterns, crepe paper balls with honeycomb centres and silver tinsel coming to life again. Joe, standing on a stool, hung the decorations in the doorways and from the light shades, then looped streamers under the picture rails, encircling the lounge room and the dining room and the hallway.

The lounge room fireplace, empty and unused all year, was transformed into the Bethlehem stable. Yellow summer grass from the verge was the stable's straw floor, and tendrils of ivy from Miss Briggs's garden circled the limestone rocks we collected to make the grotto. Finally, a shoebox containing the nativity set that languished all year at the bottom of our parents' wardrobe, was lovingly opened and the plaster-cast figures set down on the hearth. Joe arranged the statues around the empty manger, with the animals behind and the shepherds in front. Mary, kneeling adoringly and hands clasped in prayer, was placed on one side of the manger while Joseph, holding his staff, head inclined downwards looking perplexed, was stood on the other side. Finally, the Angel of the Lord was hung from wire over the fireplace arch. The baby Jesus was safely swaddled in cotton wool in the china cabinet drawer until Christmas morning.

We bought our Christmas tree from the YMCA stall at Derm Ryan's Mobil Garage down the hill. The final selection, always a sullen compromise, never seemed to meet Joe's expectations. The misshapen tree was stuffed onto the backseat of the FJ, and we drove home crammed into the front seat. The tree was given pride of place next to the Bethlehem grotto. Last year's ornaments were tipped out of another shoebox, and Joe hung them from the tips of the branches. The baubled tree and the smell of pine heralded Christmas at last.

At Midnight Mass, candles and dim lights gave the church an other-worldly, ethereal glow. The side entrance was closed off and converted into a stable, a small star with a globe in it dangled from the architrave above. Mary, calm and adoring, and Joseph, understandably worried, stared down at the baby-less manger. A cow and the donkey with a chipped ear knelt quietly behind, while the shepherds, heads also inclined in adoration, clustered along the edge of the pews so close I could touch them, their sheep safely grazing by their sides. At the end of Mass, escorted by the altar boys, old Father Kearnan carried the baby Jesus wrapped in swaddling clothes and placed him in the manger. We walked home in the dark, the streetlights having gone off at ten minutes past one.

After opening presents in the morning, we had the once-a-year roast chicken and vegies for Christmas dinner, followed by pudding drizzled with custard. The pudding came in a Mills and Ware tin, which was boiled on the stove for hours. We all dissected our portion until we excitedly claimed a threepence. I marvelled that Mills and Ware could get just one threepence so perfectly into everyone's slice, year after year. Dad was always the last to find his. We all leaned over the table, shouting and pointing at lumps of pudding in his bowl, and he groaned as each morsel produced nothing. Then, always with the last mouthful, he coughed and gagged and spluttered and, with a look of horror, pulled a button from his cheek. Every year, he got the button. The mystery persisted. How did Mills and Ware do it? He carried on gagging, and we laughed until Mum, exasperated, finally said, 'That's enough now. Stop acting the goat.' He was a good clown, readily self-deprecating, and he revelled in being the centre of attention.

Arguments between my brothers were called squabbles, but those between Joe and I morphed into hostilities over time. He always had the upper hand in a dispute, but once, having pushed me beyond my limit, I chased him through the house and flung a fork at him. He slammed the feature-leadlight lounge room door behind him and the fork shattered an ornate pane. Mum rushed to sweep up the splinters, yelling at me, 'You'll murder someone one day!' I was shocked that that was what my rage would lead to: Hell. Anger had long been forbidden at home, but this propelled it to a new level of prohibition.

When Uncle Paddy, Aunty Grace and the six 'cousins' came down from Goomalling, they stayed with or near us in Cottesloe. It meant our sailing journeys and adventures in the backyard became even greater travel odysseys, with full crews of willing sailors. It also meant there were enough of us to form a congregation for Mass. The chest of drawers, now with a good sheet as an altar cloth, was adorned with geraniums clustered in Vegemite glasses. Joe donned our mother's faded-green boarding school pinafore for his vestments, green symbolising it was a Pentecost season, which I found disappointing as I preferred the red vestments of the martyrs' feast days. I stood solemnly to one side as the altar boy, handing Joe the water and raspberry cordial, the nearest thing to altar wine, and the pieces of bread cut into circles for Hosts. My other brothers and the cousins knelt in rows on the floor. Any giggles drew a priestly reprimand from Father Joe. But once Margie, the eldest cousin, started up, I couldn't help myself and we all doubled over in stitches.

We often went up to Goomalling to stay with them in the holidays. Their corrugated iron cottage, in a paddock by a creek on the edge of town, rekindled the innocence and simplicity of my first five years of life in the town. The kitchen became a furnace as the wood stove was stoked and Aunty Grace rolled out scone dough on the deal table. We took it in turns to stamp out the circles with an overturned glass so that we could hear the sucking *slooook* as it came free from the dough. Later, she would call us, 'Will ye all come now for a scoan?' We ran and sat on the back steps, licking the smattering of jam in the middle of the delicious, hot scones.

In winter, we dammed their creek, and when it was full, sailed empty Lux or Trix detergent bottles as ocean liners. We caught tadpoles by the hundreds and crammed them into tall jars and took them up to the laundry, watching each day for their legs to grow as they lazily wriggled in their watery prison. When the dam wall inevitably burst, we followed the torrent down the meandering sandy bed as it headed towards the main road. We stopped at the bridge. On the other side was the Aboriginal reserve and we knew we were not to go there. In spring, we hiked up to the old racetrack to collect everlastings, tying them in bunches and hanging them upside down to dry in the laundry.

When a chook got too old to lay, Uncle Paddy would hold it on a block of wood and the axe dropped swiftly and cleanly. Once, the chook took off headless and ran amok around the pen, blood spurting from its severed neck, spraying a neat stripe of red across my knees. Uncle Paddy cursed the 'flamin' thing' and chased the flailing bird until he caught it by the legs. We followed him, exhilarated and terrified, as he strode to the laundry where Aunty Grace dropped the limp, white shape into the copper full of boiling water. After a few minutes, she presented it to us for plucking.

In their tiny lounge room at night, we huddled on the floor in our pyjamas and said the rosary. The hurricane lamp's wavering, yellow-tongued flame cast wobbling shadows on the pressed tin walls as flames crackled in the fireplace, leaping about the prehistoric shapes of mallee roots. After the rosary, Uncle Paddy told stories about Ireland, about the hurling and the football, and the Blarney, and the bridge where he met Aunty Grace. He was a wonderful storyteller and a very fair man. The sweet smell of the hurricane lamp and their lilting Irish voices lulled us ready for bed. The two girls, Margie and Jess, had their own room, but their four boys and us 'Perthies' all squashed head-to-toe in the cramped, freezing sleep-out.

3

My Parents and the Catholic Church

The Catholic Church, we were taught, was the one true Church traced back to Jesus, the Son of God, so naturally its rules and rituals were the superstructure of our family life: kneeling by our bedsides for morning and night prayers, saying grace before and after every meal, attending Mass every Sunday and benediction on Sunday evenings. We often said the rosary together as a family, kneeling for half an hour clutching our own rosary beads, reciting the decades and the long litany of the saints. Other nights, as our sleep-out was connected to their bedroom by a doorway, I overheard our parents saying the rosary. When they prayed together, it was the one time they were of a mind with each other.

In contrast to the fearful terms and conditions implanted by the nuns, our mother's Catholicism was friendly, familiar and pragmatic. 'Pray to St Anthony. He'll find it.' St Anthony found every parking bay for her throughout her life. What more proof was needed of his intercession? A plethora of saints solved a multitude of other problems; St Jude helping us do well in exams and St Joseph healing those who were sick, if we had asked, mind you. Mum had a special relationship reserved for St Teresa, the 'Little Flower': 'Pray to the Little Flower. She'll help you', softened many minor childhood anxieties.

Her Catholicism was also highly superstitious. If we visited a church for the first time, she reminded us to make three wishes. 'And remember to make one that you'll have a happy and holy death.'

In the same business-like way Mum ran the household, she also coached us in devotion. We could offer up any suffering to the 'holy souls in Purgatory', thus lessening their time there. Principally though, she taught us the art of accumulating indulgences. Indulgences were like building up a bank account in Heaven, deposits made by physical acts of prayer or deeds, intended to be a buffer to our, and others', inevitable suffering in Purgatory. The most devout way to accumulate indulgences was by completing novenas, the most common being going to Mass on the first Friday of each month for nine months. The Sisters at school added more methods of attaining indulgences: we could go to an extra Mass, say additional rosaries, do the Stations of the Cross, pray for the sick, double fast during Lent. At the back of my missal were listed the specific time values, in days and weeks, for each practice, in much the same way a bank might advertise interest rates. The days and months were diligently added to our own mental ledgers in our heavenly bank account. I imagined mine as a leather-bound volume, the numbers in black ink, in neat columns with a balance at the bottom of the page, just like Mum's accounts. Our indulgences, stored in that invisible bank, would aid and abet us, as well as the holy souls, getting into Heaven as quickly as possible after we died. It was a win-win. All of this was the creed of her goal for us to have a 'happy and holy death'. It would be a measure of her success as our mother.

This intensely personal and practical aspect of her religious zeal was in our DNA, and its closest manifestation was our own guardian angel to whom she guided us in praying to each night. My angel was a white-clothed, golden-haired, androgynous child, the colour of warm evening sunshine in the Garden of Eden, protecting and watching over me.

A measure of the moral tone, but also the warmth, of her Catholicism was inherent in the bedtime stories she read, like *The Little World of Don Camillo*. Set in a village in the Po Valley in Italy, the Catholic priest Don Camillo and his God character were pitted against the communist mayor, who had ambitions to prove he didn't need divine intervention to succeed. They were strong but subtle tales of 'them' and 'us'; Don Camillo, God and the Church were always amusingly and cunningly triumphant over the perennially frustrated mayor. The stories were benign in the way that the two men co-existed, story after story, essential to each other and bearing no lingering malice. It was an encouraging antidote to the fire from the belly of the nuns. You could triumph over the trickery and evil intentions of the communists and the Devil if you had God and the village priest with you, but also your commonsense wits, just like Don Camillo.

Dad's Catholicism was different. It demanded loyalty, devotion and duty, which he enacted in unctuous humility and a barely concealed authoritarianism. It was black-and-white, a binary world. There was no co-existence of opposites, as in the Po Valley story, so we probably derived our disdain of other religions, of otherness, from him. He was not overtly verbal about these differences, more that by osmosis we assumed the dutiful need to toe the party line, and it brooked no deviation. This was especially obvious when it came to religious politics. The *News Weekly*, mouthpiece of Bob Santamaria and the Democratic Labor Party, was delivered every month. It was ultra-conservative Catholic propaganda fighting a political and spiritual war against communism. Communism was portrayed as the Devil incarnate, more so than anything else that wasn't Catholic.

It happened often that on weekends, large numbers of cars parked across the wide verge outside a cottage further up our street, just past the Seventh-day Adventist's church. Dad announced one day that the men who lived there were trade-unionists and communists, and that they were holding party meetings. Such was his authoritarian tone and his anti-communist fervour, none of us questioned this muttered bombshell. Quite apart from his shyness, whenever Dad had to talk about difficult or unsavoury topics, his hand went up to cover his mouth and he lowered his voice, as though the mere utterance of such words would taint him in the eyes of the world. When he painted this sinister picture of these mysterious men whom I'd never seen, it was impossible to consider any other purpose, like they might simply be enjoying a few beers.

I was aware that Dad regularly attended meetings of the Catholic Men's League, and that he hovered in the shadowy world of the Knights of the Southern Cross, but he never openly discussed any of it. An evangelical and clandestine vein must have been pricked, activating his need to be seen to be loyal and active in the defence of the Church, because he said he'd been asked to take down the registration number plates of their cars. Not wanting to disappoint those Catholic connections, he asked Joe and I to do the spying. It was my first inkling of his fallibility as a parent. *If it's that important to you, why don't you do the spying?* The question formed but hung on my lips, where it stayed.

Heart thumping, barely breathing, I followed Joe as we nonchalantly strolled up the street past the Seventh-day Adventist church. Crossing a side street, we dropped to our hands and knees and crawled along the verge, scuttling like dogs from car to car, keeping our heads low so as not to be noticed. After memorising the numberplates, we ran helter-skelter home before we could be kidnapped and tortured by these agents of the Devil. Why else were we being asked to do something so covert? What would the blokes inside have thought had they seen us crawling along behind their cars, stopping momentarily at each numberplate, then scampering to the next one?

It was hard to reconcile these trade-unionists with the benign communists in the Don Camillo stories. Nevertheless, my father's practice now required vigilance to defend the faith from the immediacy of the Devil. My lingering feeling, though, was that he was a coward, getting his children to do his dirty work. I was to encounter this passive, cowardly side to his religious zealotry again years later, in 1989, on the footpath outside my own home. It was when I was delivering bad news about the Catholic Church and the assistant priest who had lived in the presbytery just down the road.

One evening, not long after the spying foray, we were playing out on the verge when the Cottesloe fire engine – gleaming red with its ladders strapped overhead, bell clanging furiously – roared down the highway, heaved around the corner and stopped beside us. The fireman holding the bell-rope stood up and shouted from the open cab, 'Where's the fire? Where's the fire?'

We shook our heads. How were we to know? They roared off up the street and stopped outside the trade-unionists' house. We ran to stickybeak. 'One of the chaps fell asleep while he was smoking,' a fireman told us. 'The mattress caught fire.' Everything from the adult world that filtered down to us had a moral complexion. In our family, smoking was bad enough, but smoking in bed? That was unthinkable. What more proof then did we need that communists were agents of the Devil?

***

My father was one of nine surviving children. His mother, the daughter of Polish immigrants, was born in Sevenhill in South Australia, and was apparently loving and very gentle but chronically introverted. His father, the son of Irish immigrants, also born in Sevenhill, was similarly introverted but as much as can be interpreted from remembered conversations, he was stubborn and unable to show affection or intimacy of any kind.

From my observations of my father's siblings, they had all inherited both traits from their parents.

Dad was born in 1909 at Nannine, a gold town near Meekatharra, but grew up in Goomalling where his father had moved in his job as a fettler on the railways. He left school at fourteen to work as a telegram boy in the post office and worked his way through the ranks of postal clerks, eventually moving to towns all over the state as a relieving postmaster. This itinerant job suited the self-sufficient and self-absorbed man he'd become, diligent to a fault but with no desire to settle and put down roots. He was a naturally gifted sportsman and joined social and sporting clubs in every town. He had many acquaintances but no life-long close friends, apart from Uncle Paddy and Aunty Grace. A family friend described his lifestyle as 'ever the gay bachelor', in the old meaning of the term. During the Second World War, considered to be an essential worker as a relieving postmaster, he was one of the few young men not overseas on war service. Prominent in the tennis club social world in Kalgoorlie, where he was posted in 1942, he soon attracted my mother's attention. He was thirty-three and she nineteen. When he was later transferred to Broome and Derby, she arranged a plane trip north to keep the wick trimmed on their liaison. Being wartime, with no regular flights, it suggested an unusual determination.

My mother and her older sister, Maud, were born in Victoria. Their parents, elderly by the norm for those years, were publicans in quiet rural towns and moved to Kalgoorlie when she was three. Both parents were involved in running a large hotel and in 1929, the year my mother turned six, the girls were sent to the Sisters of St Joseph of the Sacred Heart convent boarding school in Boulder, a few miles from their hotel. As the Great Depression took hold, and with the convent impoverished, the nuns (nicknamed the Brown Josephs) took out their frustrations on the girls, according to Aunt Maud. She said they were underfed and used as child labour. She told the story of a particularly cruel nun who, after Maud had just finishing polishing the wooden floor in a large corridor, inspected her work, said she had missed a bit and made her polish the entire floor again. The venom with which Aunty spat out this story exemplified her loathing of everything Catholic for most of the rest of her life. My mother expressed another sort of sadness and bitterness about the boarding school. She described standing on the back balcony of the convent watching the neon sign blink on and off at their hotel in the distance. She stumbled around words like 'imprisoned' and 'exiled', the memory of her abandonment to those cruel nuns close to her heart for the rest of her life.

The two sisters then went to the Santa Maria convent boarding school in Perth for their high school years. When Maud finished and left to go to university, my mother, once again feeling abandoned and terribly homesick, left school without finishing her matriculation and returned to work in the office at her parents' hotel. Although she talked often of her affection for her parents, her father particularly, she also talked of her regret at not having had a tertiary education like Maud. She became determined that any children she might have would get that opportunity. A life in a hotel office was not the pathway to achieve such an ambition, and so she pursued my father, who she married at age twenty-four. At thirty-eight, he was nearly a generation older than her, and quite Victorian in his limited capacity for intimacy.

In conversations much later in our lives, she alluded to the disappointments in her marriage, which to all accounts began in the first days of their honeymoon. She had asked one of his cousins, with whom they were staying in Sevenhill in South Australia, what she could do to invite more intimacy. Love and sexuality would be ghostly absences and ominous presences that would haunt their marriage.

The newlyweds settled in Goomalling, where my father had been transferred. Not only did he already know everyone, but his elderly parents were also still living in their cottage on the edge of town. As postmaster, he was now an important person. Although naturally kind, generous and cheerful, these traits were tangled up in a keenness to please, tempered by an overt humility that I suspect protected a man fearful of his feelings. Soon after they moved to Goomalling, he asked my mother to bake a cake for a social function. The women in the town told her it was easy. 'Do this, do that,' she later recounted they had said. But Mum had grown up in boarding schools and a hotel and, unable to understand the process, the resultant cake, her first, came out as a flat rock.

'Call that a cake? That's not a cake!' My father flicked his hand mockingly at the disaster.

'Righto. If that's how you feel, that's your first and last cake, pal.' She'd learned enough about him by then not to verbalise this thought, but it would tumble out in time. A tone had been set. She never cooked another cake in the fifty-eight years they were married and made a point of mentioning it. It explained why, as teenagers, my brothers and I became adept at making pre-mixed packet cakes and self-saucing puddings for our desserts.

My mother had expected an equality of spirit in their marriage, as she had seen in her parents' marriage working side-by-side running their hotel. So if his patriarchal, Victorian values precluded him from participating in the mechanics of running their household, she at least wanted an acknowledgement of herself and her feelings, and not criticism. In her way, she was an early feminist even if the bar was not very high. It would not turn out well. My father and the Catholic Church would conspire to derail her very reasonable expectations.

In a bitter moment years later, she confided to me her frustration that my father's outgoing, 'gay bachelor' manner and his generosity towards everyone else masked a stubborn self-centredness and self-righteousness that, like many men of his generation, meant he assumed himself always in the right. He never apologised, to her or to my brothers and me, for anything. But it was his inability to be lovingly intimate with her or show empathy that ultimately became her cross to bear. Sometimes on the sidelines and sometimes embroiled in them, I increasingly witnessed her struggles and watched as she sought solace for her pain in her Church. The same Church that was harbouring the man who would quietly and methodically betray her trust.

Despite the festering malaise of their marriage, they were each in their own way good, kind, generous, honest and loyal people, and they kept their parenting free of any malice. They were strict but fair, and did not punish unjustly. There was also forgiveness. Transgressions had consequences, sometimes with a cane, but were then forgotten. There was a lot of action among us boys – the chatter and banter, the comings and goings, to school, to sport, to Mass and to friends' places – and Mum and Dad were always available, totally committed to us and our spiritual welfare. Our home in those early years was a safe and mostly happy place.

My father's brand of Catholic worship had an air of performance that I thought was the way you worshipped, so I emulated it. As an adolescent, I came to see it as a construct of the self-image he strove to project. He saw himself, and made sure he was seen, as a devout pillar of the Church, especially in his time-consuming volunteer duties outside Mass. In this sense, the Church trumped our family. Visibly pious and compliant, I was easy prey to be inveigled into his service. Every Saturday evening, I accompanied him on his pilgrimages for the Sodality of Mary, carrying the large statue of the Virgin Mary to different homes around the parish. Having been at work from Saturday morning until early afternoon, it meant he was then away from home for several hours again in the evening. As well, on many springtime Saturday afternoons, I'd sit with him in the school offices at Catholic primary schools around Perth, helping him count the proceeds from school fetes. As an adult, I suspected that I'd been taken on these Catholic Men's League commitments primarily as a solidarity buffer against the vitriol he'd receive when he got home. On Sundays, after we had attended early Mass as a family, he would drive around Cottesloe picking up the children of lapsed Catholic parents, taking them to a later Mass. There would be as many as twelve kids crammed into the FJ on these mornings. He would drop them at Mass, then pick them up and drive them home afterwards, another two-hour commitment away from my mother.

His duty to the post office was a necessary and acceptable absence from family life, but my mother came to see these optional absences in service to the Church as excessive and unreasonable, even by her devoted standards. She had felt abandoned by her parents to the nuns and now she was being abandoned by her husband. She had five boisterous boys, two of whom were toddlers. She assiduously managed every aspect of home life, and clearly expected some equality in running the household, at least on weekends.

At night in our sleep-out, I easily overheard her frustrated, angry outbursts. But the Sunday her anger exploded, my parents were oblivious to my watching astonishment.

'You spend all your time off with the bloody Church. You're never here!' Swearing was a mortal sin, punishable in Hell for eternity, and 'bloody' the very worst swear word I'd ever heard.

'There's no need for language like that.'

'Oh, yes, there is!' She spat back.

He stood back from her, pulled his shoulders up, put his hand to his mouth and launched into defensive self-justification.

He had no capacity to acknowledge her feelings or simply understand her, least of all her anger. She buried her hands in the sink, furiously scrubbing. But as she too was deeply embedded in the Church, with its demand to serve, these conflicts had the effect of turning her pragmatic, materialistic devotion inwards. The Church became her emotional refuge, a place of solace where she sought succour for her domestic troubles. She started going on her own to a different Mass at Cottesloe. Years later she went to a different parish altogether in the next suburb over. In a spiritual sense, she divorced him.

As a child, immersed in both strands of my parents' sensibilities, the Church became many things – the authority that demanded servitude, loyalty and spiritual devotion, but also the place where you took your troubles and sought comfort. We were taught that the ultimate happiness of Heaven would reward us for our earthly trials. Yet what was missing in all these teachings was the legitimacy of our earthly feelings. Instead, I learned self-justification and defensiveness.

4

The Roadmap to Heaven

1957–1962

The technical specifications of the Church and the pathway to Heaven were taught by the nuns at school. On a dedicated blackboard in the classroom, elaborate chalk drawings portrayed the vestments and implements used by the priest at Mass. Other drawings illustrated the radiant hierarchy of the Godhead; the Trinity, the heavenly angels and saints, the Pope, the bishops and priests. It was a formidable, unchanging pyramid with the Holy Spirit at the apex from which golden shafts of light emanated, a beautiful, shining world that actually existed above me.

Every day was defined by the Church calendar, an unchanging rhythm of seasons. Sunday Mass was the solemn, sacred marker for a landscape through which I travelled every week, a journey to an inner, spiritual realm clothed in the mystery of the Latin Mass. The sanctuary, separated from the congregation by wrought iron altar rails, was a stage on which the imposing marble altar stood, laid out with starched altar cloths, flowers and flickering candles in large silver candlesticks. Mounted high in the middle was the tabernacle, an ornate gold-and-silver dome shrouded in silk matching the colour of the season. The implements of the Mass – the chalice, the ciborium, the paten – were precious gold and silver vessels. The priest's vestments, also coloured according to the season, were layered in an ancient assemblage of exotic splendor of albs, cinctures and chasubles. The theatre of the Mass itself was shaped by intoning undulating, sing-song phrases, '*Kyrie eleison, Christe eleison, Kyrie eleison*' and '*Sanctus, Sanctus, Sanctus*'.

However, this beautiful world was mired by a dreadful taint. We had inherited Adam and Eve's Original Sin. Eve had succumbed to the Devil's temptation and disobeyed God. Poor Adam, the blameless man like my father, was seduced by Eve and roped into her betrayal of God to eat the forbidden fruit. The pair were not just banished from the Garden of Eden forever but were made to feel shame for their nakedness.

And so penises were shameful. My father's prudishness was evidence of this homage to God. Yet playing naked in the bath with my brothers, I was at odds with this conundrum – the natural joyfulness of it on the one hand, especially getting our 'stiffies' to poke up through the suds, and the knowledge that it was not right. In itself, it didn't feel impure. The paradox this bred was only partially eased by the nuns adding that, thanks to having been baptised Catholic, my Original Sin had been put in abeyance, meaning I was safe in my childhood state, but it was still there *in potentia*. Those that gave in to the Devil's temptations and wickedly left the Church would immediately be re-immersed in their Original Sin and could never get into Heaven. It did not seem odd to me at the time (given that childhood illness and death were not uncommon) that we were being prepared for death, not life.

Although it was clearly stated that it was only your soul that would get into Heaven, the concrete, mathematical structure of the process imbued it with the physical. It was my body that did the offering up of pain and suffering, and the counting of indulgences, so it must be my body that would or would not reach Heaven. It was enough to feel the heat standing around the bonfire on Guy Fawkes night to know that Hell, deep under the earth, was physical. Heaven must be as well, up there in the sky. And the Catholic Church controlled every detail of the route and the entry requirements.

In the vacuum of emotional fulfillment created by my father, it seemed inevitable that my brothers and I became our mother's absolute raison d'être. So, in the manner that her Catholicism was material and Heaven the reward for all her suffering, it was not surprising she had a palpable fear that a child of hers would not make it. I wore her anxiety, and wanted to always be in that State of Grace.

***

Cousin Peter and I were playing in the sandpit. We wanted to move a railway sleeper so a new highway could be graded to the 'outer world'.

'You lift. I'll push,' I commanded. But his grip slipped, and the sleeper dropped on my foot.

'Fuck you, bastard!' I screamed.

Barely hesitating, he sprinted inside. I was in deep trouble. But maybe if I resumed playing, nonchalantly moving toys around, self-consciously pretending innocence, I might deflect the inevitable. No such luck. The verandah flywire door flew open and banged ominously against the asbestos wall.

'Come inside! *Immediately*!'

I limped into the kitchen, the air thick with sin.

My mother was standing against the greasy, enameled gas stove. I cowered by the door, my cousin off to one side, a smug look on his face. My foot was of no consequence.

'What you've just said is a terrible mortal sin. Where did you learn those words?'

I shrugged.

'We have to get you to confession!' Her anger speared at my soul with the imminence of Hell.

There was no mention of a hospital or a doctor. She strode up the passage to the phone and made the three rings to the post office and hung up, the signal for my father to phone home for free. I stood still, demoralised and humiliated under my cousin's holier-than-thou gaze. The rings of the return call shattered the silence, and the sorry story was conveyed in muffled tones. She hung up and her returning footsteps resounded on the passageway boards.

'You'll have to wait until your father comes home from work. He'll take you to confession at St Joseph's.'

'Your father', not 'Dad'. I was damned.

St Joseph's, the church associated with St John of God Hospital in Subiaco, was a half-hour drive towards the city. Confession was available there all hours of the day and night for the wicked to urgently confess their heinous sins. It was the spiritual equivalent of the hospital's Emergency Department. During dinnertime conversations, my brothers and I laughingly hypothesised that if we'd murdered someone in the middle of the night, we could rush there and confess, gain absolution, then happily get on with the rest of the night. But the reality was otherwise. I sweated all day, my spiritual life on a knife edge. I'd go straight to Hell if I died before making it to confession. All my indulgences would have been wasted, my imagined angelic life tainted, perhaps forever. Mum was beside herself. She would have failed in getting one of her boys into Heaven.

I couldn't look anyone in the face, imagining their judgmental eyes following me, the pariah, having to be rushed to emergency confession. People would see me being hustled into St Joseph's. They'd know I'd committed a terrible sin. How humiliating.

Dad's arrival home was mixed with the relief that I could now go to confession, but also the deepest shame. I'd committed the first mortal sin I knew of in our family. Sheepishly, I limped after him and hopped one-footed onto the front seat of the FJ, easing my bruised foot under the glove box. With all day to reflect on the affair though, I'd begun to feel secretly defiant at the injustice. Peter had said 'Fuck you, bastard' to my mother. She'd said 'Fuck you, bastard' to my father, but I was the only one who was being rushed to confession. And still no-one had asked about my foot.

We drove up the highway in silence. Stopped at the traffic lights at Stirling Road in Claremont, Dad turned and looked down at me.

'Do you know what those words mean?' It was his throaty, authoritarian voice.

I shook my head. He must have been hoping I knew as there was an embarrassed silence. Turning back, he looked straight ahead, cleared his throat more than usual and gripped the steering wheel. He started muttering.

'"Fuck" is … er … uh … er … uh …' he paused, fumbling for the words, '… er … um … a woman's breasts, and … er … um … er … uh … "bastard" is someone who has been born to an unmarried mother.'

In the ensuing stunned silence, my defiance and sense of injustice took off full-blown. Now *he'd* said those words. *He* didn't have to go to confession! Anyway, why did those words mean I'd go to Hell if I died? Aunt Maud had big breasts, though the word 'breast' was never uttered. Women had a 'bosom'. And I vaguely knew of unmarried mothers. They were talked about in hushed tones whenever we went past the Home of the Good Shepherd on the hill in Wembley on our Sunday afternoon drives. It was the ironically named, Gothic-looking institution where we were told the Catholic Church took in unmarried mothers, wicked sinners that they were, until they had their babies. But what was the connection between a woman's bosom, the Home of the Good Shepherd and my mortal sin? It was a long time before I found out. What I would also find out, decades later as the abuses within the Catholic Church began to surface, was that many of the girls were there because of rape and sexual abuse from family members, family friends and priests. The girls were blamed and pilloried, just as Eve had been. It was their fault. Sexual abuse was not, could not, be named. The Catholic Church had its own interest in it being kept under wraps.

Dad parked as close as he could to the front door of the imposing red-brick church at St Joseph's, its tall, grey spire piercing upwards to a Heaven maybe no longer attainable. Shielding me with his body, he ushered me surreptitiously through the heavy wooden doors. He clearly felt the transgression more keenly than me. One day I would get a clearer sense of his fear, that it would be *him* mentioned in Church circles if we were seen. He rushed me down the aisle towards the confessionals arrayed along the right-hand wall.

'Quick.' He pointed to the confessional with the little red light above the priest's door. Every second was critical.

'Bless me, Father, for I have sinned. I said some swear words. "Fuck you, bastard".' There, I'd said it again. I cringed. But my penance of one 'Our Father', three 'Hail Mary's' and one 'Glory Be' was the same as for my standard made-up confession on Saturdays. For this most terrible mortal sin? My terrified mind registered the disconnect. An eleven-year-old boy, six o'clock on a weekday, an emergency dash across the city, and penance over in two minutes?

But I could at least breathe easily on the way home, forgiven in the eyes of God. I had a clean slate, and soon a healed foot. My parents never mentioned the episode again.

Pondering this event years later, I understood how it exemplified my parents' modus operandi. For my mother, it was the fear that one of her children might not attain heaven, whereas for my father it was the shame I had brought on the family.

***

In 1960, the year I turned nine, I had left the convent school to begin Year Four at St Louis, the Jesuit college in nearby Claremont. The aura of Catholicism had changed from fearful subservience to one of responsible, academic duty. My moral compass became more positive. We were set on a course that was intended to take us to university. The Jesuits talked openly about our duty and destiny as intelligent Catholic boys, and the college annual devoted several pages each year to photographs of 'Old Boys' who had gained their degrees. I reveled in the challenge and discipline of college life, with its erudite priests and teachers, and strict expectations of excellence. School reports relayed a careful analysis of performance and capabilities, and I became dux of my class, an achievement celebrated with due gravitas at Speech Night.

5

The Reverend Doctor Bertram Richard Adderley

1959–1964

In the late 1950s and early 1960s, a constant visitor to our house was Father Bert Adderley, the son of old family friends. His widowed mother, Bertha, her hair curled and plastic blue, caught a taxi to our place once a week to share an evening meal. She was a welcome guest as she always brought a brick of Peters ice-cream for dessert. Father Bert's regular appearances seemed a natural consequence of our mother's generosity towards old Bertha.

Adderley had gone to Rome to receive his Doctor of Theology, so he wasn't shy in promoting himself as a cut above your average priest. He was witty, intellectually sharp and a lively trickster. And he wore plain clothes – no stuffy black suit and stiff white collar. He called Mum by her first name. Only close family friends did that. And he came in the back door like them, too. It was as though he wasn't actually a priest. He sat at the table and drank tea and told us the gossip about his parish school and about who had invited him to lunch. We were told he was the editor of, or a contributor to, the diocesan newspaper of the Bunbury diocese. It seemed natural then that he should expound on Church politics, portraying himself as the modern man in the Church.

At the end of the chatty cup of tea came the invitation.

'Who'll come to the beach with me?' I remember the cheery smile as he looked at us older boys. I liked him and was eager to be treated as special. In any case, accompanying him was an honour and expected in our family culture.

He drove his MG sports car like a rally driver and parked on Marine Parade at the deserted reefs south of Cottesloe, just north of what was then the remote Leighton coast. Down on the beach, he stripped off down to a skimpy pair of Speedos and, putting on his snorkeling gear, swam out with his spear gun while I paddled in the shallows on the edge of the reef. I was too scared to go further. The reef was a fearful place, dark and unknown. He skewered an octopus and came up right under me as I stood watching. He thrust the squirming octopus against my arm. I frantically pulled off the sucking tentacles, naive to the menace in his laughter. It was my only trip to the beach with him.

When his visits to our house stopped abruptly in 1964, we learned that the Church had withdrawn his editorship of the newspaper and moved him to a distant, smaller country parish. His demotion became a much-discussed mealtime topic. My parents reasoned that his columns in the newspaper were too outspoken on Church issues. Father Bert was smart, and had been ordained in Rome to boot. We all agreed he was being silenced for political reasons. Even at my age and in those times, I thought it manifestly unjust and a contradiction. Why would the Church banish someone so friendly, so cheerful and clever, for being intelligent? It didn't make sense. Though I did learn what might happen if you were outspoken on Church issues.

6

Sexual Abuse

March 1961–January 1964

The sexual abuse by Leunig quickly developed into an established pattern. It never happened on a Sunday and never when I was with Joe. Alone on my weekday morning, the church behind us now silent, Leunig would gesture, his index finger curling upwards and beckoning, his face lifted and tilted, chin forward in that silent command. If there was a boy from another family on my roster, Leunig would grasp my shoulder aggressively as I went past, motioning with a silent, sharp, sideways flick of his head that I was to wait in the corner of the sacristy. I stood there, with my back to the wall, while he disrobed. I knew what was coming and was powerless to extricate myself. It was inconceivable that I flee. I avoided his eyes and stared at anything else in the sacristy as he quickly laid out the vestments in the wide, shallow drawers, then pushed them shut with a dull thud. He turned and leaned back against the cabinet. The curling finger summoned me.

Again, I breathed in the smell of shaving soap and scorched, over-ironed cotton as he pulled me against his swollen belly and clamped me in his vice-like grip, reaching straight down into my shorts. His shiny cassock slid from side to side behind my head and shoulders as he rocked his body back and forth. My penis seemed small and soft in his large hand. I stared at anything to take my mind off what was happening, the leadlight windows, the ornately carved wooden cross. Out of the corner of my eye, I watched and waited for a figure to appear at the sanctuary door, terrified of being caught. It would be my fault. I hadn't refused him.

My vigilance also played out at the altar during Mass. As I brought up the cruets of water and wine, Leunig took them casually, his lingering gaze harbouring a contemptuous sneer as he locked onto my eyes. At the washing of the hands, I stood at the side of the altar with the water jug and the shallow bowl, a towel over my forearm, and he offered me his hands. I poured water over those pudgy, nicotine-stained fingers and, as he washed them, he muttered in Latin, absolving himself of responsibility as Pontius Pilate had done. He took the towel off my forearm and dried his fingers, staring at me the whole time.

He did not look at my outstretched tongue as he gave me Communion but into my eyes. I had no strategy to avoid the lure in his face and every time our eyes met, I was pierced by the momentary seizure and panic that signalled our secret was alive; a living curse inside me, trapped in an invisible chamber with no doors to the outside world.

The two priests in the parish alternated week-on-week saying the weekday Mass. I knew in advance which week Leunig would be on roster and, given the spell that his secret had cast over me, was impotent to do anything else than turn up. To refuse to serve would have raised questions with my parents that I could not answer. I had not the courage nor the resourcefulness to be deceitful or devious, nor risk tainting my pious self-image. There was simply no questioning of my commitment to the Church.

The abuse in the sacristy continued for three years. It was always a silent encounter. Once he said, 'You like this, don't you?' I didn't answer. My mother used to be the one who offered soothing words as she rubbed my back; now it was the priest. I still called him 'Father'. The more the abuse happened, the more intractable the moral dilemma, as just turning up in the sacristy amounted to consent.

When I recited the 'Confiteor', a prayer of confession in my night-time prayers, I struck my breast three times with my clenched fist: '… through my fault, through my fault, through my most grievous fault.' But guilt implanted by someone else cannot be expunged by prayer. It was outside the realm of personal control over my soul. So guilt came to haunt every minute of every day, it too trapped inside that chamber, a constant reminder of existing in an irresolvable, formless world, a real-life limbo from which there was no escape nor any hope of resolution.

The only time I remember feeling free of guilt was when I was playing sport at school, or holidaying in Goomalling with Uncle Paddy's family, or at Marty's family farm. Marty was an only child, so during the school holidays his parents always let him take a school chum to keep him company. I was grateful to have a turn and loved their farm, with its wide, furrowed paddocks stretching away to the hills, its horses and sheep, its sheds and pens and pepper trees. I was free to wander and adventure with Marty, uncomplicated by the moral morass lying in wait in the city.

Years earlier, the nuns had written lists of all the possible sins on the blackboard in the Year Three classroom. The sins were arranged in two columns, venial on the left, mortal on the right. The venial list was long, and I was comfortable with it – the stuff of family life, fighting with brothers, disobeying parents, the everyday, petty infringements easily confessed so I could return to my otherwise holy life. The mortal list on the right meant eternity in Hell if you died without confessing; thankfully, it was much shorter. Murder was number one. Swearing must have been there in some form, but I only remember the reference to 'Taking thy Lord God's name in vain.' 'Bastard' was not one of them. Nor 'fuck'. Adultery was there too, further down the list. The nuns never explained what it was. It had to do with the commandment, 'Thou shalt not covet thy neighbour's wife', whatever 'covet' meant. It was a mortal sin clearly aimed at men.

What Father Leunig was doing in the sacristy was not on either list.

Since any talk of sexuality or genitalia was taboo, it is hard to imagine how any discussion could have taken place in our family, school or Church context, unless a parent intuited and courageously coaxed out the truth. Of course, I knew it was terribly wrong that the priest was playing with my 'little man', but the pact of secrecy magnified the moral dilemma into the realm of an indefinable 'terrible' because it was not even classified as a sin.

Confessions were held at Star of the Sea on Saturday afternoons. Every fortnight my brothers and I sat squashed alongside our father in a pew outside the confessionals. We shuffled and slid along the polished wooden seat as the queue shrank, fidgeting and elbowing each other. The afternoon sun slanted yellow down the aisle and the hollow roar of traffic echoed in the solitariness of waiting.

The latch was high on the heavy wooden-panelled door. It opened easily and clunked shut. I knelt down in the tiny, soundproof cubicle, my knees knobbly on the wooden kneeler, and anxiously fingered the silken, purple curtain covering the metal mesh window. Would it be kindly old Father Kearnan, holy, humble and forgiving, with his voice cracked and faraway, or Father Leunig and his nasally voice? When the hatch to the cubicle slid open and the priest mumbled a prayer in Latin, I knew instantly if it was Leunig because the hatch snapped open too quickly and the mumbled prayer was too perfunctory. I tensed in panic but still said, 'Bless me, Father, for I have sinned. It is two weeks since my last confession and … ' I knew he knew it was me.

I had never done anything that could insinuate myself as a sinner. Intuitively, I knew that I was a good person. My confessor was the perpetrator of the only thing wrong in my life. As confession was the voluntary offering up of my own legitimate secrets, I had a real sense of not wanting him to know them. I didn't want to give him that power over me, so I consciously confessed made-up sins, cobbling together petty ones from the list on the left-hand side of the blackboard; little 'white' lies, as opposed to other colours that were not discussed. Still, I felt humiliated as Leunig sat in silence, vaguely visible through the metal screen, leaning back, the purple stole snaking around his neck and across his belly as it bulged under his surplus and cassock. He sounded bored.

Penance was intended to be my prayer for God's forgiveness. But God, along with my golden-haired, androgynous guardian angel, had disappeared and were replaced by anxiety and terror and guilt. Confession and penance could not give me a clean slate.

Waiting for my brothers to finish their confessions, I walked up and down the central aisle of the church, feeling the warmth of the afternoon sun, praying obsessively to the Stations of the Cross, thinking of the betrayal, trial, humiliation, injustice and helplessness of the crucifixion of Christ. An observer might have mused that I was a devout, though perhaps unctuous, young boy, potentially headed for the priesthood.

The awkwardness of my confession with Leunig was my first memory of reflecting on the fact of the abuse, and a consciousness of my reaction. At the time, I did not think anyone might suspect that I was being abused, nor that anyone else might be as well. I understand now that the annulment of feeling, and the mechanics of shame and disempowerment embodied in the secret, all implanted and supported the belief that I was his only victim.

Through these years, from early in 1961 to early 1964, Leunig could only have abused me, at most, one day a fortnight. I must have 'coped' with that, putting on a good face. Pretending all was well was part of the lie to my family. I was as good as I could be at school, perhaps by nature as much as compensation. I was good at sport and was captain of the football and cricket teams for a while. I was no longer dux of the class. Through 1962, report cards included comments from the Prefect of Studies noting 'an overconfidence' resulting in marks '… not representative of his real worth'. In 1963, my class position dropped to tenth and stayed there. Teachers' comments noted I was 'silly in class'.

7
The Beach
January 1964

The precarious nature of this double life, and the effort to maintain the pretense of normality, was brutally exposed one day in the summer holidays early in 1964. I had just turned twelve. Every morning, our mother took my brothers and me to Cottesloe Beach, where we swam and surfed, carefree and unencumbered by any authority. Racing out of the cold water, we'd throw ourselves onto our bellies and cocoon ourselves in the warm sand. Then we'd roam behind the beach umbrellas looking for cool-drink bottles to redeem for sixpence. Transistor radios, all tuned to the hit station 6PR, were playing 'All My Loving' from the Top 40. I squatted in the sand, squinting in the glare, listening to the Beatles, watching the coloured flags fluttering on the flagpole of the surf-shooter hire tent.

Mum was reading under our umbrella, planted at a jaunty angle near the water's edge. Occasionally she eased herself in, shuffling gingerly out into the surf, jumping up with the waves, then sinking down up to her chin, keeping her hair dry. Lying on the sand about ten yards away, I watched as she dried herself with an old towel then flicked it so it fell flat on the sand. Bending over, she crawled in under the shade of the umbrella and sat down, pulling her knees up and wrapping her arms around her shins.

I watched a man come down the steps from the promenade and striding across the sand towards our umbrella. He was wearing a small swimsuit and had a towel slung over his bare shoulder. It took me a moment to recognise Leunig, as I'd only ever seen him in his cassock. It was as though he was naked.

There was a deliberateness about him, like he was here on urgent business, not the carefree sidle everyone else had coming onto the sand. His aggressive stride and set jaw betrayed an outsider who did not belong on our beach. A stab of fear lodged in my throat. He was intruding into my private world. If everything else in my world was Catholic, the beach was certainly not. The Church had no place and no authority here. An unadulterated rage erupted, a righteous fury pounding inside my chest and my head. My mind screamed:

The beach is MY place. YOU HAVE NO RIGHT TO BE HERE! HOW DARE YOU COME HERE!

Then came the terrifying thought: *This is the ONLY place where I am safe from you.*

The rage became a trembling, sick panic. A desperate lament went around and around in my head like a stuck record. *This is the ONLY place where I am safe from you. This is the ONLY place where I am safe from you.*

My mind was crying, shocked to realise my utter helplessness. The beach – the only place where I could be myself, free from his grip, where for a few hours there were no secrets and no double life – had been invaded. Whatever my compliance in the sacristy condoned, it was an arrangement that only happened there.

Another lament then started up, pounding around in my mind in desperation: *He'll now have control over me everywhere. He'll now have control over me everywhere.*

It was the gutting, sinking feeling that he'd broken the rules. Curiously, I felt betrayed. The rage and this sense of betrayal ominously turned to despair.

Leunig reached our umbrella, leaned down and spoke to Mum. She looked up and, swivelling around, nodded in my direction. He turned and followed her gaze. He'd asked her where I was, and she'd pointed me out. As I watched them, a new panic strangled into my consciousness. While the abuse was hidden away and I'd kept my side of our pact, she couldn't possibly know what had been happening. Yet now she was part of it. It felt like a physical switch was flicked, the sickening realisation that I'm on my own in all of this. *No-one can ever help me. I'm on my own.*

I lay in the sand, motionless, awash with terror, staring back at him. His arm jerked up abruptly and he beckoned, the curling finger and the inclined nod of his head up and back, those familiar gestures of command. But this time they were aggressive. His narrowed eyes were strangely twisted in his face. He mouthed the words, 'Come here!'

He needn't have. I understood. But something was different. It was the anger. I'd never seen him overtly angry. He'd always been, well, mute. A new fear joined the panic. I knew I was compelled to obey him, but I did not understand his anger.

I stood up, angry and deeply resenting his intrusion into my only safe world. Deliberately, and consciously in protest, I walked towards him as slowly as I could, barely moving one foot at a time. I dug my toes deep into the sand so that it might slow me down even more, making the statement in the only way I could that he was breaking the rules. He stared at me the whole time. But as I reached him, my anger vaporised. I was defeated.

He gestured towards the water. 'Come for a swim, out deep.'

I followed him into the surf and another panic surged up. Cottesloe beach drops away sharply close to the water's edge. I was not a confident swimmer, so I never went out deep, always staying close to the shore with my feet firmly on the bottom, letting go only to ride up and over the waves as they rolled in.

We waded out into water up to my chest. He grabbed me in his vice-like grip and pulled me hard against his belly and swam us both out far beyond the breaking waves. If he let go, I'd drown. And he seemed so vindictive it was reasonable to fear that he might just do that. The terror felt like my body was on fire.

He floated on his back and pulled me on top of him, so I was looking up at the sky. We rose up and down as the waves swelled under us. He locked his arms tightly under my armpits and slid his hands down my stomach into my bathers and started rubbing my penis. He was showing everyone on the beach his hands inside my bathers. We floated like this for what seemed an age, but was probably only a few minutes.

He let his legs sink down so he was upright behind me, holding me tightly as I faced the shore. I couldn't feel the bottom. I stared at Mum under our umbrella.

Can she see me? Of course she can.

I looked up the beach towards the groyne, then back again. Everyone was watching as he kept rubbing and rubbing.

Can they see me? Of course they can.

I kept turning back, looking at Mum and then the crowds on the sand, to see if anyone realised what was happening. Finally, the secret would be out. People would know the truth that I was letting him have his hand around my penis. I was reeling in pure terror at how long it was going on. Surely I would be caught.

It was obvious that he didn't care what happened to me if our secret was blown. It was as though that's what he wanted, to betray me. And it tipped me over the brink. I became desperate, resisting his violent grip, squirming and kicking my legs. I no longer cared if I drowned.

'Keep still,' he commanded.

I kept writhing. He tried reasoning. 'Don't you like this anymore?'

I thrashed my legs violently. He taunted me, 'You don't want me to let go, do you?' It was the superior tone of someone holding all the cards.

I kept resisting and his voice became shrill. '*Keep still!*'

But I didn't care what happened anymore.

He let go, pushing me away with a guttural exclamation of disgust.

Scrabbling and dogpaddling frantically, I rode with the waves, my head angled up for air. It seemed interminable. I touched the shore, dug my toes into the sand and scrambled up the sloping beach, sure that everyone's eyes were following me. The humiliation was unbearable. I kept my eyes down, looking at the wet sand, keeping well clear of Mum and our umbrella.

On my own, at the back of the beach near the concrete seawall, I knelt as though in prayer and, clenching my knees together, consciously buried them into the soft, warm sand. I could still feel his hand inside my bathers. I was trying to hide my genitals out of sight, as though to reclaim or protect them.

I could not hold the tension any longer, this juggling act between my two lives. I started crying. Tears streamed down my cheeks and dripped onto the sand. My anxiety soon turned to my brothers, that they would see me crying. No-one my age ever cried at the beach. How would I explain?

I implored no-one in particular: *Please, please, please don't let them come near me.*

My entreaty didn't work. Terry came over and threw himself down in the sand beside me. I turned away towards the seawall and, as surreptitiously as I could, tried to wipe away the tears with my sandy hands. They wouldn't stop. My cheeks were covered in wet sand.

My mother never asked why Leunig wanted me. Perhaps she presumed he just wanted an affectionate play with someone. That's what she would have seen. Besides, the priest was still the pinnacle of sanctity.

But the beach as a safe haven had been destroyed. My family

could not know how unsafe I felt, and I could never tell them. I was on my own and the sense of being separate from everybody brought on a new feeling of utter desolation.

That day on the beach was the first time I'd consciously considered, reflected and acknowledged the full nature of the sexual abuse and its terms and conditions. I had previously 'coped' with them because I understood that, under the terms of our secret, my mother could not intervene to protect me. But as I'd watched her speaking to him, believing she was now on his side of my secret world, that strange separation had happened, that tangibly physical switch. In that moment, all feeling for her was erased. I no longer saw her as my mother. She'd become just another random woman on the beach, unavailable to me.

The desolation and the terrifying aloneness of the day, of feeling psychologically excised from her and my family, contributed to the trauma that I would one day come to know as Complex Post-Traumatic Stress Disorder.

Leunig did not abuse me in the sacristy again. I found out recently that in February 1964, soon after the abuse at the beach, he was transferred from Cottesloe to the chaplaincy at St John of God Hospital in Subiaco, a child-free posting with no altar boys or schoolchildren. Was his anger at the beach that day a consequence of receiving this news? Had there been complaints? Was he sent there as penance? Did he blame me?

8

My Mother's World Unravels

1964

My feeling of separateness within the family diminished as the year progressed, and I became actively involved in an unfolding family drama. My grandfather's galloping ill-health preoccupied Mum, his primary carer. With Dad always absent, I began to help her with some of the practical tasks of looking after him.

On one afternoon, she double-parked the FJ outside Ron Burt's butcher shop on Napoleon Street. I jumped out and pushed open the heavy glass door into the smell of blood and meat and sawdust to collect Grandad's old, brown Globite case, full of his shopping. He was in the habit of leaving it on the floor by the side wall while he went off on other business. Blue-and-white striped Mr Burt, leaning against the white-painted chopping block, raised his cleaver and nodded. I struggled back to the car with the heavy case and Mum drove around the corner and parked outside the Albion Hotel. She disappeared inside. Granddad didn't talk on the way back to his house. Mum carried his shopping as he felt his way in through the gate.

Later that year, he was hospitalised at St John's in Subiaco. I often went with her on her visits. Shy because he was always cranky, I stood back, well clear of his bed. I was fixated by the transfusion bottle dangling from a chrome post, capsicum-red blood feeding down a plastic tube and snaking across the white bedspread into his shrunken, stretched, alabaster body.

'I'm cold. The doctor said I need more blood.' He seemed defeated. Mum held his hand.

Leunig, now the chaplain at the hospital, would have prayed at his bedside as he lay dying, performing the sacrament of Extreme Unction. My mother would have been there too, kneeling, praying as Leunig anointed her father's forehead. Her world was disintegrating. As it turns out, the two men in front of her would be responsible for both ends of the fraying rope.

Granddad died in October 1964. Old Father Kearnan, in full priestly black suit and white collar, knocked on our front door, the proper way. He was carrying a large casserole bowl wrapped in a tea towel.

'I've had my housekeeper cook this for you.' It was a pie of sorts, grey meat and potatoes with a pastry top. He was that sort of priest, caring and considerate.

As thoughtful as it was, it could never have been enough to insulate my mother from her grief. And yet another shock was waiting for her in the solicitor's office. In his will, Grandad left my mother his house near the beach in Cottesloe, and most of what was left of his money. Aunt Maud had presumed that she would be gifted an investment property with a fine house as well, also close to the beach in Cottesloe. The sisters were dismayed to discover that their father, years earlier, after the death of their mother, had sold the property to finance his lifestyle. Maud, who was unmarried and had been boarding with him, had to move out and struggled to find somewhere to live. She disputed the will. My mother, equally distressed, wanted to acquiesce and give her sister all the money to maintain the peace. My father apparently took a hard line and pressured my mother to defend the will. The court ruled that Aunty Maud be given a greater share of the money, but the house and some of the money was to stay with my mother, as she had five children. As a result of the dispute, the two sisters became permanently estranged. After being an intimate and generous part of our lives, Aunty Maud disappeared.

We moved from our rental into Grandad's house in late 1964 or early 1965. Unsurprisingly, the house was in poor condition, having not had any maintenance since its construction in 1917. The garden was a tangled and overgrown wasteland.

'I hate this place. I hate it. I hate everything about it.' Mum was overlooking the dishevelled garden from the back window in the vestibule, her face wet, her eyes red-raw, her fists clenched. Her cries crashed around us. Later, I watched as Dad, standing apart from her in the kitchen with his hand to his mouth, did not embrace her or show any sympathy. Instead, he was chiding her.

'You're making too much of this. You've got to get over it. Get on with things.'

Then she disappeared. We were told she'd been admitted to a small private hospital nearby. Muttered reasons about 'needing a rest' was the best Dad could offer. I visited her there one day after school. She was sitting up in bed in a private ward, a bedraggled, weary woman barely recognisable as my mother. I was embarrassed. She apologised for not being home with us. No-one told us that it wasn't a rest, but it seeped out eventually. She'd had a nervous breakdown. She was away for three weeks.

I felt impelled to be responsible for some form of repair in this new family crisis. The overgrown garden seemed an accessible place to start so, working alone, I feverishly ripped out the tangled grapevines entwined over a collapsed arbor, dug up the untamed shrubs that covered the paths and tore out the neglected roses that had turned feral. Dragging the debris into a vast pile, I set it alight as though it were a funeral pyre. Flames leaped across the lilly-pilly tree, scorching the leaves. The purging of the decayed garden, I reasoned optimistically, would erase the legacy of my grandfather's death. She would have a blank slate when she came home.

I proudly led her around the now naked garden when she

returned, wanting her to see it as a new beginning. Instead, she just sobbed. She didn't say anything. She seemed beyond help, unreachable.

Although I experienced my father as a loyal, committed parent – patriarchal and authoritarian, but probably no more than many fathers in that era – his kindness and gentleness were passive and conditional. That is, so long as things were smoothly going his way. It was his intolerance of failures, moral and practical, and his predisposition to criticise us boys as well as Mum, that made her homecoming as miserable as her departure. So he continued to admonish her tears and her outpourings of grief, expecting the cause of her breakdown to have been patched and for her to carry on as though nothing had happened.

'You're overreacting. You've just got to get on with things.' There was no tenderness.

'Your mother's not feeling herself,' he kept saying to us. When he couldn't get her to follow his advice to bury her grief, it was her fault. I've sometimes wondered if he saw her inability to cope as a reflection on him, a shame that challenged his need to be seen as the perfect husband in the perfect Catholic family.

In any case, it was awful to watch, him standing apart from her and exhorting her to 'get over it'. She showed extraordinary restraint in the face of his continued denial of her trauma. Apart from her marriage vows and her Catholic duty to see it through, I understood that she did it for my brothers and me. She would weather his disdain to make sure we got our schooling, went to university and eventually made it to Heaven. We would then be together and happy. It would all end okay in Heaven.

***

Free from the abuses, my confidence stabilised as this year progressed and I maintained my position at tenth in the class.

Comments such as '... result disappointing' mingled with 'an excellent student'. 'Gerard has done very well to find a place within the coveted first ten ... Well-behaved and co-operative boy.'

9
Leunig Returns
1965

With my mother mentally fragile and my father emotionally and physically absent in service to the Church and post office, when Father Leunig turned up unexpectedly a month later, it was little wonder that my mother welcomed him without hesitation, feeling blessed that the priest had come back to visit us.

In March 1965, Leunig was appointed parish priest in the country town of Quairading, a farming district two-and-a-half hours east of Perth. The previous year, as chaplain at St John of God Hospital in Subiaco, barely six miles from Cottesloe, he had not made any advances towards me. He'd been in Quairading barely a month when he reappeared. I was thirteen but had not yet started puberty.

Granddad's old house was on the corner of two streets. The front door was hidden down one side, away from the main street and out of view, so friends and family all came through a side gate in the fence at the back of the house, and up the steps to the landing. Leunig arrived unannounced one night, knocking at the back door just before dinnertime. I stared at his paunchy figure as he stepped into the vestibule and felt the sudden deflation as the air was sucked out of me, our secret instantly resurrected. I was on my own again.

Of course, my mother could not refuse him, especially as we were about to sit down for dinner. She would have stretched the meal eight ways or gone without herself to include him. Our dining table was octagonal, a 1960s red-and-white, scatter-pattern Laminex on chrome legs, sitting squarely in the middle of the vestibule. The spare space at the table was opposite my father and, as it happened, next to me. Leunig said grace and, as had always happened on the altar, I saw him glancing sideways at me, remote and watchful. The usual chatter and chiacking of my brothers took on a greater volume, each of them talking over the others to impress Father. When dinner was finished, he became the showman, telling stories and jokes. I watched as everyone laughed, and had to laugh too lest I be accused of disrespect. And anyway, nothing bad had happened in over a year. His narrowed eyes roamed the table, back and forth. He was not just looking at me.

I remember five visits in what I now realise was his grooming of the family. On each visit he performed a new jest. The first time, he gave a slide show of a trip he'd made with a fellow priest across the Nullarbor Plain. He brought his own projector, and we watched the pictures on the vestibule wall. One was taken from the passenger's seat inside the car. It was at night and showed a flared match at the tip of a cigarette, lighting up his face as he was driving the car. He warned us that the flare from the match temporarily blinded you, ostensibly teaching us safe driving habits.

On two visits, he did the 'Craven "A" rocket trick.' Carefully disassembling an empty Craven "A" cigarette packet, he spread the aluminium foil inner lining flat on the table. Taking the tissue paper that encased the cigarettes, he folded it into a concertina shape and stood it on its end on the aluminium foil. He lit the tissue. The flames burned down until all that was left was the gossamer thin ash, still intact and upright in its concertina form. The weightlessness of the tissue ash in the rising column of hot air caused it to rise quickly, like a rocket, until it nearly hit the ceiling.

'Do it again, Father!' the young ones all shouted. I remember only marvelling at the feat.

He arrived another evening, at dinnertime as usual and again unannounced, carrying a small, dusky pink canvas carry bag, which he put on the floor beside him at the table. It was a typical meal, my younger brothers all talking at once. Dom was the loudest. Both he and Paddy, being young, were keen to have a voice over us, the domineering older brothers. When we finished dinner and the empty plates were cleared away, he lifted the carry bag onto the table and showed us what it contained: a brand-new, battery operated, Grundig reel-to-reel portable tape recorder. It was the first we'd ever seen.

'I had my housekeeper sew the microphone into this invisible pocket,' he said, pointing at a small black dot surrounded by pink stitching on the outside of the bag.

It had been running since he arrived, recording our meal together. We gathered round, leaning over the table, and listened again to our chatter. The meal had sounded like chaos, each of us clamouring to be heard above the others, especially Dom. The dinner table was his stage and his chatter hilarious. We all laughed ourselves silly, thoroughly approving of Leunig's trick.

He sat through it all unsmiling and detached in his inscrutable way, scanning our faces left to right, left to right. It was not in my nature to be insolent or disrespectful or do anything that might betray my secret. He hadn't approached me in the house nor singled me out for special attention and, as nothing awkward or distressing had happened, I laughed along with everyone else, conscious of being separate from them all. The only relationship that existed at the table was between Leunig and me. Our secret was an invisible, tight cord and I endured its tension, warily watching his eyes roam back and forth.

He was like a sorcerer, mesmerising the whole family, weaving a new spell. The invitation came quietly but landed as gently as a railway sleeper. 'Would Gerard like to come to Quairading for the weekend?'

He asked my parents in front of us all. Neither of them turned to ask me. My father would have felt honoured, proud that his family was being favoured in the eyes of the Church. Perhaps my mother did as well. But if she knew or intuited anything, she didn't breathe a word. There was no warning or hint, overt or implied, to 'be careful' or to 'look after myself'.

10

Quairading

Winter 1965

Packing a suitcase was Mum's art: the projected needs, numbers of items per day, allowances for contingencies, their order of removal, first-night pyjamas on top and next day's underpants underneath. Whether it was a school trip or off to Goomalling or to Marty's family's farm, or now to Quairading, her advice was the same and the preparations meticulous.

'Take plenty of spare clothes, just in case.'

She packed a pair of winter pyjamas and my Sunday best for Mass. She always wrote a list of the clothes, with categories and numbers in columns, and taped it inside the lid of the case.

'Remember to check everything against the list when it's time to come home.' She was careful to mind the family's limited resources.

Leunig collected me in his new Ford Falcon on a Friday afternoon. Few people we knew owned new cars, yet the Catholic priests always seemed to have them. The way he'd parked it, sideways on the steeply sloping grass verge, with the driver's side downhill, meant I had to get in on the uphill passenger's side. Resisting gravity's pull to slide down the bench seat towards him, I gripped the passenger door handle tightly.

'Why don't you sit here?' He indicated I should let go and sit beside him.

'I'm okay here.' My response was very conscious, making the statement as much to myself as to him that this physical separation should be construed as unwillingness.

We travelled up Stirling Highway towards Perth. Passing a

side road in Claremont, he pointed up to where he'd grown up. He told me about his brothers and sister and their families. I remained silent, disinclined to engage with him. The moral implications of what was happening had already started to preoccupy me.

It was a protracted inner conversation, quiet and reasoned. Even though I'd had no say in the decision, I understood that merely going away with him was giving him permission to do what he'd done in the sacristy. I fully accepted responsibility for the consequences because I also understood that, in upholding my side of the secret, I could not have expected my parents to intervene to protect me. I had an image of them standing together in the distance, silent and inaccessible. I was on my own for whatever lay ahead. As I could only conjure up a sacristy-style rubbing of my penis, I accepted I could cope with that. So, though wary and appropriately anxious, I was not afraid; a feeling supported by his many friendly visits to our dinner table, with no hint of the anger or betrayal I'd experienced at the beach.

I loved travelling in the country, and the first half of this trip was the same road my family travelled to Goomalling. The places we passed were markers of this familiar journey – huge, old gum trees that were special, the Stonehouse shop, the Mahogany Inn, the swamp behind the service station at the York turn-off – my inner map registering the distance gone and the miles left to go.

On this trip though, I only remember the inner conversation until, leaving the forest in the hills east of Perth, we emerged into farmland as night came on. The headlights fleetingly picked out patches of open grassland, fences and trees bleached in the bright lights. Leunig pointed out a place in a darkened paddock where a passenger plane had crashed after the war. He was very interested in the circumstances of the accident and described them in great detail.

I knew where Quairading was on the map, but I'd never been there. I had no idea how long the trip would take. The absence of any bearings in the darkness made the journey seem to go on forever. Eventually, we slowed, turned off the deserted road, went up a side street in the town and pulled into a yard next to the presbytery. He left the headlights on and went over to unlock the door. In the glare of the lights, the building was a blank grey, with a long, low gutter along the back. Weeds pressed up against the wall. I got out and stood beside the car. It was freezing. The night air was laden with the pungent, sweet smell of dew on grass and damp earth. A cluster of forty-four-gallon petrol drums stood off to one side between the car and the presbytery. A hand pump protruded from the screw cap hole in the top of one. He came back to the car to collect his bag.

'What are the drums for?'

'The farmers always keep the priest supplied with free petrol.' He laughed, guttural and hearty.

I stayed by the car, shivering in the freezing night air. I didn't want to go inside. The presbytery building jerked me back to my reality. The inner monologue on the journey up – that familiar voice, with its rationalising and justifications and acceptance of my fate – was no longer hypothetical. The first wave of real fear swept over me.

I don't remember walking inside, eating or unpacking my case. Memory began again after I had changed into my pyjamas. The presbytery was so cold, I was shivering. I must have been in a separate room to him, because he called me out into an open living area. It seemed completely bare, with little furniture and no signs of a home life. Being alone with him, given over and abandoned in this barren, soulless house, crystallised the fear.

'Come into the bedroom.' He was standing opposite me and gestured abruptly towards a door beside him.

A paralysing terror surged through me. The room around me disappeared and he became a distant, solitary figure surrounded by a circle of blurred vision, like I was looking at him through the wrong end of a long, narrow telescope. He was the only thing in focus, the blurring obliterating everything in my peripheral vision.

My feet would not move. Some part of me knew he did not have complete control, yet I also knew I would have to obey him. I deeply resented feeling this powerlessness, that I couldn't say 'no', however much I did not condone whatever might happen. But nothing could have prepared me for his next guttural command.

'Take your pyjamas off!'

His order rang like an alarm, shattering the silence. I couldn't move. It came again.

'Take your pyjamas off and come into the bedroom!'

This time it was brusque and cruel, a snarl with a hint of frustration that I was not obeying. He had that same rigid expression as on the beach, unsmiling, deep-set eyes unmoving and piercing, his head lifted that same way, his chin thrust forward.

To say I was sexually naive was an understatement. I couldn't even try to imagine what was to happen that required me to take off my pyjamas, what being naked prefigured, or what violation might await. I was now shaking uncontrollably, frozen to the cold, bare boards. A cascading helplessness coursed through me as though my whole sense of self was unravelling. I would have to go into the bedroom with him. I could not see that I had a choice. But to go naked was unthinkable. It was not my father's prudish modesty, nor that nakedness might be a sin; it was a personal morality. I aspired to live a life of perfection like the saints. I would not cross that line. My voice came from somewhere outside me, weak and quavering in the cold air.

'No.' It was tentative but faintly defiant.

Neither of us moved. It was a stalemate. He was still the distant figure down the end of the narrow, blurry-edged tube. Then his tone changed.

'Why won't you take off your pyjamas?' He was curious.

'It's wrong.' It sounded lame.

His demeanour was still one of absolute authority, the one holding all the cards, so my defiance seemed paper-thin. Yet his questioning gave me courage. I had a vague sense that I could seize a degree of control if I offered a compromise that at least preserved some vestige of my morality. It seemed the lesser of two evils, whatever the greater one might be.

'I'll only come if I can keep my pyjamas on.'

Any empowerment I may have clawed back in resisting him was instantly annulled by the pang of guilt at my complicity. In offering a compromise and agreeing to go into his bedroom, I was giving him permission to do something.

'Okay. You can keep your pyjamas on.' He sounded friendly.

His head inclined towards the bedroom door. I was relieved I'd be able to hold onto this fragment of myself. But what was this concession? The exchange reinforced my feeling of desolation. I had an overpowering image of myself standing alone in the middle of a frozen desert at night, shaking with the cold, with no bearings, no lights and no possible means to get help.

I followed him into the bedroom. Something in me must have shut down because I became an automaton, just following commands.

'Get up on the bed!' He was curt. But when I balked, his tone softened.

'You don't need to worry. Don't be afraid.'

The bed was wide and in the middle of the small room. It seemed to take up most of the space. There was a window on one side with beige curtains that didn't meet and a sliver of black from the night outside showed through the gap in the fabric folds. He closed the door behind him. The light was on.

I climbed onto the bed and lay down on one side. The room was so cold, I quickly pulled the blankets tightly over me, conscious that this was also giving the message I did not want to make myself available.

He was standing at the bottom of the bed, and the tunnel-vision image of him returned as he started taking off his clothes. I looked away, embarrassed. After all, he was still a priest. But as he moved to climb onto the bed, I looked. He was white and flabby, his genitals vaguely visible in the gloom below his round belly.

'Not under the blankets. I want you to lie on top.' He gestured aggressively with a sideways flick of his hand. I reluctantly started to come out from under the blankets. But it was too slow for him. He leaned over and snatched them off me. I sat bolt upright, instinctively pulling my knees up to my chest. He climbed onto the bed.

'What are you going to do?' My whole body was trembling.

'I won't hurt you. Lie down on your back. In the middle.'

I shuffled sideways and lay down in the sagging middle. He had a towel in his hand and as he leaned forward, he spread it over my pyjamas, across my belly and between my legs. I felt the resistance in my legs as he pushed them wide apart and climbed between them. It was all happening in slow-motion. Most of his weight was on his forearms, his face inches from mine. He writhed, moving his body up and down, pressing hard onto my belly and grunting. It felt complicit to watch, but I looked down anyway. His erect penis emerged then disappeared. It was grotesque. What was he doing? I felt its forbiddenness.

My mind was racing, grappling for some understanding.

Why has he spread a towel across my belly? It must have to do with hygiene.

In a rush, the irrationality of what was happening dawned on me. Someone from the town might come in. Father was back from the city and a parishioner might need to see him urgently. They would knock on his door and walk into the bedroom, and they'd see him naked on top of me. This fantasy became pure terror. I stared at the closed door, transfixed by its whiteness. It wasn't locked; he'd just pushed it shut. It could swing open at any moment. And the light was on. They'll catch me.

Then reason cut into the fantasy. Discovery was much more likely to come from the window. Someone might be outside now. They'll hear him grunting. They'll look through the window. The curtains don't meet. They can see in. The random noises of the night suddenly came alive, a distant dog barking, a car rattling down a gravel road.

In my imagining, I reasoned everyone would want to witness it, like the queues of men that lined up outside the freaks tent at the Royal Show. I looked back at the curtains. The car I heard was definitely pulling up. People were getting out and crowding around, peeping in through that shadowy slit in the curtains. And they were all men. Men, as I'd learned from my father, carried the mantle of shame and punishment.

Now I became desperate. I hadn't refused Leunig. In fact, I'd consented 'if I could keep my pyjamas on'. I was the guilty one. Naively, I could only imagine that if we were caught, I would be the one sent to prison. The sanctity of the priesthood ensured he was untouchable, and prison was the only punishment I could conjure up commensurate with the monstrousness of his act. I did not think of it as a sin, as from my mother's world. It was a crime of the taboo, of the secular world, as my father would have had it, and my guilt cemented that. I looked back at the slit in the curtains. Any moment, the horrified men would burst into the bedroom and march me down to the main street to prison. It was an image of four men, one on either side and two behind holding my arms, frogmarching me down the road.

He grunted and stopped, lifted himself up and climbed off me, gathering up the towel by the two corners on my stomach, bunching it as he pulled it off. He brushed his hand across the outside of my pyjamas, feeling my genitals.

Nothing 'awful' had happened. He hadn't played with my penis. I crawled back under the blankets. He turned off the light. The curtains glowed palely from some dim light outside. There were no shadows of men's heads on the curtains. I'd been spared. I lay there swimming in profound guilt at my complicity. It did not occur to me I could go back to the other bedroom.

A violent, ear-splitting explosion outside suddenly shattered the stillness of the night. I sat up, again shaking in terror. We'd been caught.

'What was that?'

'It's just the petrol drums.' He paused. 'When the temperature drops below freezing, the pressure difference inside to outside of the empty drums makes the tops suddenly buckle inwards.'

The drums continued to implode, one after the other, violent salvos echoing into the night. His explanation did little to ease my fear. I'd never heard of this phenomenon, and I imagined no-one else had either, so now the men would come running. How could they ignore these detonations? They'll knock on the door to make sure Father is safe and they'll find me in his bed. They'll march me away to prison. I lay awake for what felt like hours, tensed, primed to every noise, waiting for a face to appear at the window or the door to burst open.

I don't remember waking up, eating breakfast, showering or dressing the next day. Memories return later in the morning when he asked whether I'd like to learn to drive. I'd often helped my father drive, steering the FJ and changing the gears for him while he worked the pedals. Learning to drive was normal. I wanted normal. Anyway, Father hadn't harmed me, and no-one had burst into the bedroom to arrest me.

The cemetery was on the outskirts of town, on a gently sloping clearing in the scrubby bush. He pulled up in the deserted car park, got out and walked around the car. I shuffled across the bench seat to the driver's side. He climbed in and lit up a cigarette. He explained the automatic column shift, the brakes, the accelerator.

'You only use one foot when you drive an automatic.'

I huddled up to the wheel with the seat as far forward as it would go. He leaned over and adjusted the rear-view mirror. I drove around the car park tingling with excitement, stopping, starting, reversing and practising parking. He was patient and friendly. Assured of my competence, he asked whether I'd like to drive out onto one of the back roads. I was surprised at my eagerness. Ironically, it was with a different guilt and I didn't think about prison if I was caught. I wended my way out onto a gravel road lined with York gums and barbed-wire fences and drove cautiously down the middle of the road.

'Move further over to the left.'

It was hard to trust myself feeling this scared. He showed me how to line up the edge of the road with a creased indent in the front of the bonnet. I eased the car over.

'That's it.'

Smoking nonchalantly, he used his cigarette to occasionally point out farms owned by families in the parish. I was not interested. I had his permission to drive on my own on a main road. Priests were above the law, and I was a beneficiary. I would have boasted about it to my brothers, but this too belonged in my secret world.

'You can go faster if you want to.'

I looked down at the speedo. Thirty miles per hour. I pressed the accelerator and the needle crept around to forty. The car was roaring on the gravel. That was as fast as I dared go.

'Go faster.' He was waving his cigarette forwards. The speedo inched up. Fifty.

'Faster!'

I held my nerve until the needle touched sixty miles per hour. The feeling of competency and power was intoxicating. I was a thirteen-year-old illegally driving a big, new car at the country speed limit on a gravel road. It was exhilarating. I was beyond fear. Father was authorising it. I was invincible.

Circling back to the outskirts of Quairading, I pulled off to the side of the road and we changed seats. He drove back into town and parked outside the general store.

'I have to get some food for our dinner.'

He stepped onto the pavement. A group of men came over to talk to him. He stood beside the car, nodding as he talked, unsmiling and unflustered. The men glanced sideways at me in the car, and I was jerked back to the events of the previous night. The thrill of the drive evaporated. I shrank down against the passenger door, trying not to catch their eye.

I don't remember the meal being prepared, or eating it, or undressing, or getting into my pyjamas. I don't remember any night-time prayers. We didn't have a discussion this second night as he ushered me into his bedroom. I knew what was going to happen, even though I had no idea what he was doing, but it didn't lessen the fear. I was convinced we'd be caught this time. The men outside the store had seen me and knew I was with Father. They would come to make sure I was okay. In fact, they were already spying on me through the window. I had gone into his bedroom without any protest this time. I was even more complicit.

I lay down in the middle of the bed. But I kept my head and shoulders raised on the pillow and watched him undress, spread the towel out on my stomach, ease my legs apart, and climb between them. I flinched at the sudden weight of his belly as he started rubbing. I looked away at the curtains as he did it, primed for the inevitable.

The drums began imploding again, shattering the stillness of the night. Tonight, the men would definitely come and see me in bed with the priest. I lay in dread and waited. Every second held the imminence of discovery.

In the morning, as he was about to go to the church to say Sunday Mass, he casually said, 'You don't have to come if you don't want to. If you'd like, you can have a hit of golf around the school oval.' I had the feeling he didn't want me to go; and as the parishioners I'd seen on the pavement would surely recognise me, I didn't hesitate to accept his dispensation.

I took a few clubs from the bag he gave me, and headed out onto the hard, bare earth of the sloping school oval. Although it was an easy decision in the moment, it wasn't without some misgivings. I had never intentionally missed Mass on a Sunday. But Father's dispensation had such authority that the whispers of anxiety soon dissipated. I became so comfortable with my freedom, I laughed at my superiority over the parishioners who still had to be inside at Mass. It was the same feeling of omnipotence as driving his car. With Father's permission, I could do anything. I was above the rules of the road and the Church. But soon enough came a lingering unease, born from the nonchalance with which he'd given me the dispensation, and the speed with which I'd accepted.

As I chipped golf balls around the perimeter of the oval, near the bottom corner, I stopped and looked up at the church. The feeling of superiority had waned. I was relieved I didn't have to confront the parishioners, but what had they thought of me playing golf instead of being inside at Mass? Guilt had re-entered my conversation.

We returned to Perth in the afternoon. I don't remember packing my case or checking my clothes against the list taped inside the lid. I don't remember the trip, nor going into my home or any conversations with my brothers. The weekend oscillating between the night-time distress and the daytime thrills and freedom cemented the disconnect with my home life.

And there was a cost. Over the next term, my class position went from tenth to twenty-first, a crisis exemplified in Maths where, from first place a year or so before, I dropped to thirty-fourth place with a mark of fifty-six. I'd been, and still wanted to be, in the 'coveted top ten'. It was humiliating. My already struggling self-esteem was in tatters. School reports started noting attention-seeking behaviour in class, a self-destructive pattern that also extended to my peer group. I was setting myself up for ridicule, as though to give substance to my feeling of being an outsider.

II

Quairading Again

Late Spring 1965

I don't remember the invitation, the Friday afternoon pick-up or the journey back into the countryside going to Quairading a second time. It was later in that year because it wasn't cold, so it would have been closer to my fourteenth birthday. The palpable terror of my first visit had subsided and was now a vague anxiety. The men on the pavement outside the general store had kept their distance.

I knew what was expected of me, a tacit acceptance of my role. I lay quietly in his bed, in my pyjamas, while he did whatever it was that he did. I still had no idea, but my fear had lessened. I didn't stare at the gap in the curtains, nor at the doorway where the parishioners might burst in. I waited under his heavy body until it was over. The petrol drums were silent. In this absence of fear though, I felt the first stirrings of my own sexuality.

In the morning, Leunig talked about flying. He'd either obtained his pilot's licence or was learning to be a pilot.

'Would you like to see the gliders at the Cunderdin airfield? They have a meet every Saturday afternoon.'

Planes were the stuff of boyhood adventure. I'd already devoured all the Biggles books, so I readily accepted the invitation. After a long drive, we arrived at the wide, sparse aerodrome and sat in the car on the edge of the airstrip. The gliders were being towed into the sky and, after they circled for some time, came in to land, whispering in the air as they slipped over us. I got out of the car and walked over to look at some lying lopsided on the dry grass of the outfield. I got closer to the landing strip and felt the *whoosh* of air from their wings as they landed. At a discrete distance, I listened to the pilots talking with each other.

Leunig said there was an aero club meeting in another town and if we hurried, we might get there before they packed up for the day. He would try to get me a flight. It was another long drive before we pulled in beside an airstrip – a gravel runway stretching away from a wide apron in a clearing in the scrub. There were no cars or people there, and only one small plane was left, parked some distance away. Leunig walked over and talked to the pilot. There were no gestures or smiling that suggested a genial conversation. He came back to the car.

'He'll take you up for a quick flight. He's reluctant because it's late and the aero club has finished for the day.' He was abrupt.

I crossed the apron and climbed into the plane. My excitement waned as I sensed the pilot's disquiet. I wanted to tell him it was my first flight, but he hadn't even said hello. It was then that I felt responsible for his apparent coercion. It fueled a new anxiety. Someone outside my pact with Leunig was now involved in giving me a good time. And he wasn't happy about it.

He taxied down to the far end of the runway, turned the small plane around and stopped. He tested the throttle, then flicked a switch, first one way then the other, six or seven times. Unable to contain my curiosity, I asked him what he was doing.

'There are two magnetos and I'm switching between them to make sure they're both in working order.' It was a reluctant response.

He lapsed back into silence and eased the throttle out until the engine roared. The gravel runway was rough as we accelerated until that exhilarating, suspended-in-nothing feeling overcame me as we lifted off, freed from the earth. We flew a brief circuit of the town, over some wheat fields and bushland, and came in to land in the warm glow of the evening sun. I watched out the side window as the small plane approached its own shadow on the airstrip. The shadow wheels met our real ones with a thump.

Leunig was standing on the edge of the apron, his legs apart, a solitary figure in his priest's black trousers and white shirt, unmoving except for his arm occasionally pivoting upwards as he brought a cigarette to his mouth. I climbed out and thanked the pilot. He grunted, tilting his head down, not looking at me.

It was another long drive back to Quairading. In the last moments of the afternoon, yellow sunlight flickered sideways through the York gums that lined the roadside, casting long shadows across the road and into the paddocks beyond. The evening air was cool and steeped in the sweet, damp smell of the dew on dry grass, and it bit through the air vents in the car.

This experience of the sun flickering through the trees, the long shadows in the fields, and the smell of the cool, moist evening air became inextricably entwined with this new anxiety that the adventure had been a risky flirtation with an outsider. Any security I felt at not yet being discovered in bed with the priest vanished. When nobody knew, it seemed less terrible. Now there was a real risk someone did, and it cemented the guilt at my complicity.

But something else had also happened to compound this dilemma. The previous night, as he writhed on me, I'd felt my own sexuality stir, and it had made me curious.

We went to bed again. As he finished and gathered up the towel and climbed off me, I asked him what he was doing. He explained about ejaculation.

'It's called "shooting".'

What was he talking about? Guns shoot. How could that describe his rubbing on me.

'What is it?'

'It's like Lux.' Lux was a creamy-coloured, viscous kitchen

detergent. His reply was warm and conciliatory, like a teacher whose student's curiosity had finally been aroused.

'It shoots out of your dick. That's how you make babies. Don't you know?'

I shook my head.

'I'll show you in the morning.'

He may as well have been talking a foreign language. I knew nothing about the mechanics of sex, least of all how babies were made. My parents had never uttered a word. Failure at school meant I was no longer in the cool cohort of the boys that huddled together sniggering at the facts of life, where I might have gleaned the bones of it. But I did know something; I was entering the realm of a taboo.

With this curiosity, my situation with Leunig changed. I was not just overhearing a 'dirty story' of the schoolyard type. I was *in* the dirty story. As he talked about his erect penis and described what it did, I felt a tantalising urge to immerse myself in the taboo, to find out more. Yet asking these questions and absorbing the answers set down another layer onto my already overflowing guilt.

I was lying back, propped up on the pillow. Leunig was standing at the bottom of the bed.

'Who else do you do this with?' I surprised myself with the question. He was pleased. He talked about another boy who came for weekends. I recognised his name because he was at one of the other boys' colleges in Perth where some cousins of mine were boarders.

Leunig tilted his head up, a knowing nod.

'He's experienced and knows what to do.' He was boasting, as though it had been a conquest, to emphasise what we were doing was normal, but insinuating I still had a way to go before I was fully fledged.

In the morning, I reminded him of his promise of a 'Lux demonstration'. He opened the cupboard underneath the kitchen sink and took out a plastic bottle of the detergent. Opening the cap, he pointed the bottle down into the sink and squeezed it. A fine jet of pearlescent, creamy liquid squirted into the bowl, clinging to the bottom in a sticky globule. He squirted it again.

'It's like this, *shooting*.' He emphasised the word and looked at me, sensing that my curiosity meant I was becoming more malleable. The detergent oozed along the bottom of the sink bowl. I could not connect it with his rubbing on me in the night. How did this stuff come out of his penis? Penises were for peeing. Pee was watery and clear or yellow. It didn't make any sense.

His lessons and stories took his nakedness out of the realm of the 'rude and terrible' and into the 'dirty'. Without ever uttering one descriptive word about sex, the Church and our culture generally had managed to imbue sex, in absentia, as filthy and sinful. I knew that this was what was happening, acquiring sinful and dirty knowledge.

I have no memory, again, of food being prepared, of eating, washing, dressing or saying any prayers. I would have remembered prayers or the rosary had they occurred, as they would have been guilt-appeasing activities.

Sunday Mass that weekend was rostered for the church at a small, isolated siding called Kwolyin, twenty miles down the road towards Bruce Rock, to serve the remote farms. Leunig didn't give me the option to stay at the presbytery.

'You have to come with me.'

The morning sunshine shimmered on the rust-coloured asphalt. The undulating wheat fields either side had dried to a soft, fawn colour. He was silent. Only my mind talked, that inner voice ruminating on his explanation at the kitchen sink, calling his penis a 'dick'. I had been shocked. 'Dick' was gutter slang.

I still expected to hear decent language from the priest, even when he was so sinfully deviant.

The church at Kwolyin was built of red brick, the size of a large farm shed, with shoulder-high windows down each side. A crucifix crowned a little entrance porch facing the road. It was the only building there, lost and forlorn in a patch of remnant bushland. Leunig drove around a low fence at the front and up to an area of open dirt on the right-hand side. He parked towards the back, next to some rough-barked York gums.

'Can you bring these in?'

He pointed to the vessels for Mass. He carried the vestments from the back of the car, and I followed him across the dusty ground to the back door of the church. In spite of everything that had happened, I still thought it was special to be allowed to carry the chalice and the other precious objects. I stood outside the door to the sanctuary and passed them to him. I peered in at the empty pews beyond. He leaned towards me.

'You don't have to come to Mass if you don't want to.' I again sensed he'd be happier if I didn't. He flicked his head towards the bush. Relieved, I walked over behind his car towards a long, low-hanging branch on a leaning York Gum. I sat down on its rough bark, facing the road.

The farmers and their families began arriving, parking in front of the low, metal railings strung between the squat, red-brick piers of the fence that divided the road from the church. I was in full view, sitting on the horizontal tree branch. The women and children got out on the far side of the cars. The men got out on my side and, as they put on their coats, stood and stared at me, their faces quizzical. As they filed into the church, some kept looking back towards me. My inner conversation started up again.

I know what they're thinking. This boy has come out to Kwolyin with Father. Why isn't he inside serving on the altar or at Mass with every Catholic for miles around. Why is he outside under a tree? It's a mortal sin not to go to Mass. Isn't he a Catholic? If he isn't, why is he with Father?

I felt transparent. They could see right through me to my guilt. It was the same uneasiness that I'd experienced with the pilot. I had the hour of the Mass to reflect on my situation. The inner voice was strident now, talking clearly and logically.

It's not about missing Mass and committing a mortal sin. Father's dispensation seems rock-solid. It's what it says about me and my values: that it's easier and less shameful for me to sit out here, on a tree in the middle of the bush, looking and feeling ridiculous, than be inside with those men who clearly saw me and were wondering what I was doing. And, asking questions last night, means I'm implicated in what he's doing.

I sat there, swamped with this new guilt. A line had been crossed. I didn't know the words then, but it was about moral integrity.

I don't remember the end of Mass or everyone leaving. I don't remember the drive back to Quairading, packing my suitcase, checking items against the list. But I do remember every nuance of the inner conversation that began on the two-and-a-half-hour journey back to Perth that afternoon. It was the opposite of the conversation on my first trip up to Quairading. This time the voice was haunted, pursued by the moral implications. I knew what had to be said. Over and over the words formed, only to shrivel in silence. When the outlying houses of the city started to appear in the rugged hill country to the east, it signalled we were close to home. The time had come. But still I kept putting it off. I had to say it before we got home. I knew that once we were there, I would not be able to refuse another invitation. I could not involve my parents.

Feeling physically sick and staring straight ahead, I finally spat it out.

'I'm not doing this anymore.'

His brooding, angry silence filled the car for the remainder of the journey home. I turned away and stared out the passenger window, enduring the agony of his mood. He dropped me at home with no platitudes or goodbye, discarded like litter. This time I remember going into the house and putting my case on the spare bed in the middle bedroom.

***

A few months earlier, in September, Normie Rowe, a well-known Australian pop star, had been charged with the carnal knowledge of a thirteen-year-old schoolgirl. As the case was prominent in the papers and magazines, and I rather liked him, I was intrigued and looked up 'carnal knowledge' in the dictionary. To my dismay, many of the elements of the definition had happened to me in the sacristy, on the beach at Cottesloe and in the presbytery in Quairading. One afternoon some time later, on my way home from school, as I was walking along Napoleon Street past the shops, it dawned on me.

What Leunig has been doing is criminal.

Discovering that I had been complicit in criminal conduct added yet another layer to the morass of guilt. It raised the stakes on the secret. Reporting the abuse, as though that had ever really been an option, was now an impossibility.

12

A Normal Life

1966

It was the first full summer in our grandfather's house. I was old enough to go to the beach on my own and, with Terry in my charge, we took the short cut up a back lane to the golf course, wending our way across the fairways down to the beach, our towels around our necks and our painted Coolite boards under our arms. Afterwards, salty and sunburned, we walked home and made ourselves sandwiches. We lay around in the cool of the lounge room watching the television Joe had persuaded our mother to hire for the holidays.

When the sea breeze came in, we played backyard cricket on the path up the middle of the garden. Fast bowlers began their run-up inside the rat-infested shed at the bottom of the garden, and spinners from behind the boobiallas. A giant frangipani tree grew in the slip cordon. A snick hitting a branch was 'out'. If it evaded the labyrinth of branches, it was 'four'. The tree had a swathe of limbs missing where wild off-cuts had flayed it. After work, Dad bowled to us until we were called for dinner. 'Just one more over' he'd call. But it was always half a dozen, because he loved playing sport with us.

Having turned fourteen, I was now legally employable by the Postmaster-General's Department. I started work as a Saturday morning telegram boy at Dad's post office, riding an ancient, iron-heavy, red bike down the leafy streets of his district, my leather pouch full of suggestive wedding telegrams. Earning my own money was a lifeline to independence. A Commonwealth Savings Bank account book replaced the long-abandoned indulgences credit account.

Terry, who was eleven, and I formed a surfing club with our neighbour Matty, who was thirteen and also an altar boy at Star of the Sea. We were the 'Junior Australian Boardriders'. The 'Jabbers' met in secret in our garden shed, painting the letters 'J.A.B.' on the inside of the weatherboards, the meaning never divulged to curious siblings.

Our disposable income, traditionally sourced from cool-drink bottles returned to the corner store, soon bypassed the sixpence lolly bags in favour of cigarettes. We walked to another corner store suitably distant from home so we wouldn't be recognised, then hid behind the grass trees down by the railway line, the illicitness fostering a camaraderie as we smoked. We didn't talk about anything personal, like girls or sex or 'shooting' or 'Lux'. I knew my mother could smell the tobacco on my breath when we came home. She obviously cut us some slack to experiment, as in a throwaway line sometime later, she mentioned bronchial scarring and the dangers of smoking. By now she had regained some equanimity as, in her acquired wisdom, she didn't confront the menace in the authoritarian way my father would have. I never smoked again.

Adolescence meant healthy obsessions with Holden cars and beautiful women, Julie Christie in particular. I couldn't bring myself to talk to any of the girls my own age, surreptitiously staring at them across the pews at church, at the bus stop, or as they walked up the hill past my room. Except Ann. She was very pretty, the nearest to an embodiment of Julie Christie, and lived diagonally opposite us. I talked to her once after school, on the verge outside our house, until her father, a bear of a man, came out and called her home. It was much easier to talk with older women. Jenny, the mother of five children, lived in the house next to Ann. We often used to stand on the verge between our two houses, talking for what seemed like hours. She was interested in me and asked questions about my thoughts. She wasn't a Catholic, but she was interested in religion as a philosophy. I liked her and felt her equal.

For some years now, Mum had gone to a different Mass in Cottesloe, but she now began going to Mass in the neighbouring parish of Swanbourne. This became her new spiritual home. I understood even then she was making a statement about her marriage and Dad's excessive devotion to the Church. Her independence of worship was never discussed nor was it offered as an option for us to accompany her. We remained with him at the Cottesloe parish. But I now found his unctuous, self-conscious humility embarrassing. I began to separate myself, not only from this style of worship, but also from his roadmap to the adult male world. In the secret world I lived in, immersed now in fantasies of girls and sexuality, I was free to do whatever I liked, however inappropriate or delusional.

In 1966, a well-known interstate footballer had come to Perth to play for a local team. He and his family moved in near us. As it happened, they were Catholics, and I recognised him at church on their first Sunday in our parish.

He was tall, strong and handsome, if a little aloof, and his wife was petite, with smiling, blue eyes and a shock of tousled, blond hair. They had three young girls who fluttered around them like ducklings. After Mass, I hovered with the men who gathered around him, animatedly talking football. She and her children stood awkwardly off to one side in the car park. I kept eyeing her and her apparent abandonment by her husband and edged over to talk to her. We relaxed into an easy conversation, talking about her girls, her husband's football career, her home in the Eastern States and how she felt moving to Perth.

Within weeks, I'd become infatuated. Sunday was an eon away each week, the time in-between spent constantly fantasising about her. My brothers and I always sat with Dad at the front of the church, the pews occupied by the conspicuously devout. I anxiously watched for her family to come in the side door, hoping they would not choose to sit at the back, and was always relieved when they sat in the same row, just behind me on the opposite side of the aisle, close enough so that when I turned, I would be able to catch her eye. She would sense my look and, smiling, linger her gaze long enough to fuel my fervour. The rugged footballer sat at the far end of the pew staring straight ahead. Their girls squirmed and wriggled between them.

After Mass, he stood under the peppermint trees in the churchyard, the centre of attention for a large cluster of men. She and I stood in the open, her girls hanging off her skirt. She was homesick for her family and this became the emotional bond between us. She whispered about her husband's intolerance.

'"Buckle down and get over it",' she told me he'd said.

I understood this vacuum of empathy, so I knew how a husband should respond. I had no thought of inappropriateness, either on her part as an adult or mine as a fourteen-year-old. Her hand would gently touch my forearm to emphasise her feelings, sending shivers through me, sweeping me away in the delusion that I was more understanding than her husband. Her fear of him was betrayed in her anxious glances towards the huddled group under the trees, and then her plaintive looks back at me as she left each week. Describing her homesickness one Sunday, her hand rested on my arm and tears trickled down her cheeks. She was a small, delicate, brightly-coloured bird, too young somehow to have three children. I wanted to protect her, to stay talking forever, but the men dispersed and he called out to her in a gruff summons. She edged away reluctantly, glancing back, smiling a goodbye as she moved to join him.

The next Sunday, their pew was empty. My bird had flown.

I was bereft. I made discreet enquiries, though perhaps not that discreet for a teenager. It seemed the family had only been renting until they found a more suitable home closer to his club. The self-confidence I had begun to feel talking with these older women was reflected at school. Year Ten, in 1966, was the first full year free of abuse. My school marks improved dramatically, and I climbed from twenty-first back to ninth place. Being back within the 'coveted top ten' brought comments, such as 'Well done indeed', from my teachers. In the exams at the end of the year, I passed all subjects, including Latin, with a near-distinction average.

Another event happened around this time that dampened the chatter around our dinner table. A boy who had finished at our school the previous year, and who was a keen surfer at Cottesloe, had 'got' his girlfriend pregnant and they were having to quickly get married. His family attended our church, so the shame had a more immediate, geographical impact. The moral tone of the discussion sputtered on amid red faces. Dad was silent. Mum, glancing around at her five sons, attempted to head off a similar shame on the family, describing the 'dangers of experimenting'. Without uttering one word about sex, she managed to convey this sorry story of damnation and its consequences.

13

A Confrontation

Early 1967

My infatuation with the footballer's wife reflected an optimism about life and my sexuality that seemed to have quieted the moral dilemmas created in Quairading. But beneath the surface, a yet-to-mature, volcanic rage was simmering. Its eruption would shock me.

I had just turned fifteen. I was coming home from the post office after a Saturday morning delivering telegrams. As I rounded the corner and headed down the side path towards the back gate, I saw Leunig's pale blue Falcon was parked out on the verge.

Rage tore itself loose, spewing up from the depths.

HE'S BACK! HOW DARE HE? HOW DARE HE! I was running by the time I reached the gate. I didn't have a plan.

Leunig was standing in the kitchen, which overlooked the side path, and saw me coming. As I flung open the gate, he rushed out the back door, ran across the back landing and leaped down the steps two at a time. He stopped in the middle of the bottom step, his feet wide apart, blocking my way. He was wearing his black trousers and a white shirt.

I stopped just inside the gate, only a few feet from him. I had grown because I was level with his face. His eyes were narrowed and squinting, darting left and right, checking me out. I stared at him, reading his expression. His eyes betrayed him.

'What are *you* doing here?' My voice shook, the 'you' laced with contempt. My heart pounded somewhere near my throat. The rage felt fire-red in my face.

Seconds passed in awkward silence, only the voice inside me was shouting.

He's afraid. Why is he here? Why did he rush out to stop me coming inside? How does he have the gall to come back? I thought I was rid of him forever.

'I've just been talking with your mother. Your parents are happy for me to take your brother away for the weekend.'

With this, his tone changed. The fear I'd sensed in him became a triumphant sneer. His face lifted the way that I knew, the irresistible authority in his chin. The raging voice in me wavered helplessly at his presumptuousness and his arrogance. He sucked me out of myself until there was nothing left, sick to the pit of my stomach with the feeling I would never be free of him.

'Which one?'

'Terry.'

Naming my next youngest brother unleashed a spasm of fury. Terry, the happy-go-lucky, gentle, uncomplicated, cuddly one. My Jabber mate. My only mate. My eyes shot at Leunig, boring into his pudgy face.

'If you dare touch him, I'll go to the police.' I was scared witless.

He was silent. His eyes went back to scanning. He was thinking. He turned and went inside.

I can't remember any of the next hours.

In Quairading, terrified of being sent to prison, I had not fantasised about being punished by the police. In my imagination, I'd been marched away by a secular authority administered by four men. The secret pact with Leunig had been forged with respect to my parents, not the police. The police belonged to the world outside the Church. They had no jurisdiction inside our religion or over the priests. They did not operate in the world of the Ten Commandments, or in the lists of sins, or even on the gravelled back roads of Quairading. In this stand-off with him, invoking the police was an instinctive, gut response, blurted out in panic; the only consequence I could muster of sufficient gravitas to potentially stop him. I had Normie Rowe's carnal knowledge charge to thank for this consciousness.

I'd always thought I was being protective of Terry. And I was, mostly. I understand now that I also did it to protect my secret. It was safe while the chronicle of abuse stayed with me. Despite the entrenched shame and the guilt of complicity, I had come to manage a life where it was contained enough to allow me to live. But it also had to stay there. Leunig abusing Terry would risk it being exposed. After the weekend, I didn't ask Terry if anything had happened. If nobody said anything, then my secret was safe. I had to believe he wasn't abused, because it would be my fault if he was, as I'd never warned anybody about Leunig.

14

The Honeysuckle Moment

1967

My home had become a home in name only, its place as a haven long lost. This confrontation with Leunig opened up those old wounds. The next wound, the night of my initiation into puberty, would bleed for many years.

Since withdrawing from the abuse in Quairading, curiosity about the facts of sex had gone underground. My self-imposed exile at school still precluded me from joining the jostling of boys whispering puberty's pleasures. The alternative, a healthy sex education for Catholics, was a contradiction in terms, both at school and at home. Given my father's Catholicism and Victorian prudery, my mother was the only option, but it was a bridge too far for both of us. In this vacuum, knowing nothing, I could not have anticipated or understood the moment. I was drifting off to sleep in my bunk bed when I was overwhelmed by the warm pleasance of ejaculation. Alarmed, imagining 'it' would be a steady stream like peeing, I rushed to the toilet. Instantly, I was dragged down into the deepest shame. It burst into my consciousness with a viciousness that stripped away any veneer of coping.

My mother, perhaps observing my late-night rush outside or perhaps intuitively, moved me to a separate bedroom. There I succumbed to obsessional nightly masturbation, trying to find the unknowable 'something' inferred by Leunig. Each time I swore that this was the last time, but I couldn't stop and often cried myself to a distressed sleep. Of its own accord, the swamp of guilt that had been laid down in Quairading now metamorphosed into pure shame. At first, I didn't know that that was its name, but the moment I did remains as vivid as the afternoon it occurred.

***

I was coming home from school, down the familiar pathway beside the house when I stopped outside the side gate, transfixed and unable to go through. I was staring at the honeysuckle creeper that climbed in a tangled skein across the trellis next to the gate. I could not go through the gate into the house, that repository of guilt and secrets and sexuality, that crucible of unresolvable moral dilemmas.

My entire consciousness was swamped in a cataclysmic shame. Every fibre of my body was so intrinsically and intractably riddled with shame, I knew I could never purge it. It was now my life. My mind flailed around, desperately trying to see beyond it, to grasp a future not submerged in this morass of shame. But nothing could remove it, nor anything new replace it. All I could see in my imagination was a swirling, opaque fog. The future had disappeared, consumed in the fog. The desolation and helplessness and nothingness of this vision was so overwhelming, I knew that my life as I'd known it was over. It had run its course. It was over.

The implications slowly sank in. If I could not imagine a future, what was there to live for? It was the moment of absolute despair. There was no God, no Christ, no parent, no friend, no possibility of redemption. It was terrifyingly lonely, and it bred an ominous dread. I would have to live in this grey nothingness for the rest of my life.

I'd been staring at the honeysuckle creeper all this time, and it has become the lifelong motif of the desolation of that realisation. I would come to know it as my 'honeysuckle moment'.

Eventually, I walked through the gate, up those steps and into the house.

In a paradoxical twist, the school chapel became my refuge. Every morning before school, I knelt in its emptiness and prayed to no-one in particular. It was a quest for solace and, in the way that being the only one in a church legitimises aloneness, it worked while I had that solitude. But outside, watching the groups of boys who had once been my peers, I experienced my isolation day after day.

I was standing outside the chapel one of these mornings, unable to move. The in-group of my class were chiacking on the lawn, playing keepings off with a tiny white football with a string attached. They scuffled and teased each other, strutted and swaggered brazenly like men. Some of them had started shaving. Some had their driver's licence. Not only did I feel alienated from them, but I also felt myself arrested in childhood. I would not have a future like they would. I would never mature to be like them.

My world disintegrated. In the term exams, I slumped to thirtieth out of forty in my year. Comments such as 'Very poor effort' appeared alongside failed subjects. My Maths score had slumped from fifty-six down to twenty-five. An eighty-seven on the French exam five months prior had become a forty. 'Very poor paper and term's work.' I was so humiliated I asked my mother if I could leave the Jesuit college and go to the local government high school. My father was not part of the discussion. She refused, not surprisingly, but didn't ask why or enquire what had gone wrong to get such awful marks. I could never have told her in any case. Mere survival required the suppression of all consciousness of the abuse and its aftermath. I was soon to encounter, though, the ruptures in her own life that might explain why she couldn't embrace my failure.

I was now angry at what my life had become. I'd been a top student and that had collapsed, along with what was left of my self-esteem. I'd had to endure the abuse on my own and had to stop it on my own. I would have to fix this disaster on my own, too.

At the beginning of 1967, a new Jesuit priest, Peter Quin, had arrived at the school. I rang and made an appointment. Quin, not knowing me from a bar of soap, was curious that I had come to see him of my own volition, especially given my disastrous marks. Where was the fuming parent behind this lazy boy? He was openly sceptical and cynical of my intentions when I told him I believed I was a much better student than the report indicated. Nevertheless, he established a mentoring program. He gave me a book to read, and thereafter a new one each week. They were adventure stories by Alistair MacLean and Hammond Innes and we discussed them in one-on-one sessions during the term. I embraced this new regime and looked forward to our meetings.

The results were dramatic. By the end of term two, I had climbed back to twelfth place in the class. In the essay exam, I had written a visually rich, imaginary story inspired by our childhood holiday rambles up to the racecourse in Goomalling. Quin, still obviously sceptical, accosted me the day after the exam.

'Your essay was very good. Where did you copy it from?' His mouth was set, his lips tight, his head inclined in accusation.

His words flicked like a whip, stinging as they arced across my face. He waited for an answer.

'I didn't … it's mine …'

The pauses were stunned and humiliated silences. Secretly, I was proud. I felt a smile inside. It balanced the stigma of being called a liar. In the term report, he commented, 'A good essay. Full of personal touches and humour.'

Quin was a new breed of Jesuit priest, worldly and pragmatic.

As Prefect of Studies, he was able to direct the curriculum and introduced sex education in our year, in place of the usual Religious Doctrine. It was helpful to hear and finally understand the mechanics of intercourse and the descriptions of a healthy, balanced sexual life. Pleasure in sex was openly discussed. I found that reassuring, even though shame still swam around me day and night. It never occurred to me to tell him about the abuse. Puberty had formed another shell around that secret.

My immaturity in Quin's classes reared its head often and I continued to ask silly, irrelevant questions. He almost sprinted towards me once, his voice hissing and gravelly, his eyes narrowed and piercing, 'You must be more mature!' He was passionate, impelling us towards our destiny as intelligent and forward-thinking adult men. He paced back and forth in front of the class, his fingers tightly bunched up in front, holding this imaginary thing we were to grasp and run with – maturity. This was our future. But I did not have a future. Subconsciously, I wanted whatever it was he was offering. Perhaps intuitively, I knew he was the only person that might be able to lead me there. And it would seem that the only way I knew how was to try to please him. Wanting to be liked was the only way that any sense of myself could be acknowledged. It frustrated him endlessly.

That year we also began dancing classes with the girls from nearby Loreto Convent. On Friday nights, the boys from several year groups arrived at the convent, swarming outside the hall, critiquing the girls, pretending courage. The doors opened and we filed in and stood nervously, snatching sideways glances at those we'd established as our favourites. The nuns, progressive by Catholic standards, maintained a relaxed oversight from the stage. Their folded arms and unmoving faces clearly declared the boundaries. I was the least likely target of their vigilance. Each week I simply looked forward to the chance to be with a girl.

The girls rotated in an inner circle and the boys in an outer until we were commanded to stop randomly at our next partner. Tongue-tied and awkward with the much-discussed girls, I enjoyed talking to those who had 'issues', according to the other boys – too tall, too curly, too plain or too shabbily dressed. I felt safe with these girls. We were the outliers.

The schoolyard was abuzz with who we would take to the school dance. Ann, my neighbour from across the road, would have been my choice, but I was too scared to ask her. I was surprised when she agreed to go to the dance with a boy I thought awkward, certainly another outsider. I could have had a chance. I invited one of the boarders, Sally, a quirky, somewhat anarchic country girl. Arrangements were made over the phone. Come the night of the dance, Mum drove me to collect her from the suburban hotel where she was staying for the weekend with her mother. I waited anxiously in the car across the road for what seemed hours, Mum placating me with an early attempt at mindfulness. 'Take a deep breath.'

Finally, Sally appeared down the stairs into the hotel foyer, dressed like the queen, her mother an aide-de-camp proudly by her side. A fluffy, white fur wrap enveloped a glittering sequined dress in which there appeared to be traces of the girl I'd danced with in class. Faux jewels dripped from every fixed point and a twisted, fragile beehive was topped with a tiara, the whole so high, she had trouble easing herself into the car. In dancing classes, she'd been casual, good fun and boundary-pushing. That suited me. But on the back seat beside me was a fragile concoction unable to move her lips or face for make-up. She daren't move a muscle lest the entire construction disintegrate. I looked out the rear window as we drove away in stilted silence. Her mother was waving hopefully.

Sally spent the night in the ladies, adjusting and tinkering, or talking with her friends at other tables. Timidly asked about the possibility of a dance, she carefully shook her head. In a way, I was relieved. Taking the lead was not a strength. Eating Cheezels, I listened to other boys' chatter about discreet mini-conquests. The night's failure, mired in adolescent angst, cemented the feeling I didn't have what it took to be a man. I didn't know it then, and it would be many years before it was named, but I was suffering from depression.

It was a word not talked about by anyone, and certainly not acknowledged in our happy family. But something must have been obvious to my mother because it was arranged for me to go to Goomalling to spend the two weeks of the upcoming holidays with Uncle Paddy and Aunty Grace. They had leased some of their land to an oil company to build a roadhouse, and had become the proprietors of a restaurant and petrol station.

The building had just been completed. The site was built up and terraced into a series of platforms on what had once been the tennis court where, as youngsters, we had played our games. The terraces needed to be retained and lined to prevent erosion. Uncle Paddy borrowed a small truck for the fortnight and each morning we drove out to a nearby quarry and collected granite rocks. Working methodically and carefully, we placed the stones in interlocking patterns, forming battered, dry-stone retaining walls against the sloping soil of the terraces. Uncle Paddy let me maneuver the truck around, turning and backing up to unload the stone at the next section of terrace. He didn't ask where I'd learned to drive.

'Back her up, man. Hold her there.' He hitched up his flannel trousers.

I liked the physical work and the feeling of accomplishment. I assumed an ownership over the project and gave him advice on how best to build the batters. He quietly let me have the lead.

'You're the boss, man!' He talked to me as an adult, all the while his eyes twinkling.

At the end of one of the terraced sections, he needed to build a loading platform. We had a robust discussion on how best to make it. I'd watched how reinforcement was used on building sites, so I had firm ideas. He acquiesced and agreed to build it my way. The platform was a success.

I was deeply satiated by our joint labour, and by Aunty Grace's fussing and cooking by the wood stove at night. And I'd had two weeks of distraction from my ever-present shame. The retaining walls are still there on the terraced slopes, fifty-five years old, monuments to resilience and Uncle Paddy's Irish wisdom, and a temporary antidote to depression.

The next school term, Margie, our Goomalling 'cousin', came to stay with us. She had been boarding at the Presentation Sisters convent in Mosman Park and needed time away from the pressure of rules in order to study for her final exams. She had always felt like a sister to us boys and, now living with us, it was like having a real sister in our family. I felt very close to her.

15

Another Teacher in Our Kitchen

1967

Dennis had been one of Terry's form teachers at the Jesuit college, one of a growing number of lay men at the school. He lived nearby and, many afternoons after school, would drop in for a cup of tea. My mother welcomed him, as any teacher who taught one of her sons was highly regarded. When she wasn't home though, he would let himself in the back door, put the kettle on and make himself a pot of tea. My father was never there.

One afternoon, earlier in my high school years, he was standing in the kitchen leaning against the stove as was his manner, his arms folded across his tight white shirt, his face twisted. He had probably asked my opinion on something.

'You boys are philistines.' He threw the words at me.

I didn't know what the word meant, but I felt its insult. I resented his presumptuousness, his condescension, his derision at naive comments, his belittling, sarcastic retorts.

'Think for yourself. Where do you get such stupid ideas from?'

It was teacherly banter, he would say, to elevate our consciousness. But my compulsion to be liked overruled intuition and I was drawn into his sphere, simultaneously feeling angry with myself that I uttered such mindless nothings, while groping for something of substance to say to appear worthy of his approval.

Later in 1967, careers counsellors had come to school to talk to our year. The nihilism of my 'honeysuckle moment' was an aching, living presence. I lived one day to the next, struggling with the nothingness, unable to even imagine a future, let alone the ambition of a career. Exam results continued to bellow 'abject failure'. Though demoralised and angry, I still put on my happy face for Dennis.

He was standing in his usual proprietorial position in the kitchen, his arms folded, his legs casually crossed, his dark blue trousers tight and bulging in front, his pointy, black shoes angled outwards like daggers. The electric kettle bubbled away behind him. His penetrating, dark eyes were hard and remorseless.

'So, what are you going to do then?' His tone was laced with contempt.

Joe had started studying engineering at university. I had an interest in cars and machines, and I understood retaining walls, so perhaps I had a genuine leaning towards becoming an engineer. Or maybe following Joe was all I could conjure up in my vacuum of ambition.

'I'm thinking of doing engineering.'

'You're just a mindless copycat,' he sneered, 'It's typical of younger brothers. It shows how unimaginative you are.'

I squirmed at the toxicity of his scorn. If the idea of engineering was the foundation of a future, it became shrapnel in this fusillade from his acid tongue. In his perverse way, though, he was right. I was fifteen and the ability to discriminate or act decisively for myself had been paralysed. But his approach could never have guided me to a place where I might have discovered some solid ground. While Peter Quin was, by this time, a positive mentoring adult, Dennis was the destructive opposite.

When he later moved to a house on the outskirts of the city, his afternoon visits stopped. But now came the invitations to help him work in his new, semi-rural garden. Again, I did not have the wherewithal to explain a refusal to my parents, and still craved external approval. I went there alone and laboured in his overgrown garden.

Then came the news from school. Dennis had been arrested for molesting a youth.

My family were sitting at the dining table, the evening meal not yet wound up. Dad cleared his throat, the call to attention for something important. When there was a suitable silence, he began.

'Dennis was in hospital for a small procedure. He apparently got to know a lad when they were sharing a hospital room. The lad invited himself back to Dennis's place. Now he's gone to the police and reported Dennis, saying he'd been molested. The lad is obviously lying. He's trying to blackmail Dennis.' There was no elaboration on what 'molested' meant.

Dad was emphatic that nothing had happened. Dennis had been set up. In the tradition of family discussions about injustice, especially after Adderley's infamous exile, my brothers and I now railed at this new instance. It animated our dinner conversations, how easily your reputation could be ruined by malicious accusations, and blackmail to boot.

Later, Dad told us a date had been set for a trial. Having accepted my father's position that Dennis had been set up, this news seemed a contradiction. Why would there be a trial when it was so clear that the boy was lying and trying to blackmail him? Dad explained that Dennis had asked him to be a character referee. After dinner one night, he curiously read out his reference. I remember one phrase: 'We have always trusted Dennis implicitly with all our five boys.'

He could never have known otherwise since he was never there when Dennis was around. Neither had he asked me or any of my brothers if anything had happened.

Dennis was given a good behaviour bond and moved away.

16

Our House

1967–1968

The tension in our parents' marriage had become more transparent. Dad's lack of affection and empathy, and his unreasonable extracurricular activities in service to the Church, continued to infuriate Mum. But it was his passive 'always right' posture, and his denial of her feelings, that made her anger finally boil over. That forbidden anger. He would then censure her for it, the implied criticism that she was not all-suffering and self-controlled like him. Trapped in this dilemma, she compensated by maintaining a clenched-jaw façade of her marriage as a happy one and, in the absence of a shared intimacy with him, she turned to her sons. We became her sole raison d'être. It had been nurturing when we were young, but as it morphed into needing emotional fulfillment, it became a double-edged sword.

Late one afternoon, I came into the kitchen as she was standing by the sink. The syrupy, yellow light of the setting sun slanted through the window, glowing on the side of her face. She was clearly distressed and muttering to herself in a not-so-soft voice. I went towards her, but stopped and stood apart, not wanting to have to take on the burden of what was troubling her. She didn't turn around but addressed me as though I was an apparition.

'You don't notice me. You boys ignore me just like your father does. You treat me like a servant. It pains me to think one day you'll become a husband like your father.'

She was right. The spasm of guilt cut to the quick, but it quickly turned to anger. She was criticising and blaming me. Yet her pain was so palpable, compassion overrode my self-centredness and resentment, and I stayed by the stove, separate from her but close enough that she could construe my presence as a willingness to hear her complaint.

'You have to practise being a good husband. When you come home from school, you have to give me a kiss, hug me and ask me how my day has been.'

Despite my hostility, and my resistance to being told how to behave, I didn't want to become a husband like Dad. So I followed the regime for months, entering into it with a genuine sense that it would make me a better person. Every afternoon after school, I went into the kitchen and put my arms around her. She turned her head, and I gave her a kiss on the cheek. Our eyes didn't meet.

'What have you been doing today?' I don't remember her answers.

After each perfunctory enactment of de facto husband, I retreated to my room, deeply resenting being controlled and unable to 'speak', especially as I did not feel anything like love for her. It was a visceral reaction to the control. First it had been the priest. Now it was my mother. I pitied her though, and her scheme had the opposite effect of reinforcing my feeling of alienation in the family, separate from her yet inextricably entwined in her unhappiness. This drama continued to play out for most of our lives.

Joe, now at university, rediscovered the self-directed, strong-willed boy who had roamed free when we were young. He embraced university life with vigour and more than once tempted disaster. He challenged the authoritarian, Catholic family ethos to the core. Mum charged Dad with controlling his behaviour, but he had bolted through the gap under the gate. Joe, also resistant to being controlled, did not retreat sullenly down the passageway to his room like me. He bucked. They'd never had the tools to harness the creative side of his restless energy and, falling back on their brand of antiquated authority – and the forbidding of anything negative – was never going to work either. Rather, it impelled him further afield to find whatever it was that stirred inside him. Now they were at their wits' end.

The family phone was on a small table in the hallway outside my bedroom. I couldn't avoid overhearing my mother's frequent calls to her close friend Pam, complaining bitterly about my father's failings as a husband and his ineffectual efforts to control Joe. After an hour of desperate conversation, the receiver clattered down and she ran to her bedroom, sobbing inconsolably. I could not insulate myself from her anguish, and though a part of me was scornful of her 'weakness', I still went and sat on the edge of her bed, which was squashed against the wood-veneer wardrobe where my father's suits hung in full view because the latch was broken and the door swung open. Holding her hand, I listened to her rage, pitifully offering excuses and consolation, all the while staring at my father's suits and avoiding her eyes. I never questioned where he was on those evenings.

I was helpless myself, thrashing around in the collateral damage of not having any sense of my own feelings, so I recoiled at the vehemence of hers. I reacted and defended my father, though I was ambivalent about him, too. I thought that she was the unreasonable one. But I held her hand and she clung onto my arm, her fingers digging like talons, until her grip went limp. 'Go. Do your homework.'

I returned to my room confused, anger mixed with scorn and pity, a very troubled empathy. On the one hand, I didn't care what happened to her, but at the same time I was deeply troubled by her pain, thinking that I was the only one who seemed to care.

The previous year I had started writing poetry, compelled to express in some form what was happening, both in my family and in my day. Some poems described beauty that I'd glimpsed. More were nihilistic. Most were of the desolation and alienation I experienced around my mother.

One night, shouts echoed from the kitchen. She screamed. A pot banged. Footsteps thumped on the lino. There was a blinding crash. Then another. And another. Shattered china was hitting the floor, tinkling like a thousand thin bells. Edging down the passageway, I peered around the door. Scattered shards speckled the floor and amidst them my mother sobbed, her eyes flashing red, black and wild. I tiptoed back to my room and wrote an emotionally detached and unsympathetic poem describing the sounds of the shards as they sprayed across the floor.

Another night, I heard her rush out to the landing after screaming for several minutes, slamming the back door behind her, like a cannon exploding. The car engine roared outside on the verge. There was a deafening crash. The engine sputtered, then roared back into life and faded away into the night.

'I remember that night,' Terry told me, fifty years later. 'She rushed past me, out the back door, screaming she wanted to kill herself.'

17

Matriculation

1968

I finished the previous school year in twelfth place, but a mark of thirty in a Maths exam underscored the fragility of the recovery. I was advised to have Maths tutorials. Tutorials were for the not-so-bright boys, and I knew I did not deserve such failure and humiliation. Nevertheless, I began my final year, having just turned sixteen.

The school dance was early in the term and I decided to invite a girl from Methodist Ladies' College who lived five houses up the street. Ali and I sometimes caught the bus to school together, and several times her dad had picked me up as he drove past the bus stop. She was softly spoken and sincere, and I liked her. With just a week until the dance, I plucked up the courage and phoned.

'I'll have to ask my father.' The following night she called back. 'He said I can't go.'

I was angry with her father, but secretly relieved. I was not going to have to take responsibility for inviting a non-Catholic. I concocted an excuse for the few who asked.

At the same time, the Maths tutorials began. The tutor parked his Studebaker outside my window and, for most of the session, I stared out at its peculiar shape. The abstract x2 + y2 being coerced into my consciousness had lost all meaning. My heart had lost its moorings. This aimlessness, just going through the motions and unable to rouse any enthusiasm for life, was another symptom of my depression. I felt sorry for the tutor.

I dropped to eighteenth place in the class after the term exams, the 'mocks'. I failed Chemistry, a subject that had so far survived the carnage. I also failed Latin. Back in 1964, the year free of abuse and before I was taken to Quairading, I had been dux of the Latin class. I told my mother I wanted to withdraw from it to concentrate on passing Chemistry. Again, on my own, I arranged a meeting with the Rector. Latin was synonymous with the 'intelligentsia', so the Rector's disappointment at letting down the school's expectations only added more shame to my already bursting swag. I had once been a responsible, hard-working and successful student, yet even in the face of immaturity and abject failure, I still wanted to uphold these attributes. Now I was angry at what I had been reduced to. I was acting from self-preservation and would do whatever it took to salvage my education. In the final exams for matriculation, I got an average pass in Chemistry. I was pleased I'd made that decision for myself. I scrabbled a low-average pass in the other subjects when they should have been a doddle.

The results were only sufficient to be awarded an Advanced Education Scholarship to a technical college or the newly formed Institute of Technology in Perth. I had not won a scholarship to university. The trajectory of my Jesuit education had been a failure. With no ambition or even an idea of a career, the future wallowed formless. Someone suggested architecture. 'You've always liked watching houses being built.'

My mother arranged a careers counselling appointment in the city. After a day of exhaustive testing, I was told architecture was the least suitable profession. I don't remember what I had shown aptitude in or what careers were suggested. I had come close to winning the essay prize at school, but that wasn't a matriculation subject and wasn't considered an indicator of a future. I knew I was intelligent and deserved something of substance, and I had always felt destined to study at tertiary level. In the vacuum of ambition, and against the advice of the counsellor, I enrolled in Architecture at the Perth Technical College. At least it was called a profession.

Part Two

18

The Perth Technical College

1969–1970

The Perth Technical College was a collection of imposing heritage buildings on St Georges Terrace, in the heart of the city. Behind its façades, rows of prefabricated, corrugated iron huts crowded together in twisted and rough lanes down the hillside. In one, rusty and hot, was my first-year studio. During breaks in the nine-to-five, five-day-a-week routine, I wandered aimlessly around the city. I peered into buildings and arcades and shops, down seedy alleyways and back lanes with chainmesh fences and locked gates and dented rubbish bins, slipways to other seedy lanes. I was looking for something. I could not know that it was a search for my lost self.

Wally Greenham, the studio tutor in that basic hut, was a free-thinking spirit, the first I had encountered. He was also a Japanophile and had a sensibility for materials and simplicity that he brought to his teaching, challenging the conservative brick-and-tile status quo in thoughtful and artistic ways. I was intrigued, without having any understanding of what it was he represented.

Men, and a few women, of every social background were at 'The Tech'. It was a new world that, alongside Wally, soon drew me beyond the culture of my upbringing. Although still feeling like an outsider, there was space to begin discovering something of myself. Leaving the Jesuits and entering this secular world struck an optimistic nerve that foreshadowed freedom. After a late-night social event at Wally's Japanese-inspired house early in this first year, I arrived home in the wee hours of the morning to find my mother sitting on the back steps, sick with worry. She berated me with a passion. Humiliated, I probably defended myself against her realistic concerns. But in this new world, away from that angst-riddled household, I had discovered legitimate freedom and it offered a future that roared loud with self-worth.

When I easily passed the final exams at The Tech that first year, I felt encouraged. I applied for and won a cadetship with the Commonwealth Department of Works that paid a weekly wage. The terms involved a five-year post-study indenture to the Department, the idea of which was so paralysing, I saved the entire next year's wage, sure I would withdraw at year's end, as I had no passion for anything architectural. The money saved could be refunded to the Department.

Until this year, Mum had never had any paid work outside our home. I encouraged her to follow up an advertisement for an occupational therapy assistant role at a nearby disabled children's special needs residential centre. She got the job and went on to work there for the next twenty or so years, becoming a second mother to some of the residents. In a sense, it rescued her from her depression. She carved a meaningful new life for herself that legitimised and lauded her role as a mother, allowing her to express her natural kindness and generosity. The new job meant she was no longer isolated in her thankless, unappreciated and unpaid home duties. Her ethos of equality in the family re-emerged and as a result, changes were wrought.

'First one home peels and puts the potatoes on.' She hired an ironing lady first, and then a cleaner who came once a week. Mrs Whyatt became a fixture in our lives, knocking on the doors of late risers, scolding the untidy and turning her nose up at beery smells. How refreshing to be pulled into line with a dry wit and a wry smile, and not judgment or criticism.

I was let go as 'de facto husband'.

The city now began to reveal its spirit and, with the unfettered imaginations of my studio cohort, I worked away at loosening the family strings. We started frequenting a pool hall every lunchtime and, guiltily, I tagged along into the gloom of the city's underbelly.

Next door was an auction house and, at the one-hour lunchtime auction, goods were bought and sold at machine-gun speed. We bought an old sofa on wheels for two dollars and pushed it down King Street, taking turns riding on its plush, wide cushions. Piled high with waving youths, the sofa careered across St Georges Terrace, bringing traffic to a standstill. We hauled it up the stairs to the common room. It had little to do with architecture, but I was having fun. It infected my mood for study, and my results that second year were exceptional. My inner voice re-emerged with a long-lost, affirming clarity, vindicating my intelligence.

19

University

1971–1973

I kept the Commonwealth cadetship, paid my parents a year's board and bought a car with the balance. Another student encouraged me to apply to university for third-year entry to the Architecture course. I was selected for one of twenty places. I had finally reached university. I quickly relished the intellectual rigour and discovered a particular interest in heritage buildings.

For the first time, I began to experience friendship and to live a life further apart from my family. Home became merely a place to sleep. I shared nothing of importance with my parents and little with my brothers. I had no idea what they were doing or who they had become, a cruel fact I was to realise fifty years later when Terry apprised me of what these years had held for him.

He had come last in his class in Year Eleven and had to repeat the year. Humiliated, he used to get off the bus at the Ocean Beach Hotel after school, pull a jumper over his school uniform and, being eighteen, go in and have a few beers. He'd then walk home. What I also didn't know was that our other Jabber mate, Matty, had started going 'off the rails'. A few years later, I learned he committed suicide only a few metres from the rat-infested shed that had been our clubhouse. For the three days before he shot himself, he kept coming over to our house and asking Dad where Terry was. Terry, having struggled after he left school, had gone bush.

'He's gone away, working out on a remote sheep station.'

'When will he be home?'

'I've no idea. We have no means of contacting him, and we haven't heard from him in a long while.'

***

The Department of Works sent me to Canberra with other cadets from Western Australia during the summer vacation of 1971. Over the Christmas and New Year break, we travelled up to Sydney and performed the rites of passage in Kings Cross. Deep underground in a club with a pink 'X' flickering above the entrance, we huddled among a seething herd of loud, young men. I hung back guiltily as the throng jostled at the edge of the runway. Like the boxing tents at the Royal Show, it was a meat market. A young woman teased her way down the platform to catcalls and howling and cries of 'Get it off!'. She pushed her pelvis towards the leering heads and, accepting a twenty-dollar note tucked into a very private part, she let one tousled head lean in. A roar went up. The boy-faced victor turned and shouted back into the throng, 'I did it, Spider. I did it!'

The time away from home softened my feelings towards my mother, and when I was due to leave Canberra, I invited her to meet me in Melbourne so we could drive home together across the Nullarbor. She was ecstatic, but on the journey, alone with me, she slowly reverted to her possessive self. It was subtle to begin with.

'You're lucky you still have your faith. So many have let it go.' That was the first part of her mantra. Then it shifted to the secular, to her. We were standing in the roadhouse at Mundrabilla, halfway across the Nullarbor, in the middle of the desert. She was holding my arm, like we were on a date, but firmly as though I might try to escape. She was reclaiming me as her de facto husband with such a vengeance, I recoiled in an onrush of déjà vu.

***

The next summer, I took leave from the Department to travel with a mate, Don, for a three-month odyssey through Europe on a student's wage. After a month in London, he and I set off for the Continent with Eurail Passes and a budget of five dollars a day. Don, a dedicated architecture student, had a long list of places to see and, previously oblivious of these wonders, I tagged along happily. We travelled at night, sometimes sleeping on the train, so that we would arrive in cities at dawn. We then wandered through the day, breathless in Gothic cathedrals, entranced in galleries and medieval city streets, traipsing down misty, cold, cobbled alleys and country lanes to find these architectural icons. We slept in youth hostels and in waiting rooms, ate cheese and ham on chunks of bread, and paella and risotto in cheap restaurants.

I kept a daily diary in a carbon copy receipt book and, every week, tore out the pages and posted them home. As in the previous year, I was comfortable relating to my family from a distance. Away from the angst and my mother's possessiveness, I again discovered charm and delight and adventure, so the diary was cheerful, passionate about the discoveries, the people we met, the places we stayed and the food we ate. Mum had her friend Pam type up the pages as they arrived back in Perth. After three months, it had become a substantial travel manuscript.

I hoisted my backpack, heavy with gifts and dirty clothes, onto my bed when I arrived home. Mum stood in the doorway, clutching the typed manuscript to her chest. Neither my brothers nor my father were around.

'Thank you. Thank you. Thank you. This is the most treasured gift.'

Travelling had offered a world free to roam, to be myself and write. It was intoxicating. I had rediscovered a childhood magic, unencumbered by rules or religion. I had a voice, and it was in the written word. It had tumbled out freely when I was away.

Now, standing by my backpack, the tone of her statement stung me. In 'owning' my manuscript, it felt like she was trying to own me. There was no room for me. And I bitterly resented it. Even as I grappled with the guilt, I was angry at the resurgence of this one-way nature of our relationship. I was now an adult, yet I had no voice with her nor any power. I could only feel that she was sucking those words back out of me.

I understand now that she too would have wanted to be free, to roam, to experience the world's marvels away from her responsibilities and her troubled marriage, and that vicariously she could do it joyously through my writing.

***

My final year at university in 1973 was spent mostly in the studio and the library, only returning home late at night to sleep. My thesis was an exploration of the natural world as it impacted architecture and urban design, particularly the aspect of topography, and I used much of the material I had photographed in Europe to underpin my work. It would prefigure a turning point in my life.

20

Bound Upon a Course

1974

After graduating, I joined a large architectural firm in the city. They were generous giving me experience and I learned the basics of the profession, for which I was grateful. But the working day was dissected into fifteen-minute slices with Musak piped through the office. When the music stopped, at five-fifteen, there was a mass exodus down the stairs. The staff seemed passionless. My poetry and short stories began to describe the office as a prison, five-fifteen the moment of night release.

Serendipitously, I picked up a book at our local library, *Bound Upon a Course*, by the Irish scholar and writer John Stewart Collis. I stood at the bookshelf and read the first few chapters before I took the book out. I was captivated by the trajectory of his life through his years of scholarship, as a conscientious objector during the Second World War, and his subsequent rural life of solitude, reflection and writing.

I had been called up during the Vietnam war and had my national service deferred until I graduated from university. By 1973, the Whitlam government had been elected and both 'Nashos' and the Commonwealth Cadetship indenture system had been abolished, so I was free of both commitments. I identified with Collis in more ways than one. I photocopied page 202 and pinned it above my desk. It has travelled with me ever since, the last sentence underlined: 'It occurred to me that the answer to the riddle of the world is to be able to *see* the world; and that instead of worrying about salvation we should recognize that vision *is* salvation.' (1)

Collis prescribed a surrendering to an unequivocal trust to

experience the mystery and wonder that unfolded in each moment, an optimistic surrender to circumstance and the fulfilment that came from being fully conscious, mindfulness before it had that name. During my travels, exploring and writing in Europe the year before, I had already, unknowingly, been following these principles and had been awakened by them. Conscious surrender to the creative stream in everything was the key to the vacuum of ambition in which I still existed.

It was as though his writing was addressing me personally. I ordered and read all his books. *The Worm Forgives the Plough* and *Down to Earth* were collections of his observations while living a semi-rural life and working as a farm labourer in lieu of active service during the Second World War. He wrote of a connectedness to the natural world and, with a rush of identification, I could imagine and trust myself in such a future, however unknown. It was my first conscious feeling of release from the nihilism of my honeysuckle moment, which had permeated the previous seven years.

In the expanded optimism and freedom encouraged by Collis's world view, I began to go to art-house movies. One was Ingmar Bergman's film, *Scenes from a Marriage*. I was dismayed at the depictions of marital hypocrisies, chauvinism and denials of the woman's feelings, conflict after conflict, so familiar from my childhood. In one scene, after an unresolved confrontation with her impassive and unyielding husband, Liv Ullmann's character agitatedly swept the floor, lifted a rug and swept the dirt underneath. It had a profound impact.

Mum was standing at the sink in the kitchen, her back to the door. She was furiously scrubbing, her bobbed hair shaking back and forth. Something was wrong. I leaned against the doorjamb, well apart. In hindsight, it was not a good moment to choose to discuss the film. She half-turned to listen as I described in detail the circumstances that led to Liv Ullmann's housewife sweeping the dirt under the rug.

'You should take Dad to see it.'

Ironically, I wanted them to be open and honest with each other, assured that telling the truth would make her life better. In my self-centred empathy, I had no understanding of her fragile boundaries or my father's intractability. And I had forgotten the golden rule in our family – to name or express discontent was forbidden. Were she to agree with me would be an admission of the failure of her marriage. I could not have anticipated that, given what I'd listened to in her many long nights of anguish, she would now feel criticised.

She turned, her face drawn tight, her eyes coal-dark, bruised recesses, her arms hard against her side, fists clenched like she was plummeting downwards.

'We're a happy family here. Don't bring your unhappiness around here. If that's how you feel, you can leave.'

There was no need to hit me. Her words did the punching.

You misunderstand me. I'm talking about you and Dad, not me. I'm offering you help, a film to show him up, a strategy to get to him to change, to heal your marriage. My inner voice pleaded with her in silence. I wanted to help.

'I'll never marry. Marriage is a farce.'

I spat it out, in equal and opposite fury. I was shocked to hear myself. Where had that come from? I'd never been overtly angry with her before.

'Well, you can always live like Uncle Steve.'

He was one of my father's brothers, a confirmed bachelor, living what looked to me like a lonely, self-centred life. He, like my father, was similarly stricken with a paralytic inability to express feelings. He boarded with one of their widowed sisters. He only ever talked about cricket, golf or bowls, and then in muttered, critical tones, a bit like Dad – that sense of superiority that nobody could do it as well as he.

'I'll never live like Uncle Steve!' I stormed off down the passageway.

I had no idea what I was saying. I had never articulated the thought before, that Catholic marital options were black and white only. I had just alluded to another colour. A dissenting voice was not possible. It was the beginning of the end.

We had been happy as young children and that had probably carried my mother in her early years of unhappiness with my father. But things had changed. Our relationship had been compromised, and I was as vulnerable and unconsciously trapped inside my secret as she was inside her marriage. Neither of us could know the way out of our dilemmas towards each other and, without the truth, we would both just keep jousting with air.

I shudder now at my cold-heartedness in the face of her fragile mental health, but at the time it was everyone for themselves. Without understanding anything of my own position, I had reverted to survival mode and she saw this as treason. The tenuous thread that bound me to the family gave way. I was on my own again. It was only a matter of time before living at home became untenable. When the time came, there were no goodbyes, just relief as I fled.

21

The Share House

1974–1975

During the last two years at university, several students in my faculty had formed a folk-blues band, often jamming in the studio as we worked away. The band matured to eventually play regular gigs at venues across the city. I liked their music and followed them wherever they played. Affirmed by their generosity, I'd begun to accept invitations to meals at their share house. It was a lively forum, and their house gradually became a haven, free of emotional baggage. At first, I felt like an interloper, a fraudulent bystander, a child among adults. I had no inner authority or template of trust in friendship, but I grew into a life with them, and with that came a legitimacy about belonging. There were three architectural students, an English scholar, a public servant and an arts coordinator among them. One was Jewish. One was a very ex-Catholic. It was a mixed-gender house, and several had partners who often stayed over. These couples argued freely and openly, discussed feelings and expressed negativity and got upset with each other … and then got over it. I was an onlooker to functioning relationships.

In long evenings over shared meals, talking about poetry, philosophy, music and literature, I discovered I had opinions and thoughts. People listened. No-one criticised or was sarcastic. They were supportive, encouraging, positive.

Six months into my new working life in the architectural firm, barely a month after the Bergman incident, the group invited me to take up a spare room. I moved out of home at twenty-two, the first of my siblings. The relief was so overwhelming that

I did not have any contact with my parents or my brothers for several months afterwards, even though the move was only a few kilometres to the next suburb.

Years later, I came to understand that, metaphorically, I had left home long before and had been living there as an outsider for twelve years. Despite my father being the initial and continuing source of my mother's pain, it was her criticisms, her possessiveness and her attempts at controlling me that had turned her into the enemy. What I could not comprehend at the time was that it was who she had become – the silencer of my attempts to forge my own truth – that I was escaping, not my family. I risked nothing in leaving and the exhilaration and feeling of liberation was proof. However, the collateral damage in my escape was the loss of the possibility of a deserving thread of camaraderie with my brothers and my father.

In leaving home, I also unequivocally left the Catholic Church. I never again went into any church in an act of faith. I still loved the Mass and had been co-opted onto the Cottesloe Parish Council in the previous two years. I had become interested in the liturgy in the post-Vatican II climate and wished to discuss this at the last meeting I ever attended. The parish priest at the time, Father Robert Healy, only wanted to talk about raising money. He treated my interest with condescension. My experience with Healy made me realise there was no longer a place for me in the Church as I'd come to experience it. The sexual abuse did not consciously figure in my decision. The share house – with its secular values, warmth, laughter and genuine friendship – had supplanted the authoritarian values of the Church and my need for a place of solace.

I'd discovered an intoxicating new life in the physical world, in the sense John Stewart Collis had described. I never once felt the guilt that ex-Catholics who are lapsed often express (such a judgmental and possessive word, 'lapsed', that one is still 'in' the club but not paying their dues). Rather, it was the throwing off of a sticky and tangled yoke; of a Church that had become a place of business, unsafe and unwelcoming; of a Church that was inextricably entwined in my mother's grief, and so much to blame for the unhappiness and lack of fulfilment in our family; of a Church that had allowed and sanctioned the source of my still-buried trauma.

Two months later, having made no contact with my family, I came down with a flu and was bedridden for over a week. I never found out how he heard, but Dad came to visit me, the only time anyone from my family visited the share house during the year I was there. He was shown to my room. He stood in the doorway, holding up a can of Heinz tomato soup.

'I thought you might need some nourishment, fella.'

I was deeply touched. Our relationship had always been practical and superficial; about cricket and football scores, about work, about the weather, about farmers and their crops, about events. It had never been about feelings. This can of soup was his unconditional love, and it told me that my absence from, and apparent rejection of, the family had not diminished his caring. This was the man I'd naively defended at my mother's bedside. But my warmth towards him lasted barely a minute. He leaned over the bed, lowered his voice conspiratorially and covered his mouth.

'Mum doesn't know I've come to see you.' His visit was to be a secret.

I was impressed that in his love he could spirit a can of soup from their pantry cupboard and sneak out to visit me, but appalled at what he was admitting about his marriage. I was more shocked though to infer the extent of Mum's anger about my departure, and it put her possessiveness into perspective.

I could not have known that there would be no half-measure in leaving. My need for what turned out to be a complete and irreversible rupture was intuitive; it was enough to have escaped intact.

In my own compromised way, I had tried to care about her when I was at home. But I had fled to protect my individuality, the self that Collis had alluded to, which was expanding rapidly to fill this new world. Much later I came to see how monumental her pain was at my abandonment of her. She was left to live in the vacuum of my father's lack of intimacy and, more significantly, in the unconscious fallout from the many years of betrayals.

***

The musicians among my housemates were the highlight band at a dance being held at the annual York Fair in September 1974. Their funky, bluesy music was irresistible, but for now I was sitting it out on the straw-bale bleachers, people-watching with one of my housemates, Frank. There were two young women also sitting it out farther along our row. I was entranced by the closest one and kept turning and not-so-coyly staring at her. I nudged Frank.

'Let's ask those two girls to dance.'

He nodded in his laconic way.

'I'll take the dark-haired one closest to us. You happy with the other one?'

It was a rhetorical question. We climbed down from the bleachers and went up to the girls, the dark-haired one and her friend. Louise and Nola introduced themselves and happily joined us on the dance floor.

Louise and I danced and talked the rest of the night in an exhilarated outpouring of shared feelings about family, travelling, music, our new lives as professionals and our new homes away from our parents. Unused to this brazen method of meeting, I didn't have the presence of mind to get her phone number. The next morning, serendipitously seeing her walking along the main street, I shyly asked her for it, then rang her at her work the next week and we met for lunch.

One of the women in my share house had taught me to cook an authentic spaghetti bolognaise. I cooked one for Louise on our fourth date, before we went to the art-house movie *A Swedish Love Story*. It was a positive film about relationships and young love, the opposite of Bergman's palette of discord and marital hypocrisy. Sitting on the wooden back steps at the share house afterwards, the evening air was warm and still, and we were chatting comfortably about the movie. The warmth and trust inherent in the sex in the film seemed to give me a licence.

'I was sexually abused when I was young. By my parish priest.'

I hadn't planned to tell her. It just came out, calmly and without affect, surprising since it was the first time I had told anyone. She listened quietly and didn't react. Since we'd danced, I had felt a joy and an immediate trust that Louise reciprocated. It foreshadowed loyalty and an intimate friendship. It allowed me a door I could open away from the shame of the abuse.

Our life together was to be a long road from that moment, and it would not be easy. I had no compass with which to navigate the waters of relationships and intimacy, and I had never witnessed anything in my childhood home like what I was feeling, nor had it ever been described to me. I did not have the words to name it. I was swept away by an unbridled love. The anticipation of seeing Louise eliminated the rest of the world. She introduced me to classical music and hearing Handel's *Messiah* in the new Perth Concert Hall was like climbing Mount Everest to my ears. We cooked for each other, we went to art house movies, we disappeared for weekends camping, exploring the forests and the beaches in the South West. We sailed to Rottnest Island on the little yacht I'd bought, singing songs as we skimmed in and out of the back bays before turning back and sailing headlong home on the sea breeze, saturated in spray. The afternoon sun behind me reflected in her eyes, shining with exhilaration. We talked into the early hours. We slept together. We enjoyed the dangers of experimenting.

I did not take her to see my family for quite some time. Louise belonged in my new life and intuitively, I felt its fragility and did not want to risk exposing her to my mother, whose possessiveness and ever-present toxicity I feared. I could not identify the feeling then, but it was her anger I was really afraid of, and its capacity to silence me if I tried to assert myself. I did not want my mother to own Louise, too. That she was not Catholic was immaterial.

As all-consuming as these early months were, inevitably I hit multi-faceted roadblocks. The absence of a family model of intimacy precluded an understanding of its mechanics, of its give and take. And, as a consequence of my family's forbidding of negativity, I had no words to know or hold difficult feelings. The trust and emotional resilience that might have underpinned them had died in the sacristy. Louise merely expressing discomfort, or countering something I'd said, was enough to trigger a reaction. Perceiving it as blame or criticism, like my father, I became defensive. In turn, she felt I was trying to control and silence her feelings. Her honesty was frightening. Stung by her angry response, I would withdraw in sullen, angry silence. But I did not have any words for, nor could I identify, the anger. And I did not know the meaning of an apology. Louise would withdraw in sadness and confusion while I felt overwhelmed by the intensity and rawness of failure and loss.

The days following these episodes were immersed in grief. When we would tentatively approach each other again, I was relieved it wasn't over and wanted intimacy immediately. Louise, for her part, wanted me to understand what had happened and to acknowledge the root of the rupture. But the tools I'd brought to our relationship were ancient and abused. I was taking baby steps as an adult, learning not to defend the indefensible. When time resolved our rift, we experienced a rush as our feelings were rekindled.

Louise was a free spirit, mercifully unencumbered by the folds of medieval Catholicism that enveloped my family, even though she had been reared in a strict Methodist household. Eventually, I did take her to meet my family. I wasn't sure which was more confronting for them: her Protestant upbringing; her modern, feminist, independent views that she was comfortable expressing; or the fact that we clearly had an intimate relationship I was keeping separate from them. I had stepped outside the black-and-white Catholic mould into colour. My mother just tolerated Louise; she still wanted access to me.

Louise had long planned a trip to London and, barely six months after we'd met, she left her job and her own share house and set off with a friend. Inspired by her leap to freedom, I soon quit the oppressive architectural firm and took a job at the West Perth Markets in a John Stewart Collis fantasy of being in touch with nature. Without her though, I was bereft. The three a.m. starts at the markets lasted a month. Louise was writing passionate letters from London, about travelling and exploring. And about love. It was the first time I'd heard the word. At a loose end, I again sought out the only people available for solace. Aunty Grace showed me to the spare room. Uncle Paddy offered me a beer.

'Get this into ye, man.'

Aunty Grace chatted and fussed in her comfortable, mother-hen way. I told her about Louise.

'Ye sound like ye're in love. Ye need to go after that girl.'

I was startled, surprised to hear the name of what I was feeling. I thank her still for my life with Louise. I sold my car, my yacht and a few possessions and bought a one-way ticket to London. There was a two-day lag between vacating my room in the share house and the departure day. Naively, I didn't think I had a choice but to stay with my parents. It had been over a year since I'd moved out and, on the few occasions I had returned, I thought I had thrown off the mantle of its strictures.

My possessions dispersed down to a few essentials, I carefully packed what was left into a new backpack. I had learned how to pack a good travel bag, but now with no need for a list. I was brimming with the anticipation of reuniting with Louise, of being free to roam the world at will with her. I got a lift to the house, knowing it was a stopover and no longer my home. I leaned the backpack against the end of the bed in the spare room. I could not abide staying around during the day and disappeared into the city, ostensibly to buy traveller's cheques. While I was gone, without asking or inviting a discussion, my mother unpacked the backpack, took all my clothes, washed and ironed them and then started sewing on name tags, including on all my underpants. When I came home late that afternoon, she was sitting on the bed beside neat piles of the categories of clothes, the empty backpack against the wall. She had a needle in hand and the ancient roll of Cash's name tags coiled beside her, my name stitched a hundred times in red, thread letters.

'What are you doing?'

She explained her mission.

'I don't need name tags anymore. I'm backpacking. I'm responsible for them now. No-one else in the world needs to know who they belong to.'

I could see my rage curdling midair, my fear of her anger

reshaping the words into politeness. What backpacker ever travelled with Cash's name tags on all their clothes? It was humiliating.

Eyes down, through gritted teeth, she hissed. 'This is my job, as your mother.'

It was a one-way street. I said nothing. But in that moment, the penny dropped. This was how it had been. I had a voice in my share house. I did not and could not have a voice in this house, and was why I had deserted. I did not have the wherewithal to challenge her and it shocked me to realise how disempowered I felt.

Six months later, settled in the south of England, I came to understand she was making the statement that, no matter how I behaved, I would always be her son. She was doing what was innate – naming and claiming me. But there was no room for 'me' in her script, even though I had been an important player in her tragedy that had involved love, loss, betrayal, denial, anger and exile.

22

London, Europe and the Middle East

1975–1976

Louise and I met up in London after just six weeks apart. Striding across the dry summer grass in Hyde Park, seeing her stand, open her arms and run towards me, brought a cascade of overwhelming love. We confidently rented a bedsit in Earl's Court. It being the first time we had shared a place, the impoverished foundations of my capacity for feeling soon re-emerged as a scrambled and anguished mess. I was still reactionary, unable to know let alone own those feelings, and emotionally paralysed at conflict. I could not talk maturely through issues. As the unnameable anger rose, and unable to face Louise, I walked the streets of London, self-indulgently and morbidly writing a story of myself stranded in this doubly alienated world, alone in myself and in this vast city. My mother's lessons in 'practising being a good husband' had no traction. That well-meaning template she had tried to impart was fraught with contrivances that concealed an honest expression of feeling. I had no tools to navigate the messy history I was bringing to a live-in relationship.

We thought it might be better if we were travelling and camping, not cramped into a tiny bedsit in the whorl of the city. We bought a tent and sleeping bags and set off, only getting as far as Oxford before our relationship fell apart. I told Louise I needed space, and this left her bereft at the uncertainty of my love. We parted company, travelling separately onwards. I went west, Louise north. I cried for days, sitting on local buses, leaning against the window in abject misery. We left the door open to meet again in Scotland. Communication was via letters to poste restante in anticipated towns. We finally met a few weeks later at the Stirling Youth Hostel, a large, grey converted castle. The same open arms and warmth of our meeting tamed the cold and stony foyer. We walked and talked for hours, wandering hand in hand through the surrounding pine plantations, our feet barely touching the beds of soft needles. Hitching north, we ferried to the Orkney Islands and, in the sense that Stewart Collis had described, we both experienced the immediacy and timelessness of simple living in a remote place. We thought to hibernate in the south of England for the coming winter and hitched south down the rugged highlands along the west coast of Scotland.

An old aunt of a friend of Louise's lived in Glasgow and we were invited to stay for a few days. She came to pick us up in the city. While we were waiting, we found a not-so-discrete corner in the designated city park and indulged in some passionate kissing. Caught in this embrace, the old aunt positively scolded our 'canoodlin' and we were promptly assigned separate bedrooms upstairs in her house.

Over the next few days, we waded in a moralistic undercurrent of Scottish and Protestant glares and asides. It affirmed for us how comfortable we felt in who we were and what we had together, free of those religious and societal strictures. But we were responsible guests all the same and, to push the point home, offered to help around the house. The kitchen was clearly out of bounds, but she was comfortable dispatching us out into the Glasgow-grey, autumn cold.

'Can ye plant out my bulbs in the garden?'

It was a question but technically read as an order. The garden bed stretched sideways across the front of the house, dividing an angled entry pathway from a small, despondent lawn. Our wee

Australian humour excited an anarchic response. In the spring, when viewed from our two upstairs bedroom windows, the daffodils would boldly spell out F-U-C-K.

We hired a car and explored the villages along the south coast of Cornwall and Devon and discovered Primrose Cottage for rent in East Portlemouth, a hamlet on the picturesque tidal Kingsbridge Estuary, by the sea in south-west Devon. We bought a small car, filled the backseat with books and a load of coal and retreated to this obscure corner of the world. This time we settled into a safer place together, enabling us, as it turned out, to dismantle the complexities of our upbringings and attempt to construct templates by which we could live wholesome lives. We walked the sea cliffs and rambling lanes by day as Collis had done, and by night, we read books to each other by the coal fire, among them the radical psychiatrists R.D. Laing and David Cooper. Cooper's *Death of the Family* described a 'madness' in the way families functioned in Western culture, painting pictures of 'happy families' riddled with dysfunction and hypocrisies and betrayals. The book named the script of my experience with my mother. I could stand outside what I'd witnessed and peer into its madness. But, as affirming as it was on one level, it did not offer any understanding of the roots of my own discontent and served only to further alienate me from my mother. I wrote her a long, perhaps too unkind, letter expressing my frustrations and anger.

At the times when Louise had challenged me to take responsibility for what I was feeling, but I couldn't identify what that was, I quickly became enraged and saw her as the enemy. Now, in the safety of Primrose Cottage, my mother was cast back into that role. This was cruel. The blame for the root causes were my father, who I was ambivalent about – not a good husband but a loving and kind father – and Father Leo Leunig.

I was conscious enough of my anger to attempt to deal with it.

With Louise's encouragement, I registered for the first of several weekend Encounter groups in Exeter, just north of where we were living in Devon. The group promised self-awareness through confrontation and self-disclosure. The facilitator talked about the legitimacy of negative feelings. In the safety of that room, it wasn't long before I was overwhelmed by a frightening rage, directed squarely at my mother's stifling possessiveness. Watched by the astonished participants, I tore off my clothes and the sewn-in name tags, fiercely stating I did not belong to her. I was quivering and seething by the time I got down to my underpants and, twisting around, ripped the tag off. Ironically, labels were not enough to protect my genitals as a parent would want.

The Encounter groups fertilised an embryonic sense that something serious was wrong, but there was no wisdom guiding me to the source. The sexual abuse was not on my radar. But the groups did lead to some degree of equanimity and repair. After her death, I came across the next letter I'd written to my mother. It was considerably more understanding and conscious of our respective pain, but without any attributions to the origins. There was a gentle tenderness towards her, even as I still asserted my need to express my individuality. The first letter was not there. She had burned it in a blind fury, Dom told me recently. 'I was there. She told me what she'd done.'

It took becoming a parent myself to understand parental identity, a function of oneself relative to a child. Her identity as a woman and a wife, already diminished by my father, had been recast solely as a mother to her sons. The Encounter groups gave me an insight into the way that had thwarted my identity in my family. But it was my identity that had been hijacked when I was nine that underpinned my true quest, and I was intuitively trusting the impulse to rediscover it.

***

It being the times when all young people had to have a sojourn in England to explore their cultural roots, our Goomalling cousins, Margie and Jess, both visited us in our cottage in Portlemouth. Margie's presence as a sister figure and confidante grew in these sojourns, a role that was to become increasingly important in later years as she shared my journey towards the truth.

Louise and I left England in the spring of 1976, hitching across France to Italy and Greece on our way to Israel. We were drawn to the socialist, utopian philosophy of the kibbutzim. The few months living and working on the communal kibbutz in the Negev Desert adjacent to the Gaza Strip were wonderfully experiential, but also eye-opening. We encountered Israel as a flawed state. As fighter jets patrolled overhead, I watched black-clad women fossicking for wood in the dry earth on the other side of the razor-wire fence to Gaza while I drove a large, modern tractor cultivating vast, irrigated fields of lush green. The Palestinians who lived in Israel seemed to be second-class citizens living in inferior townships compared to the new villas of the newly settled Israelis. I saw women and children digging through the soil of the potato crop after the harvester had gone through, searching for missed potatoes. On excursions away from the kibbutz, our busload of volunteers was guarded by men with machine guns. We slowly came to the realisation this was an apartheid system at work and it troubled us deeply.

I still could not interpret Louise's anxieties as anything but criticism, so our troubles reignited and we split up in Jerusalem and returned to London separately, she via Turkey and me via Greece. We reunited two weeks later and had a happy month living in Islington, exploring London and going to classical music concerts and art galleries, and discovering the new wave of vegetarian restaurants, a culinary tradition we had enjoyed on the kibbutz.

London in 1976 was the charming, living history book of our colonial upbringing. It was also now the epicentre of a new wave in world politics; the freedom to protest, the deconstruction of colonialism in Africa, the rise of feminism, the birth of Amnesty International, the injustices levelled on the oppressed and disenfranchised in the world. We were drawn to these political rallies, especially after our experience in Israel. We actively participated in one at Conway Hall in Red Lion Square, the heart of socialist foment in London. Outside, men in trench coats sat on park benches around the square, conspicuously reading newspapers held high in front of their faces. My politics had moved down the street, siding with the trade unionists on the other side of the Seventh-day Adventist Church. My father would have been horrified that this was where spying had led me. The trousers on these spies were not sullied by grass stains; I imagine their job description did not include crawling to read number plates.

My passion to express myself at these rallies was partly fuelled by a revulsion at injustice that had survived my childhood, but principally by a maturing of those values that had begun in Primrose Cottage – a rejection of the oppressive, controlling strictures of my Catholic upbringing. I was finding my voice, and it was angry.

23

A Fremantle Life

1976–1983

Louise and I returned to Western Australia and rented a large house in Fremantle that we shared with university students. Encouraged by how our relationship had steadied, and with a small pool of savings, a year later we bought a tiny, run-down terrace house in South Fremantle. We were drawn to live among Fremantle's diverse immigrant population, a milieu we'd experienced and loved in Europe. I was offered a job as a building site supervisor, a role that allowed me some self-sufficiency. I learned the manual trades of bricklaying, plastering, carpentry and roofing – an immersion in the physical world as Collis had described, but in an urban context. The owners of two worksites became interested in my qualification as a graduate architect and asked me to design some buildings and so, on the side, a quasi-architectural practice grew. The work affirmed my interest in heritage buildings, so I rented a seedy, paint-peeled room above an army surplus store in Fremantle. I had no intentions of establishing a practice and it seemed an interim existence that also happened to earn a little money. Some months we subsisted solely on Louise's wages from her job.

We lived an alternative lifestyle as a couple with no vision of a married life nor a vision much past each week. I slowly restored the terrace house – a mostly positive, therapeutic experience, the laying down of roots, the creation of order out of apparent chaos. We formed a strong bond with the now rapidly changing community of like-minded couples and families in our neighbourhood. We became urban guerillas, pulling up paving slabs from the footpaths in the bare streets around us and planting trees; paperbarks, olives and small eucalypts. We nurtured and watered them until eventually the Council took over their care, no-one asking where the trees had come from or if permission had been sought. We watched our corner of the city transform into a leafy, shady enclave.

Living together openly and unmarried demonstrated to both our parents these new values, at odds with their traditional Christian views. When we occasionally attended family functions, Dad shook my hand warmly, 'Welcome, fella! Good to see you.' Mum could not be that embracing, instead averting her eyes and making her clenched-jaw conversation perfunctory.

Those Fremantle times were buoyant and happy, as long as I did not feel controlled. However, as Louise was the sole organiser of our social life, it was inevitable that anything she suggested that did not coincide with my vague and unrealised sense of purpose caused more than a ripple of resentment. In these moments, realising I was a passenger, I would revert to silent mode, and those silences hovered as an ever-present, threatening cloud, a storm that could be triggered by the most benign comment.

Louise went away for a time to stay in a friend's cottage, saying she needed a timeout from the burden of my moods. Wallowing in desolation and loss, I self-indulgently wrote a story about what I imagined it would be like to commit suicide. As my imagined life slipped away, I didn't care about the loss because there was nothing more to lose. Ironically, writing was a way of feeling in control. It externalised the feeling, however self-pitying and narcissistic. Being able to reflect on feelings was a start, but it could only happen when I was alone. When Louise returned and we needed to make even the smallest of decisions together, I stumbled and stuttered, and it frustrated her endlessly. Her anger in turn triggered mine, and in these moments, I deemed it to be her fault and she became the enemy once more.

I did not want to live life sweeping resentments and anger under the carpet as my parents had done, but I had no tools and no trust in my legitimacy to exist in relation to someone else. I could not understand that living solitary in a relationship was an ailment. The diagnosis was missing. I circled it like it was a spectre, sensed but invisible, with no words to give form to what would engender legitimacy. In those moments of unnameable anguish, I would withdraw again in sullen silence for days.

This circling beast eventually had a name: angry depression. But I hid it from myself and the world for many years. It was insidious and unpredictable and thrived on fragile self-esteem and unknowable feelings and set me on a path that, years later, had Louise and I sitting in a psychiatrist's consulting room.

Louise for now encouraged me to get help. Prised out of my resistance, I reluctantly trudged off to therapy and counselling, but it never went to the core of the illness nor named its roots in the sexual abuse. I had so effectively concealed that in the coping strategies that Louise and I never talked about it. Shame, I would one day learn, now controlled the public portal to its exposure.

So it was my head that went to those sessions, not my heart. The signs on the doors of the therapy rooms rotated through a number of brands over many years: Encounter groups, transactional analysis, Gestalt therapy, Vipassana Buddhist meditation, yoga, Jungian analysis, rebirthing, psychology, psychiatry, clinical psychology and counselling. I was always calm and rational, making sure I projected my happy self to the therapist, in the tradition of my early family life. In one counselling session, in a 'New Age' Uniting Church clinic in the late 1970s, the counsellor fell asleep. I didn't blame him.

I was talking around in circles, circumnavigating the volcano I couldn't name. I didn't know the pathway to its core, nor did anyone else, it seemed.

The most redemptive therapy occurred during several years of Jungian psychoanalysis. For the first time since leaving the Church, I felt deeply nourished. The immersion in mythology, archetypes and dream analysis was a meaningful, symbolic and profoundly personal world. The analysis did not address the abuse, my suppressed and not-so-suppressed rages, nor the continuing stand-off with my mother. But it did open the door to an inner world that I could inhabit, in the way that Catholicism had created an inner landscape in my childhood, and in which I could travel freely and reverently every week. The psychoanalysis was a stage in rediscovering an aspect of my childhood, that part whose spirit had been annulled. I still maintain a dream journal, noting daily moods and events. It has proven an invaluable resource for self-awareness, as well as the tracking of the history of rage and depression.

The psychoanalysis was a positive enough transformation for Louise and me to talk about having children. To contemplate having a child was to be able to imagine and trust in a future, and it conjured up all that was optimistic and generous about living but also all that could so easily be destroyed. Louise wanted to be married to give a child a secure home. Paralysed at this prospect at first, I eventually relented, the measure of yet another step in developing trust. Given our family histories, and our journey to this point, neither of us could embrace a public event. We married secretly in the Registry Office, with two of our dear Fremantle neighbours as witnesses. Some weeks later, we went to tell my parents.

We were all standing in that theatre of angst, my parents' kitchen. Slightly in front of Louise, I shuffled awkwardly sideways, then forwards, then back, a physical anxiety I would later come to label 'squirming'. Finally, I stepped towards my mother, curiously feeling a sheepish joy at the prospect of telling them, a profound gesture of acquiescence.

'We have some news. Louise and I got married.'

My mother exploded past me and hugged Louise, crushing her to her chest.

'Thank you, God. Thank you, Our Lady. Thank you, God. Thank you, Our Lady.' She was in a religious ecstasy. 'I asked Margaret when she was visiting Lourdes to pray to Our Lady that you'd get married.'

She rushed to the pantry cupboard and rummaged around in a frenzy until she found a small plastic bottle of water. She hugged it to her heart. 'Thank you, Our Lady.' She unscrewed the cap and splashed liberal quantities of water all over us both.

'It's Lourdes water.'

She did not touch me. The water wet my shirt and splashed across the lino. Our marriage seemed to resolve an inner conflict of her faith, proving the power and success of prayer, the power of Lourdes. We were incidental, supplanted by God and Our Lady. Naively, I had thought our marriage would be a gesture towards reconciliation, and had expected some generosity, or at least acceptance. Instead, I felt pushed aside and angry.

My father brought some level of joy back. Standing quietly off to one side, he smiled and shook my hand.

'Congratulations, fella. That's wonderful.'

When we told Louise's parents, they were gracious, relieved and congratulatory. It was a good resolution to their quietly withheld Methodist apprehensions. Their God was a more redeeming and forgiving one than the one I'd grown up with. After the initial gasps, her mum moved quickly to the pragmatics.

'What did you wear?' She would have given her right arm to be part of any wedding preparations.

***

Louise had been trying for years to get me to visit my parents more regularly. Whenever I relented, the moment we crossed the railway line at North Fremantle, on our way to their house, something in me was tripped.

'You've gone somewhere. You're not here,' she would state in frustration.

That railway crossing was the trigger for me to 'split off' at the prospect of being with my mother. I could not be myself when I was with her. I became mute. Louise would instantly feel compromised.

'I need you to be there with me when we see her,' she'd say.

Nevertheless, Louise continued to encourage me to be more proactive with them. I still had a notion of goodness and forgiveness, and it was from this that I could embrace the idea. I had no understanding of my condition nor an ability to name the disempowerment in the dynamic of our relationship, but nevertheless I offered my mother opportunities to be involved in our lives. We could not have imagined the consequences. She began to arrive uninvited to 'help'. After some brief pleasantries and without asking our needs, she would slip out to the laundry and disappear quickly out the back gate with our washing. Her intrusion annoyed us but made us realise it had nothing to do with us and our needs, and everything to do with her. For this reason, Louise insisted we establish some boundaries. It came to a head when she discovered my mother in our bedroom, with the drawers open, putting away our underwear. Louise rightly felt violated and objected.

'She's your mother. Stop her! Deal with it!'

I could steel myself to Louise's anger, resentful but knowing she was right. But I was paralysed by my mother's anger, unable to counter her pleading cry to let her be a mother. I didn't have the boots to wade into this quagmire, so I said nothing. I had no authority with her, even in my own house. My powerlessness made me seethe, impotent in the face of her inappropriateness and intrusiveness, and my rage went underground into that simmering volcano.

***

It was unplanned, but we saved ourselves from more angst by escaping. We used money we had saved for renovations to go to Europe for three months to immerse ourselves in the different world of the C.G. Jung Institute in Zurich. We free-audited at the Institute and had psychoanalysis with very experienced analysts. It was another step along the long journey of rediscovering a sensibility from my childhood that had meaning beyond the merely personal and physical. In this inner landscape, there were no strings attached, no promises of a better life after death, and no punitive old men or nuns peering down at me and stoking guilt.

Not long after our return, Louise became pregnant.

24

Our First Child

1984

Our son was born in December 1984. Holding this tiny, fragile baby ignited a spark that fulfilled the promise of renewal. We were delighted. Louise, feeling especially vulnerable as a new mother, renewed her expectations of me to make clear, collaborative decisions to establish boundaries with visitors, especially my mother. I alternated between the joy of our new baby, and anger at Louise's disappointment that I could not assert myself. The moments of delight occurred when I felt no expectations. When challenged, I struggled.

We had not named the baby after three days. We wanted to know him first, to let his name come naturally. He was my mother's first grandchild and, swamped by her Catholic superstitions, she was terrified the baby would die unnamed and go to Limbo. On the third day, she swept into the hospital room, picked him up and announced, 'I'm going to call him Thomas. He's Tom for today.'

Louise flashed her eyes at me and jerked her head towards my mother. But I was neutered by her presence.

We eventually settled on the name Harry. The days became weeks which became months and years. I was determined to be a good father, practical and useful in the mechanics of the days around the house, but not to be a husband as my father had been. Like him though, I had no connection to my feelings, so I could not see things from Louise's perspective and reacted angrily in her frustrated moments.

Nevertheless, Harry filled my life with a richness and redemption and, given the journey of the previous ten years, holding him was an affirmation of possibility, a rekindling of a nurturing, caring side from my childhood. I went back to work part-time, and Louise and I share-parented him. I loved my days with him, full of whimsy and wonder.

There were many photos taken in these first years, and they relayed happiness. I am smiling and relaxed. In one, Uncle Paddy and Aunty Grace are sitting on our patched and re-patched couch. Uncle Paddy, his eyes tired but still glowing a serene blue, is holding Harry. Aunty Grace leans comfortably towards the two of them. She said they had to insist that my mother bring them down to see Harry. She had been reluctant to bring them, Aunty Grace said, because Harry wasn't baptised, and never likely to be.

There are no photos of the occasions of my silent, passive-aggressive stand-offs when Louise morphed into the enemy. Had they been X-rays they would have shown my inner, raging core seething and erupting in spasms, my confused child-adult struggling for a foothold.

As a result of a serendipitous meeting, I trusted myself to suggest we sell our tiny terrace house and buy a run-down cottage on the same street. It had a large garden, an oasis in which we could plant vegetables and fruit trees and build cubbies. We lived there for a year with our toddler while we planned a new house. I took a year off from my on-again-off-again architectural practice to build the new home. It was a wholesome project to house our new family. The structure had an open plan with a cathedral-like, vaulted ceiling and when we moved in, we revelled in its spaciousness. On Sunday mornings, we moved the furniture aside, turned up Paul Simon's 'Graceland' and the three of us danced wildly. They were mostly happy years, and the angry depressions receded.

Brian Klopper, an architect acquaintance in Fremantle, invited me to join his co-operative practice. He was deeply interested in history and cultural identity and often encouraged the poet in me. The co-operative office enabled me to work alongside colleagues yet maintain a separate practice and responsibilities. It was a good resolution to my inability to trust any type of partnership. My practice grew and I took on staff. I had managed socially and professionally by not taking a passionate position on anything, modelling myself as the reasonable one. In truth, I was a fence-sitter, avoiding both conflict and responsibility for difficult decisions – a fraught model when directing employees or builders. I coped when they were loyal, compliant and cheerful, but when leadership was required or conflicts arose, I baulked, my vacuum of personal authority exposed. In my office, I kept the lid on the resultant rage, but it fomented under the surface until it overflowed at home.

25

The Psychiatrist

July–October 1988

I laboured under the anger in silence, knowing it was wrong, and that I could not be the good husband and father I aspired to be if I could not name or own the feelings behind it. Louise would not resile from attempting to make me take responsibility. 'It's not fair on our family. We do not deserve your anger.' She pushed and prodded for a feeling response until, in frustration, she would inadvertently press the button that triggered the volcano of suppressed rage. I once kicked a chair until it was dented. Another time I smashed plates the way I had learned from my mother. Louise cowered in the doorway, terrified of the monster I'd become in those moments. I would then disappear, driving aimlessly around the city for hours. She admitted years later she was fearful I would harm myself. When I slunk back in, I walked with my head down, and it would take days for me to emerge semi-intact.

We still didn't know the name for this angry depression with its passive-aggressive silences, its extreme and raging responses to criticism or blame, and its blaming of everyone else for the conflicts, but we would one day understand it as Post-Traumatic Stress Disorder. When I did raise my head again, I could not apologise or confront the problem. It had not been my fault. I was the aggrieved one. Someone else had unleashed my anger. I had no understanding of its mechanics.

Louise would try to reason with me. 'Your anger is out of all proportion to what I say or do. It's off the scale. It's not all my fault. I'm not that much to blame.' Then later, if things were calmer. 'You have to take responsibility for how you feel.'

But I did not know what I was feeling. I angrily denied being angry. I justified, I defended, I ducked and weaved, but I did stay, and so did she. Somewhere, somehow, we knew we were safer with each other than out alone in the world. We had charted a course together creating a family, but I had no ownership of it. My marriage was what filled the absence of knowing anything else, yet it was essential for my survival. I trailed helplessly and angrily in Louise's wake as she tried to live a 'normal' family life. She implored me to seek help. She was suffering from the stress of tiptoeing on unreadable, fragile ground.

She arranged an appointment for us both with a psychiatrist. I reluctantly had to acknowledge my problem, and if that was where she pushed me, then I would comply. The intermittent psychologists and counsellors I had sat with over the years had missed the target. To be fair, the abuse and its debilitating secret were held so close to my chest even I could not see them. I could not reveal what I did not feel.

I sat in silence with Louise in the psychiatrist's waiting room, humiliated it had come to this. After an excruciating wait, the psychiatrist opened her door and stood back. We filed past her, and she directed us to side-by-side seats before retreating to the safety of her desk on the other side of the large consulting room. The gap between us seemed vast.

I watched her eyes as they scanned my face. She was judging me. *Because you're here, you're a failure, aren't you? You're a man and you're a failure.* The inner voice then struck up the age-old mantra, desperate to be seen as normal, but unsettled by the silence in her intense gaze.

I soft-pedalled my story, describing it as a series of aberrations, angry and negative reactions, because that was not the real me. I could not describe the feelings behind the reactions. Louise prompted me to talk about the rages, suggesting there was more to the story. I said nothing. An hour went by, and the session was over. Nothing had happened.

'I want you to come back again.'

Why? The voice was indignant. *There's nothing more to do here.*

Louise followed up with two sessions on her own. The fourth appointment, late in 1988, was for me alone. Louise insisted I talk about the abuse, intuiting it was at the root of my rage and passivity. I didn't agree. The abuse was well dealt with years ago, I told myself. Nevertheless, I told the psychiatrist. It was the second time the story had seen the light of day. My face must have been red because it was burning. I gouged out the words from within the deep pit, half-hoping they did not make it across the room to her dispassionate, judging ears. She was silent. She seemed flummoxed.

'I've never had a case of male sexual abuse at the hands of a priest. I'm not sure what to suggest. I'll need to consult some colleagues. I'll be better able to advise you then.'

I was surprised and deflated. I had wanted to hear something tangible, a solution. I had no notion of the depth and stickiness of the abuse trauma, its embeddedness in my body, its intractability cast into my foundations. Parcelling up the abuse and keeping it well buried seemed the usual way victims dealt with the catastrophe. While the secret surrounding the abuse remained intact, it precluded any understanding or integration of the myriad effects: the inability to know feelings; insecurity expressing love; the inability to trust, especially men; disempowerment with anyone in authority; being an outsider; not belonging. This psychiatrist's room was the first significant step in the thirty-year dismantling of my armour, the necessary carapace to protect the me that was on my own in the war of the abuse.

Much later I understood that these symptoms that emanated from the depths were manifesting like a real war. I mostly blamed Louise as the outer enemy. The therapists could not see the inner enemy. When another psychiatrist would eventually label the symptoms as Complex PTSD, it would be the diagnosis given to many war veterans who felt vulnerable in the constant, impending threat of an unsafe life. Louise described the hunted look in my eyes when I spiralled out of control. Had I looked the same way as a hunted adolescent on Cottesloe Beach?

At our next appointment, I was waiting for the solution to my 'unknowable' condition. The psychiatrist swivelled in her chair. She seemed softer, closer across the chasm.

'The advice I've been given is that you must tell the archbishop. You need to officially report the abuse to the Catholic Church. You must also tell your parents and your brothers. This is important. It will explain a lot of things to them.'

Her words detonated in my chest. The shell closed in. The long-buried secret had been forged in relation to my parents and had alienated me from them. Given the fraught terms of our relationship now, how could I simply slice it open like a melon?

I stared at the psychiatrist in bewilderment. Shame resurfaced, raw and untreated. I did not understand what this thing was that I was carrying, nor that I had rights to an explanation and to help. She sensed my panic. She repeated.

'You need to tell your parents. They need to know because it will explain things for them.' Her words will always linger in my mind. It did not occur to me to imagine what it would explain, but I took strength from the way she said it. She was authorising it. She did not mention reporting the abuse to the police, nor that it would be helpful to have specific counselling. She did not identify my depressions and prescribe medication. The issue seemed to be an administrative one, simply addressed by telling the archbishop and my parents. Everything would then be resolved and, as shameful and difficult as that might be, I felt impelled to go through with it.

26

Tell the Church

1989

It seemed easier to tell an outsider before I told my parents, but for months I shied away from contacting the Church. Finally, I rang the office of the Catholic Archbishop of the Perth Diocese. His secretary was haughty and authoritarian, probing insensitively for the reason for the appointment. I nervously held my ground and refused to discuss it.

'It's personal.'

A few days later I pushed open the heavy door of the archbishop's palace and stepped into a large, imposing foyer. The secretary, seated off to the right, was mostly hidden behind her receptionist's desk, just her head moving above it, shaking like a puppet. She gave me a dark look. I was in her realm now and she asserted her authority.

'What is the reason for your visit?' Her lips were tight, the words punched out.

'I'm sorry. I can't say.'

'I must know. It's usual for all matters concerning the archbishop.' She was hissing now.

'It's personal,' I reiterated.

She pointed to a seat opposite. Her withering, judgmental eyes followed me as I turned and sat down. I scanned the room, attempting to quell my anxiety. Her brow furrowed and her face puckered whenever my roving eyes alighted on hers. I was still primed to react to that look, reminded of a schoolroom with a nun in a voluminous black habit, of a pulpit and a priest sowing guilt.

The door beside me opened and a large man stepped out into the reception area. Archbishop Foley was wearing a priest's black suit, but a magenta splash of silken fabric peeping from under his coat hinted at his rank. Smiling, he extended his hand and said, 'Welcome.' He ushered me into his lavish office.

He showed me to a seat on one side of his large desk. He walked around and sat down, leaning forward with his clasped hands on the desk, then gently asked me what I wanted to talk about. I alternated my embarrassed gaze between his big hands and his eyes as I told the story. I named the places and the times, but the physical details were still too shameful to divulge. He was silent. He nodded. He seemed very present and to understand perfectly what I was describing. He did not seem shocked. He gently posed the question.

'Who was the priest?'

'Father Leunig.'

'I'm so sorry. Your story explains a lot.'

He told me Leunig had left the state and moved to New South Wales. When he had repeatedly asked Leunig to return to Western Australia, Leunig had refused.

'I was desperate for clergy, so I went to see him when I was on a trip to New South Wales. I finally managed to entice him to come back to the West. But he came back with great reluctance.'

His hands gestured upwards, as though that might explain things.

'I'm truly sorry about what has happened.'

I hadn't expected this. He was visibly troubled, and I sensed it had brought on a great sadness. He stood up and accompanied me back out into the foyer. I walked quickly outside, a sidelong glance at the secretary. I momentarily stood on the pavement. I was relieved.

My fear had been that I would be judged, not just because I was finally breaking the pact of secrecy, but because my shame was entangled with my perceived complicity. It had been fourteen years since I'd had any contact with the Church and, despite my indifference to it now as an institution, absence had not quelled a lingering fear of its authority. I had anticipated disbelief and defensiveness, even hostility and blame. The secretary in the foyer had foreshadowed it. Instead, I found empathy and understanding and, in that brief moment, it felt good.

I often think about that conversation. Foley expressed a genuine sorrow at my abuse, but his concern quickly moved to explain things from his point of view and his issues with clergy numbers. My visit had become an explanation for the Church's difficulties with Leunig. Foley hadn't indicated action would be taken to put a stop to Leunig's ongoing ministry, or suggest he or I report Leunig to the police. He did not offer counselling. The prevailing culture in the Church then was to deny or bury any mention of the abuse as quickly as possible, as though there were no consequences for the victims, carefully avoiding any responsibility for the past actions of the priests. The abused had to deal with the ramifications and get on with their life if they could. If they couldn't, it was their own fault. The complex mechanics of the secret preserved the trauma solely within their heart, ensuring they blamed themselves or, in my case, everybody else, for not being able to make a go of it. It never occurred to me that I had any right to ask Foley for action for myself. All I could muster the courage to do was to follow the psychiatrist's advice, which seemed to suggest that telling him would deliver some sort of resolution.

In the ensuing years, I came to understand that the ability and the desire to tell the truth is at the heart of a moral life, and being forbidden to tell the truth so early in my life contributed to the loss of personal and moral authority. So, when nothing came from my visit to Foley, I was in no position to demand appropriate justice.

I also sensed that the damage from my childhood sexual abuse was intrinsic and structural. It, and the subsequent secret, felt like the poisoning – or worse, the annulment – of my capacity to trust, and the annihilation of this trust was the effective dismantling of my identity. Without a sense of identity, my ability to imagine and shape a future was incapacitated, and it permanently separated me from my parents and my brothers.

An apology cannot repair these losses, and their restitution would have to be a tangible, physical and psychological journey. Foley's words, though a relief at the time, brought no lasting solace. His 'sadness' was meaningless.

Archbishop Foley died in 1991, a relatively young man. I must have still expected something from him because when I heard of his death, I sensed a door closing.

27
Tell Your Family
1989

Neither the psychiatrist nor Louise had suggested taking an advocate or witness for support, especially as I was reporting criminal behaviour. The prospect of telling anyone was shameful enough so I instinctively dealt with it on my own, as I had done as a child. I was now beginning the same arduous journey with my parents. Given the tenuous state of our relationship and the family taboos, it would be difficult for us all. I mulled over it for weeks, every day rehearsing the scene and dreading the prospect. Steeling myself at last, Louise and I invited my parents and brothers over for lunch. Joe did not come.

We were standing around talking after the meal. Singling out Paddy first, and then Dom, I took them aside and quickly blurted it out.

'I was sexually abused by that priest Leunig. Did anything happen to you?'

They shook their heads, embarrassed perhaps, or perplexed. They did not ask what had happened, or even empathise. The silence that followed was painful, as though I was confessing to a transmissible disease. And it was in a way. Shame and silence around feelings and emotional pain was a family disease and it reinforced my separateness from them.

Next, it was Terry's turn. Fearful to hear his truth, I briefly told him about my abuse and my confrontation with Leunig on the back steps. Twenty-three years of wondering fuelled me.

'Did anything happen to you that weekend in Quairading?'

'No way.' He was emphatic. 'If he'd touched me, I would have told him where to go. There's no way I'd have let him touch me.'

Relief flooded through me; my threat to tell the police had at least deflected Leunig. I felt ashamed that I hadn't asked Terry back then if anything had happened, trusting at the time that Leunig would have been honourable. I understand now that my silence was to protect my own secret. In effect though, I had abandoned Terry to his fate then, and had been carrying that guilt all these years, impossibly tangled up with my own guilt. He didn't ask about my experiences and seemed not to register what I was telling him. But of course, he wouldn't know what he'd been saved from.

Finally, my parents. I had left them until the very end of the day. Given the history of their marriage, and their extraordinary inability to share intimacy and listen to feelings, I could never have contemplated telling them together. On a pretext, I took Mum out into the garden. We stood outside the back door of our new house, under the shade of the jacaranda tree. She was a metre from me. Her head was down, still unable to make eye contact.

'I've been seeing a psychiatrist about something that happened years ago in Cottesloe and in Quairading. She's advised me that I should tell you what happened.' I paused, a twenty-five-year pause. 'I was sexually abused by that priest, Father Leunig.'

She gasped, then let out a desperate, soft wail, the cry of pain of an injured animal. Tears burst from her eyes like they had been primed. Her hands clutched at her face, then down again, trembling with what looked like profound grief. Her head bent further downwards as though the weight of the world was on it. She was sobbing now. In between the sobs, she started muttering a bitter, angry lament.

'I knew. I knew. I knew something had happened. You changed. You changed. You changed.' The words came out as bitter, angry shards, the emphasis seemingly laced with judgement. '*You* changed. You *changed. You* changed.'

Her bitterness was like a thousand darts as the implication dawned on me. Her anguish was not towards the priest. It was me. I was being blamed for having 'changed'. It was my fault. Any possible feeling of a connection with her snapped like a frayed hawser. It was sudden and violent, worse in some ways than on the beach at Cottesloe when I had understood I was wholly on my own dealing with the abuse.

I was so bewildered by what was happening, I just stood and stared at her. She didn't ask questions or say anything to try to understand. She didn't move to bridge the chasm, to hug or touch me, or even look at me. She became a stranger again.

Her sobbing subsided to a soft muttering. She retreated inwards, morose and unreachable. Had I misread her response? Was she angry at me for not confiding and trusting in her? At herself that she hadn't followed her feelings when she 'knew something had happened'?

Suddenly she looked up. Loudly and clearly, she said, 'I will pray for the priest. He will need our prayers.'

My mind reeled backwards in this rush of rejection, the awful realisation that I was incidental in her life, that once again her Catholic beliefs trumped her feelings for her children.

Aside from the impossibility of a discussion about the negative, the awful or the difficult, if she was learning this truth for the first time, why hadn't I been met with disbelief or incredulity, perhaps even horror? But her spontaneous wail and admission of 'knowing something had happened' was at the front of her consciousness. Had she suspected it in 1961 but felt powerless to intervene, such was the power and control of the Catholic

Church in her life? She was already conflicted and angry inside her marriage so I can only imagine what new layer of resentment was put down that first day when I came home from the church 'changed', when I withdrew from her and never returned.

The absurdity of her response suggested anything might have been possible at the time. Her belief in her happy family, and her Church with its promise of Heaven as a reward for her suffering, had become her credo, and nothing at this moment of truth could be allowed to divert her from that.

Considering how seriously and competently she'd run the household and mothered the five of us, it did not seem possible that, in her 'knowing', she had chosen to ignore her intuition. But pray for the priest? If I wasn't betrayed then, I was now. My news seemed to be just one more nail in the incessant suffering on her own cross, and perversely, a further impetus towards her Church with its promise of salvation.

Neither she nor I ever mentioned the abuse again, though she lived for another twenty-six years.

It was now Dad's turn. In the practical manner of our relationship founded on his inability to express feeling, we hadn't ever shared our emotions with each other, or for that matter, our hopes or dreams or troubles. Not only had my capacity to talk about them been neutered by the abuse, I had also inherited a good dose of his passivity. And he was shy, so anything to do with sexuality was taboo. To talk about my sexual abuse seemed an impossibility. All I could focus on was getting it over with. I'd left it so late that he was about to get into the car. Taking him by the elbow, I guided him aside. We were standing on the footpath next to our neighbour's fence.

'I've been seeing a psychiatrist. She's advised me to tell you that I was sexually abused by the priest Father Leunig. She also said that I need to tell the archbishop.'

He twisted sideways like a corkscrew, hunched over then pulled up straight, finally shifting from foot to foot. He threw his head back, the way he did when he was challenged, covered his mouth with one hand and wrapped his other arm across his chest as though to shield himself. His face burned deep crimson. Then he leaned in towards me, the pre-emptive movement of complicity in a secret.

'You mustn't tell the archbishop.' The air froze.

'I already have.' I didn't understand where this conversation might be going.

His head snapped back in a whiplash, and he arched backwards like he was ready to strike. He clicked his tongue in ferocious *tch tch tchs*, outraged in a way I had never seen. His arms flailed outwards like a drowning swimmer's.

'You shouldn't have done that. That was the wrong thing to do. You shouldn't have done that!'

He was almost shouting. Then, as if every second counted, he blurted out, 'You *mustn't* tell anyone else about this. You *must* keep it to yourself. It will shame the family name if it comes out. You *must not* tell anyone.'

I understood that merely mentioning sexuality was crossing a line, but the passion in his outrage left me speechless. His family name and the image he projected to everyone in the Church was more important than the crimes committed against me. I was not shocked that he felt shame, but I was that he was so fearful. He expected me to maintain the secret to preserve *his* good name. Was this the emotional abandonment my mother experienced in his unctuous service to the Church?

Like my mother, he was not dumbfounded by the news. The shame of sexual abuse was already at the forefront of his consciousness. He knew its terms and he was ready with the strategy to maintain its concealment. The crime was in exposing it.

Whatever was howling in his mind, I was committing treason. This was how generations of priests in the Catholic Church were able to abuse children with impunity. The secret and the shame, with their power to maintain silence, were not just a function between the child and the priest, but of everyone who submitted to the supreme authority and influence of the Church.

We stared at each other. Not a word. At least he was looking into my eyes. We were at the border control of no-man's-land, stranded on either side of the barrier. After a minute, he leaned in close again, across the bar, lowered his voice and muttered conspiratorially.

'Whatever you do, don't tell your mother.' Mother, not Mum.

'I've already told her.'

His face screwed up crimson again. He covered his mouth. I stared at the sunspots on the back of his hand. He was so distressed he could only click his tongue again. His *tch tch tch*s entwined anger and regret with a pity that surprised me.

'You shouldn't have done that. It will break her heart,' he hissed. 'Heart' trailed off with a surprising tenderness. It wasn't the moment to tell him that I had experienced her heart being broken long ago. And anyway, why wasn't my heart part of the story?

I walked beside him back to their car. He didn't shake my hand as he would usually. He didn't touch my elbow as he might if he felt affectionate. He didn't say, 'It'll be alright, fella', as he would have had I broken my leg.

The psychiatrist must surely have imagined a different outcome, perhaps one that was an invitation for my parents to function fully as parents. 'It will explain a lot.' Having done what she'd advised, I felt even more marginalised. It was a measure of how the abuse had established our estrangement and exposed the structures that had maintained it in the intervening years.

Later I asked myself why I hadn't had the courage to challenge their responses as I'd challenged Leunig on the steps of our family home. I know now it had to do with finding the words, to have the voice that could override the family taboos. My father, incredibly, had just exposed another one. 'It will shame the family name if it comes out.'

His response echoed around me until one day, years later, while standing at his grave with my eyes brimming with tears, I told him he did not have to feel the shame anymore. I'd found it difficult to reconcile that this man who had played sport endlessly with us, who always 'acted the goat' and got the button in the Christmas pudding, who snuck in some soup when I was sick, who loved playing games and tricks with his grandchildren, could be so self-centred with my truth when it exposed evil in his Church; that he might have understood that he was the one responsible for protecting his child from sexual abuse, and feel regret, sadness, betrayal or even 'sorrow' like Foley. But anger and blame?

In the same way he could not deal with conflict in our family, his shame was such a passive position to take, as though the priest had nothing to do with it. The weight was to remain firmly on my shoulders.

My parents had loved us, each in their own practical ways, saying and doing the things good parents say and do to protect their children from harm and to nurture them into healthy adulthood: 'Speak nicely', 'Tell the truth', 'Don't fight with your brother', 'Be kind', 'No play 'til your jobs are done', 'First one home peels the potatoes', 'Don't drink and drive', 'Don't smoke'. But now they had both abdicated in favour of their Church's tenets.

***

Nevertheless, telling my parents was the first step to bridge a great divide with them. However inadequate the disclosure of my abuse had been, merely telling them had been empowering and enabled me to have my voice. I thought it might lead to a more mature relationship. I assumed Mum also wished for some sort of reconciliation, as she had asked for a key to our new house. But it was a ruse. She let herself in when she knew Louise and I were both at work and, with no discussion as to our needs, took all our washing away and brought it back ironed one, two or, on one occasion, three weeks later. Conscious of her fragile mental health, I rang her and gently mentioned we'd run out of clothes. She didn't apologise or rush back with the cleaned clothes.

'I'm not finished yet!' It was a non-negotiable statement.

I vacillated between voiceless fury and a genuine attempt at empathy. It took some time before I mustered the courage to confront her. I fed the news out tentatively like I was trying to corral a frenzied animal.

She whipped around, eyes flashing, and again let out that soft, animal wail.

'You're not letting me be a mother!'

There seemed no possibility of a compromise. I offered a convenient excuse – that someone had broken into our house and we'd had to change the locks. I resisted her demand for a new key, weathering the guilt of this new, perceived rejection.

28

Positive Turns

1986–1995

The ability to be more open, honest and empowered relating to my parents signaled another quantum shift. The depressions that had careered in and out of my life became less debilitating and I took greater ownership in our family life. Louise and I had travelled to a more secure place, one that led to another life-changing conversation – the contemplation of having another child. I worked feverishly on weekends to finish building our house and garden.

Tash was born in the spring of 1990. Dancing around the living area on Sunday mornings took on a new meaning. Dad took a special delight in her, tickled by her growing charm, and we began to see my parents more frequently. This seemed to quieten the waters and, perhaps in a gesture of reconciliation, Mum asked me about their home, my grandfather's house, where I had lived in my adolescent years. It had had no maintenance for many years and the upkeep was now beyond them, and the steps too dangerous for my father. Could they build a retirement villa in the large backyard?

I agreed to take on the project and oversaw the approval and construction of a new aged-persons villa where we had once played cricket. It became as tangible a truce as could be expected, albeit benign. She was overtly proud of what I had achieved and talked endlessly about it to everyone in her vicarious way. Curiously, I only felt vague ownership of, and no pride in, the person she described, the architect. I was uncomfortable with praise, as though I had no rights to it.

But the new house did herald a new era. When the old house was sold, with it went the theatre of our struggles. In this sense, it was a redemption. We now frequently joined my four brothers, their wives and small children, on Friday evenings for fish and chips. Tash especially enjoyed getting to see more of her cousins.

On these occasions, my mother insisted on a photo of her five sons. 'Just the boys.'

Louise and I bristled, but I reluctantly complied. We asked that another be taken with the boys and their wives.

Around 1986, another journey had began. A colleague, also a Fremantle architect, was dean of the School of Architecture at the university. They were establishing a School of Fine Arts and needed enrolments to justify their existence. Would I sign up for a unit? I was passionate about art, so agreed and enrolled in Nineteenth Century Art and Architecture. On the first day, sitting in the lecture theatre, the lecturer described firstly the arc of the art segment, but then, as he outlined the architectural component, I had an epiphany. *What was I doing studying architecture again? I would rather study writing!* For the first time in my life, I had the extraordinary feeling of empowerment, that I could choose my destiny. At the end of the lecture, I scampered across the campus to the Arts building and presented at the faculty office.

'I'm already enrolled in an Art and Architecture unit in Fine Arts. Can I enrol in an Arts unit as well?'

The secretary quickly thrust a form in front of me. 'Certainly. We need the numbers. Sign here!'

And so began the slow quest of an Arts degree, one or two units per year, until 1992 when I completed the course, majoring in Australian and American literature. At the graduation ceremony, I stood proudly this time for a photograph.

29

Leunig in Court

1994–1995

In 1993, Louise and I moved to East Fremantle, closer to Harry's school and next to a family with twin girls in his class. The day of the move, the two families excitedly looked for a convenient place to make an opening in the dense hedge along the fence line between the two houses. Peeling the foliage apart at a logical spot, we found an old gate rusted shut on ancient hinges. Removing it, the children freely raced back and forth between the gardens. Louise and I had extended ourselves to the last penny to buy the house so there was little left for renovations. We worked instead on the very large garden, carving out and creating a small paradise for the children and ourselves. A new and close community with our neighbours grew around shared parenting, the pets, the gardens, the play and holidays. It became a solid framework for the normalisation of adult friendship.

Despite my 'happy face', from time to time irrational rages surfaced, seemingly from nowhere but always in response to a trigger. Unable to understand the source and so express my anger legitimately, I would retreat to the anaesthetic of long days in sullen, passive-aggressive silence.

In 1994, an article appeared in the *West Australian*, Perth's daily newspaper. As I scanned down the right-hand side of the page, a spear punctured inside my chest. The Reverend Father Leo Leunig had pleaded guilty to the sexual abuse of three boys in the late 1960s. The inner conversation, silent for years, started up.

It's other boys he's been charged with abusing. What he's done to you is exempt. You're fine. You've got on with your life, haven't you? You're managing well. You don't need to do anything.

But it niggled away. Another voice – a new one – intruded meekly. *Don't you think you should go to the police and add your name to the indictment? Seek justice?*

Another, longer article appeared in the *Sunday Times* beside a photo of Leunig going to court. He was alone, dressed neatly in pressed trousers, a sports coat and tie, easily recognisable behind the ubiquitous dark glasses. He hadn't changed. There was the upturned nose, the pudgy cheeks and the bulging belly. He was given a four-year prison sentence. The reasonable voice took up the baton.

You can relax. You've been let off the hook. Someone else has broken their pact of secrecy and exposed him. You don't need to do anything now. They've done it for you. That's good. You can let it go now. No need to go to the police.

I had a vague idea about what they'd 'done for me' in bringing him to justice. But as avoiding responsibility for my feelings was my way, I got on with my work. The niggles, though, lay fallow, like seeds waiting for spring so they could sprout in good time.

A year later, in 1995, another article appeared. Another man had come forward and Leunig was charged with further multiple counts of sexual abuse, and again pleaded guilty. I couldn't pretend to conceal the abuse from myself this time. The meek voice now became strident, belligerent and demanding.

See? He came forward and told the police. That's what you should have done. Declare yourself now, demand justice! Go to the court on the day of sentencing. Yell out, 'He abused me too.' Stand up for yourself. Look down at him and the judge. Shout it out!

I couldn't, of course. That voice still struggled for authority. An older, more familiar voice, the passive one I'd inherited from my father, responded instead.

You're a good man, upholding Christian values. You're being reasonable and forgiving.

When Leunig was given a further prison term, adding one year to his original sentence, the conciliatory voice felt vindicated.

Leunig has got his just desserts now. Serving another sentence for this next lot of abuses will resolve it for you once and for all.

***

The public exposure of this second tranche of abuses was troubling. I'd abdicated again, but this time I was angry at my inability to act. It took my rages to a new level. Incredibly, but perhaps predictably, I still hadn't made the direct causal link between my fury and the sexual abuse. One incident still shames me.

We were preparing to go south for our annual family camping holiday, but the preparations had gone awry and we were running late. It would have been something between Louise and I, perhaps my loss of control, perhaps a criticism. We set off, me immersed in that angry, punishing, silent rage that silenced conversation.

I gripped the wheel, my anger festering until it was volcanic. We were passing a car park outside a shopping centre, and I looked at a light pole on the edge of the road. I had the real thought that I should drive into it and kill us all. The fantasy was so terrifying, I had to pull over, get out of the car and walk away. I could have kept walking and never gone back. I stood sheepishly out in the open for a few minutes, shameful of my inability to deal maturely with my troubles. Back in the car, I felt humiliated but at least able to acknowledge how lethal my anger had become. I didn't mutter an apology. The act of stopping and getting out of the car was enough to have felt some degree of self-control. By the time we reached the camping ground I had returned to 'normal'. The holiday was always healing; two weeks sharing a campsite at a remote beach hamlet with one of Louise's colleagues and her family, who had become familiar, long-term, caring friends. We discarded shoes and roamed in bare feet, slept in a tent, cooked on a wood fire, had long swims, went for walks in the earthy-smelling forest – a reconnection to that distant echo of John Stewart Collis. I returned to the city unburdened and energised, reluctant to leave that undemanding, conflict-free life and resume the ambivalent cycle of my working life. And wearing shoes.

I still had no consciousness of the abuse as it smouldered away inside, only experiencing a pervasive gutlessness when challenged, disempowerment in its raw form, and I would scrabble around trying to defend myself. I appeared to run a successful architectural practice but in essence I was still a fugitive, grateful for those days when I could find some respite from the war that raged within.

30
The Gallery
1999

The Fremantle Arts Centre, on the outskirts of the port city, was built in the nineteenth century as an asylum. Falling into disuse, it was reassigned during the Second World War as a hospital for American servicemen. Abandoned again after the war, it was saved from demolition in the 1970s, restored and adapted as a community arts centre. Louise and I often took the children to listen to Sunday concerts and see the art exhibitions, especially the annual Print Award. Built around a series of high-walled, limestone courtyards, the Centre was a sanctuary, one of the few places in Perth where I found quiet refuge.

It was 1999. I was forty-seven. Louise and I were at an exhibition of etchings in one of the smaller galleries. The room's whitewashed stone walls soared up to an impossibly high ceiling. Tall windows lined the long, south wall and a vast fireplace and chimneybreast the north. The light from the windows flooded into every corner of the room, illuminating the soft, linen-textured whiteness of the walls. Although not overly large, the room had a scale that always made me feel small. The solitary, low, narrow doorway to the rectangular room was in a corner at the east end. We were standing at the far end, looking back towards it.

In an instant, the room was stripped bare, a haze of white silence. A single figure had walked in. Leunig. A dagger stabbed at my suddenly pounding heart as it thumped in the vacuum of expelled air. An indescribable panic was unleashed, as once had happened on the beach at Cottesloe. Now, too, this once safe place had been violated. With an arresting urgency, the screaming in my head started.

This is MY space, MY realm, MY Arts Centre! How DARE you come into my world, how DARE you pretend to like art!

A mantra soon started: *I mustn't let him see me. I mustn't let him see me.* He was wearing the usual open-collared white shirt with black trousers. He was short and overweight. I didn't remember him as short, unable in that moment to process that it had been thirty years since I'd confronted him on the steps of my childhood home.

I pushed back against the unyielding wall. He took a few steps toward the midline of the room, stopped momentarily, then walked slowly down the middle, not close to the etchings like everyone else. His eyes drifted from side to side, left to right and back again, disinterested. He paused, then moved a step forward. He seemed to be just going through the motions.

Four or five paces behind him was a companion, dressed casually but with the demeanour of a priest. They seemed to be together but were not close. Leunig had been in prison. I pictured him in prison greens.

Why is he here? Is he on parole? Is that a parole officer? Is this part of his rehabilitation? How wrong to think that art would help his rehabilitation?

Eight metres away. My heart, cut loose of its moorings, crashed around inside my chest. He was between me and the exit. Tensed, I felt like prey as the predator approached. I froze, pressing harder against the wall, my mind reeling at his imminent menace. I could not risk letting him see me.

Seven metres. He rolled on his short legs, short steps. He was bald. It betrayed his age. His skin was pudgy and flaccid still, his snub-nose turned up, his still-curling lip arched in that permanent sneer, the set jaw, pointed and lifted upwards, the demand to come still there. But his mouth was grim set. Something was missing. Gone was the anger and the calm air of power. He seemed defeated. He said nothing to his companion.

Six metres. His narrowed, beady eyes, recessed and unsmiling, oscillated from side to side. He hadn't seen me yet. But I'd recognised him, so why wouldn't he recognise me?

I mustn't let him see me.

Five metres. I was trapped in the cul-de-sac. I would have to go past him to escape. I judged the gap and watched his every move, ready to avert my eyes if he saw me, ready to flee. I edged sideways out of his trajectory.

He was halfway down the gallery. Four metres. Three metres.

Terror seized me like a hunted animal. I leaped left, brushing past Louise and muttering, 'I have to go.'

I squeezed by, barely inches from his white shirt, feeling his presence. I looked away to the wall on my left as I scrambled out of the room, terrified his eyes would catch mine. I veered left through the doorway and out an exit into the central courtyard, across the lawn and through the colonnade around to the back of the building. Louise caught up, breathless and quizzical.

'What's up? What happened?'

'It's him. The priest. In the gallery.' I was laughing in an embarrassed way, happy to have escaped. How bizarre and cowardly. Why was I so fearful of him seeing me? I felt diminished.

'Which gallery? What did he look like?'

I described him. She went back but soon returned, unable to find him.

'Aren't you going to do something? Find him and confront him?' She was outraged.

'I can't. I can't let him see me.'

I stood for a few minutes, contemplating the absurdity, before we left by the back gate.

For years, I've picked away at the encounter, trying to dissect its effect. It was as though the master puppeteer had returned and the strings, once attached to my paralysed limbs, were now attached to my shame and guilt, those entangled feelings cemented into the depths. At that moment, Leunig was the only person who could see right into my soul, who knew the sordid truth of my 'complicity'. If I let him see me, it would be like shining a light into my own heart of darkness. He *was* my well-hidden shame and guilt. The counsellors and psychologists over the years had never managed to illuminate that truth. I only had to see him for a moment for it to be instantly floodlit.

I punished myself for being gutless. That voice whispered in defeat: *The way you fled, you're afraid of him. That's why you can't report him to the police.*

The conciliatory voice tried to bring back the argument of reasonableness: *You're justified in your inaction. He's suffered enough. He doesn't need any more prison time. You're showing good Christian values: compassionate, mature and reasonable.*

Yet the rages still erupted, unabated and unacknowledged. Another bout of therapy began; this time with a male clinical psychologist. The surface issue was a growing paranoia and my confidence in tatters, but the undercurrent was my lack of authority. I'd become unsure and mistrustful, projecting that onto Louise. I told him about the abuse and its effects on my adolescence and into my adult life. He didn't get down to the sticky repository of my supposed complicity in a personal moral crime and, like all the other therapy seasons, there was no intrinsic resolution. The seeming restoration of a semblance of order masked the mistrust that festered away, recorded with an increasing frequency in my dream journal, as things slowly took a turn for the worse.

31

Rage

2004

The volcanic rage was now an alive and animate beast, and crashed unapologetically into my office, overwhelming my passive and inadequate management skills. I had asked a young architect to vary our standard documentation terms for a special client. He resisted the request as it meant changing a particular part of his style. His refusal seemed contemptuous, and a stand-off ensued. Speechless at his obduracy, I stammered around in circles, searching for solid ground, for authority where it was legitimate and necessary.

I could never admit fault, the blame always being attributed to someone else – a builder, a planning officer, Louise or, in this instance, the young architect. Furious to the point of distraction, I talked about it endlessly to whomever would listen. The lava of anger overflowed at home, singeing everyone on the way down. Louise impatiently sidestepped the incessant flow and stopped being receptive.

'You have to act. Talking without acting will not resolve it. And it's affecting your parenting. You're becoming irrational with the children. It's not fair on them; *do something*!'

She was right. It had become a family issue, especially for Tash, whose normal adolescent expression of her growing individuality pressed those same buttons of loss of control and blame. I projected my silent rage onto her. Unable to own my anger, I would cut her off. The dynamic had become toxic.

Louise insisted I needed counselling support and, as it now involved the family, she said we should go together. She did the footwork again and found Bridie, a family psychologist. It did not take Bridie long to home in on my thinly concealed rage and she astutely dissembled the charade of happiness I habitually presented. Prodded, still resistant to the truth, I sat in her clinic room, squirming with shame. I didn't mention the abuse.

'You need to deal with your anger independently of you and Louise as a couple. I can recommend a male colleague who you'll be able to work with.'

Whereas others had not been able to circumvent the persona of composure to expose the roots of my anger, Bridie had clearly and boldly named it and pushed me towards an acceptance of it. Humiliation was now added to my stockpile of inner baggage.

With the usual anxiety, but careful to still preserve this image of integrity, I summarised my life to the new male psychologist, wondering where this next attempt would lead. He put down his pad, aligning his pen beside it on the desk.

'You're depressed. Very depressed. It will be difficult to work with you while you're in this state. I'd like you to start a course of antidepressants. Once they've had time to take effect, then we can start therapy. Can you make an appointment as soon as possible with your GP?'

He gently dropped this bomb. Depression? Medication? Anti-depressants? How would I tell my doctor? My pretenses were slashed in one sentence, and my inner voice that pretended control flailed around the room a failure. He arranged for our sessions to start in three weeks when the antidepressants had taken effect.

A June 2004 diary entry records the doctor's visit and the start of the antidepressants. I write a note of 'an interest in seeing what will happen'. Two and half weeks later, the same despair that permeates the diary is still described, but this time with the observation that it doesn't have an emotional effect: 'I can keep going as if all is normal, but watching this feeling that it is not.' Then, a few days later: 'Overwhelmed this morning by the panic/anxiety feeling – but as above, it is not crippling, though today, more so than yesterday, it left me almost breathless.'

Louise encouraged me to tell the psychologist about the abuse and, as shameful and embarrassing as it was to tell the story, I did as she asked. But in following her instructions, I did not yet have a truthful insight myself, so the disclosure lacked authenticity, as though I was describing an ingrown toenail.

Over the course of fourteen sessions during 2004 and 2005, he listened well and administered advice that at least empowered me to act more authoritatively in my practice. But I was acting on his instructions, not from an intrinsic understanding of what was causing the rage that drove the mayhem. That malevolent seed, the sexual abuse, remained cemented in place. Slowly, my barely serviceable coping strategy – the happy face – began to wilt. Paradoxically, this allowed the much quieter, positive voice to slip in, empowered enough to whisper: *Justice?*

32

Sexual Assault Therapy

2004–2011

Working with the psychologist and talking more openly about the abuse now began to open doors to that dark place of the war-torn landscape. I felt less ashamed and, for the first time, talked seriously about reporting Leunig to the police. Louise, sensing I needed an advocate, encouraged me to talk to my brother Dom, a lawyer, and we met at a seaside café. Squirming unmercifully on the cold, steel seat, I told him the bones of my story again. He still did not flinch. A few days later, he rang with the best contact and the number for the Police Sexual Assault Unit.

Why hadn't I had the wherewithal to follow this obvious and simple course?

This question, a flicker of my inability to comprehend the disembodiment inherent in abuse, was demoralising. I couldn't understand that I did not yet have an outer voice to claim justice for myself.

I jotted the number down on a slip of paper, toyed with it, folded it and put it in my wallet. In the ensuing months and years, I came across it from time to time, fingered it and put it back. On the good days, I didn't want to stir up that hornet nest. It was on the depressed and angry days that I wanted to ring the Unit, but those were the days I was least able to do so.

Finally, desperate and determined to act, I hunted through my wallet. The slip of paper was gone. I could easily have looked in the phone book and called the Unit myself, but I didn't. I slipped back into the rhythm of coping, putting on the face. Louise commented that I now walked with my head down all the time.

Harry had moved to Sydney in 2004 to study engineering. Now an adult, his role in my life had matured to one of sharing bigger ideas and interests. Louise and I began to commute to Sydney frequently to spend time with him. Returning from one of those visits, on the plane journey back to Perth, came my watershed moment. Floating free above the world, the cauldron burst. Tears streamed down my cheeks as I tried to conceal the helpless sobbing. I turned to the window, humiliated and bewildered, before I surrendered to the chaos of that moment.

As startled as I was by the feeling of being gutted, I did not, and could not, understand it. It seemed the more I talked openly of the abuse, the greater the automatic impulse to keep the lid firmly closed. The perverse rhythm of this turmoil swelled and ebbed for another five years until it became toxic. I threw myself more deeply into work as a distraction, until that too felt poisoned. The working week became one of barely contained resentment. I looked forward to weekends when I would have no responsibility for anyone or any project. But the week's simmering anger started to overflow into Saturday. And then Sunday.

Five years later, in 2009, it was at four o'clock one Sunday afternoon when I had the first insight. That familiar and nebulous rage and resentment, plus the accompanying dread, had been building all day. The weekend had not fulfilled its promise of freedom. The second insight came seconds later – it had been like this every Sunday afternoon for years, almost to the minute at four o'clock.

This moment of lucidity, about having to put on the 'happy face' and be responsible for staff and clients and their buildings when I had no intrinsic authority and no sense of ownership of that responsible architect, instantly triggered bitter resentment of my work. This was catastrophic. Architecture was the scaffold on which I had built and padded out a modestly competent identity as a professional. It was the glue that held together my fragmented shards.

With an uncharacteristic sense of urgency, I knew I had to report Leunig to the police. I opened the telephone book and looked under 'Police; Sexual Assault Unit.' It didn't exist. There was no reference under 'Police.' I looked under 'Sexual' and found 'The Sexual Assault Resource Centre'. I called in the morning and a woman answered. She was discreet and asked for a few details.

'You'll have to come to our Centre and see a counsellor first before we can take any further steps.'

I was at a loss. Should I mention that I wanted the police? Maybe this was the police 'sorting house'? I went ahead and made an appointment.

The Sexual Assault Resource Centre was an anonymous, single-storey building with only a street number. I parked away from it and walked a roundabout route so I could approach it quickly and obliquely, afraid I might meet someone I knew. It felt familiar, like how my father had shielded me as we rushed into St Joseph's church in Subiaco, fifty years before. I was directed to a waiting area in the foyer. A counsellor soon came and took me to an interview room. She was sensitive and confident, and told me the clinic was a Health Department service, a specialised unit for sexual abuse victims. It had nothing to do with the police.

'A counsellor will be appointed in due course,' she said. 'We'll notify you when a place is available. In the meantime, you're to call immediately if you're at risk of self-harm. Here's the twenty-four-hour number.'

I agreed to follow up with the counselling they were offering. Anything was better than nothing. I was at the end of my tether. The police report fell to the wayside again.

The first sessions with the counsellor were unremarkable. There was a recess over Christmas, and when the sessions were due to recommence in February, she was on leave. My new counsellor would be James. A fist clamped my heart and pushed on my airways at the prospect of sharing the sexually explicit details of my abuse with a man.

Sitting in the waiting area again, I squirmed on my seat as people walked past. I still couldn't put a name to that reaction, the same as had happened in the art gallery. It was the notion that I was transparent – they knew why I was there and could see right through me to my shame.

James came out to meet me.

He's too young to understand what I've experienced.

I followed him down a maze of dog-legged corridors to a bright, sunny room. He was friendly and welcoming. I eased into my story, surprised at the way he simply validated the facts. There was no talk of remedies or strategies to help me cope, all of which implied a known end. Nor was there mention of antidepressants. He seemed to be simply granting me licence to traverse my inner landscape, without the expectation of a solution.

In therapy, I'd never known what to expect, except to hope to be rid of the symptoms of this unknowable, malevolent yoke that manifested as rage. The 'problem' never had anything to do with me. I would be fine if people would just leave me alone.

The fortnightly visits now brought on a deep anxiety. In the early sessions, I sat on the mustard-yellow couch and felt fraudulent.

You're too old for this. How presumptuous of you to think you're important. Stop wasting his time. There are much younger, more deserving people needing his time; young women who really have been sexually assaulted.

And then, after a moment. *You're an impostor. What happened to you is not that serious. And anyway, it was nearly fifty years ago. You've got on with your life pretty well.*

I still talked in circles, trying to sound genuine, but James didn't go to sleep. He was not particularly interested in what I was thinking, yet he didn't dismiss my thoughts, merely letting them go, noting them with a faint smile and a nod. As I squirmed in discomfort, he would look at me. I would come to understand his gentle smile as he watched. He was noticing and registering that something physical was manifesting in me.

'What do you feel when you say that?'

I shook my head. I had to think about it.

'I don't feel anything.' I orbited what I couldn't name yet still I talked.

He would stop me and query odd words and throwaway comments and, seizing on them, he would coax them to where my feelings might lie. Then he would watch patiently as I circled, all the while reminding me to breathe. He made sure I stayed present. He had an uncanny ability to know when my mind had fled and gone spinning off out of the room, and he gently invited me back. There was no judgement, just the reassuring half-smile at the corner of his mouth.

In one of those moments, he said, 'What's happening now?'

'What?'

'Where did you go just then?'

A dream image from the previous night had come back to consciousness and pushed everything aside. It must have made my eyes look up at the noticeboard above his computer where there was a poster about trust saying 'It's okay to tell'. I hesitated. He was confident to follow my lead.

'There are Catholic priests and monks chanting in a cathedral. They're lined up along one side, deep inside the shadows of an alcove. I'm standing on the opposite side of the nave watching them. The cathedral has a dark, mysterious, medieval aura. I'm attracted to the singing, so I go over to the group. When I get to them, they're all dead. Their bodies have been piled into a heap, a tangled hillock of woollen habits. Inside the monks' hoods, their faces are grey and expressionless. Several nuns in habit come by. They're cleaning up. I follow them to another part of the monastery that is attached to the cathedral. We walk around a cloister where there's more light. I follow the nuns past the carved stone columns that mark the inner perimeter of the cloister.'

As I told James the dream, a deep longing welled up, swelling like a monsoonal storm. It wanted to burst out. I described it and said it must be an aching for the music and religious life of my childhood. James didn't go to any meaning.

'Feel the source of the longing. Put your hand there. Keep it there.'

It was a pressure in my chest, around my heart. I self-consciously raised my hand. It felt contrived, until a moment later when an overwhelming panic drenched me in a saturating, blinding flood of terror. My mind raced away trying to escape the demand to know.

'Stay here,' he said, 'Stay with that feeling under your hand.' He was staring at me, unmoving. 'Stay here.'

Minutes passed in silence, my hand over my pounding heart. I took comfort from the stillness in his face. As the panic subsided, it was replaced with the same feeling I had experienced on the plane – exhausted of life, reduced to a hollowed-out shell.

I left our sessions breathless and squinting into the too-bright afternoon light. I would hesitate before I crossed the road, the speed of the cars difficult to judge. I was in slow-motion and they were racing. I took time out to sit on the grass in the park opposite and watch the birds as they fossicked around, slowly and purposefully exploring the earth, feeding on found morsels. Sometimes I sat in a back corner of a nearby coffee shop, waiting for the world to slow down. Though it was still early in the afternoon, I couldn't go back to my office.

Over the coming months, slowly and methodically, we revisited the episodes of abuse – the terror of discovery in the sacristy as Leunig's hand encircled my genitals; the humiliation and betrayal on the beach at Cottesloe; the dark nights of terror and aloneness in the presbytery at Quairading.

'Where do you feel it?'

It was always a pressure over my heart or deep in my chest.

'Put your hand there.'

And so I came to link the feeling with the event, and new words emerged to express what had happened.

The abuse and its aftermath were traumas. I held them deeply in my body. We were revisiting these traumas, the manifestations of Leunig's cruelty and predation, and the terror, the betrayal, the humiliation, and then finally the shame and guilt. My mind could deny them, but physically they remained locked in my body. I was now beginning to feel them, to watch and work at whittling away their concreted mass on which I had built my shaky adult house. I was also starting to name them. Lying terrorised on the bed in Quairading, I had been subject to non-penetrative, simulated rape.

I had laboured to and fro for decades, approaching then fearfully retreating from this intransigent mass locked in my body. Now, James had led me to place my hand on it, easing and prodding, waking the 'unfeeling'.

He encouraged me to do a mindfulness course, which would help me to be focused and stay in the room, since we were about to embark on a new phase: exposure therapy.

Exposure therapy would be the process to guide my mind down to those places of terror, and not just put my hand over where they were interned but to voice them again and again until they lost their grip. One by one, we revisited them. It was easy to be led there as they were all still vivid technicolour movies in my mind.

'Imagine yourself in the sacristy. Now tell me what you see. Tell me what's happening.'

Fury fuelled the first telling of each encounter.

'Tell me again.'

'Tell me again.'

Over and over, I described the scenes until they became boring. The day on the beach at Cottesloe was the most gruelling. I trembled at Leunig's invasion of my only safe place, the feeling of betrayal, his anger and the cruelty of his brazenly deliberate abuse in the public's gaze, and in front of my mother, at my powerlessness and humiliation, at his taunting, and then the feeling of defeat and utter aloneness, isolated from everyone.

'Keep your hand over your heart as you tell it. Tell me again.'

His eyes stayed fixed on mine, unwavering. I held his gaze and took heart. I swallowed and started again. As I did so, the memory of the convulsive sobbing that erupted on the plane journey in 2004 pushed its way into the story. Was that also a release of the trauma of that time?

I told the story of that day on the beach over and over, trembling each time. In one retelling, the memory of my recurring nightmare surfaced. I had had it again the night before. The remembered terror was so real, I squirmed vigorously on the couch. James and I had come to understand that squirming as my body trying to release its secrets.

James leaned forward. 'What just happened? Just then. Something happened.'

It took me a minute to connect the squirming with the memory of the nightmare.

'Tell me,' he said.

'There is a terrible war all around me. It has been raging unabated for years. I'm on my own, being hunted and shot at. The shooting is incessant. Whatever side I'm on is in a state of perpetual defeat. Terrified, I scramble across fields devastated by the fighting, hiding behind mounds of earth, diving down into bomb craters, crawling along behind shattered brick walls. It's all I can do to avoid being hit by the sprays of bullets whistling past. I can't see anyone else on my side. Nor can I see who's doing the shooting. The unseen enemy pursues me relentlessly across these devastated landscapes. I'm mute, unable to shout out or call for help.'

This same nightmare had occurred so often, over so many years, that I had stopped writing it down. In the latest dream, the shattered brick walls I was crouching behind, usually a stone colour, were red.

We talked about 'shooting'. It was a metaphor, its genesis probably in Leunig describing his ejaculation. Perhaps that had become a dream symbol for the sexual assaults. But the essence was that there was war in my psyche, with the prevailing feelings being on my own, in mortal danger and vulnerable with no-one on my side. It occurred to me now that the motif of being 'in a state of perpetual defeat' could describe the patterns I had observed for so many years: those weeks and weekends feeling unfulfilled; of being sucked helplessly along in the wake of events, at work especially, unable to be in control. In other words, as in these dreams, I had no voice.

To escape the helplessness and hopelessness in this war, I could see how surrendering might be the only escape, hoisting a white flag with drugs, alcohol, violence or suicide. And if those options were a bridge too far, then unquenchable rage. This had been my very difficult highway, but in a strange way, it and Louise had kept me alive.

Now the metaphor of war exploded to the surface in every session. James watched carefully as I ducked and ran from the shooting, fleeing the enemy, uncovering a life lived in a state of perpetual defeat. It painted a new picture of my reaction to flee the gallery as Leunig approached.

But alongside the terror, James identified moments of optimism and hope in my stories, moments that had been swamped by the superior matrix of isolation and rage, and the impending threat of danger. We came to call them the 'Uncle Paddy' moments. Had he known, Uncle Paddy, now long dead, would have advocated for me against the injustice and cruelty.

When I despaired at the relentless, incessantly surging feelings of panic, James would gently invite Uncle Paddy to come and sit with me.

'Tell him what's happening. What does he say?'

I was good at inner conversations. 'He' became a key figure leading me to a place of trust and safety. Uncle Paddy became the first 'person' I saw on my side in my inner war-torn landscape.

Steady there, man. Ye're not to blame.

Another pivotal breakthrough occurred some months later when retelling the experience of my 'honeysuckle moment'. James was watching me intently, as he always did. I launched into the scene, my hand over my heart and my lungs.

'I'm standing by the side gate of my childhood home. I'm looking up at the honeysuckle creeper climbing across the trellis. I'm consumed by shame. It fills every part of me. There is nothing else. I'll never be able to escape from it. It'll be in my life forever. The future has disappeared. I'm trying to see a future, but there is only a swirling, grey fog. I have no future. I feel only dread. Desolation and dread.'

The despair and hopelessness were once again overwhelming. I breathed into this monumental panic as it rose and tried to crush me. This one seemed to trump all the others. Again, we both watched in silence and waited until it subsided, my hand clutching my chest. However empowering it might have been to name and feel it, the experience led to a sobering and distressing realisation. Suicide might have been a justifiable release from the utter desolation of this gateway to nothingness.

Our fortnightly therapy sessions consumed the months, and the months stretched into years. One night, my family was cleaning up after dinner. I said something funny and we all had a good belly laugh. I could not remember when I had last laughed like that. The liberation from the past was overwhelming, but with it came a new feeling: grief. Grief for the loss of the innocence I remembered before I became separated from my parents and brothers, and for my life only half-lived ever since. Even as I felt this liberation, I knew there was a part of me still holding back from seeking justice.

Why don't you go to the police?

33

Tell Your Children

2010–2012

The months of gruelling dismantling, telling the stories over and over, had forged a resilience to the unending landscape of war, and James sensed a time had come.

'You must tell your children. Somehow they'll know all of this, if only from what's not been said. You owe it to them to explain.'

I felt the same excruciating stab as I'd had in the psychiatrist's room twenty-one years earlier. I could not conceive of telling my family then, nor my children now. I wanted to protect them from the horrors of the world.

I'd consciously tried to be my best as a parent, but I'd not been strong, secure and fearless. My vulnerability contaminated my generosity and love. I now owed them the truth about my sullen, passive-aggressive anger, that I was afraid to get angry because I wanted them to like me; but when my rage finally upended me, why I walked out without a word.

Six months passed. Harry, now in his mid-twenties, was home on holiday. Summoning the courage, my face flushed, I finally seized a moment alone with him to squeeze the words out through a portal of shame.

'There's something I need to tell you.'

'Yes, Dad.' He was lighthearted. But these were new words, a tone I'd never used, forewarning something dire. He frowned. 'What's the matter?'

I told him the story, along with the litany of after-effects and the issues that had dogged me, but also how counselling with James had nurtured an optimism.

'It explains why sometimes I've gone completely off the deep end and have become irrationally angry and upset, especially after an argument with Louise, and I'd disappear for hours.'

'That's awful, Dad! Who was it? Why didn't you tell us? You could have told us.'

He was simultaneously shocked and caring, angry and inquisitive. I wanted him to hug me. I tried to say the word 'shame', but couldn't. I muttered instead how I hadn't known what I was feeling; about emotional immaturity, about recoiling from difficulties and conflict. I was in explanation mode, talking from my head and not my heart. I didn't think to say, 'I'm sorry. It wasn't my fault. And more importantly, it wasn't yours. I'm really sorry.' I wasn't afraid that dissembling the shell of my happy persona might diminish how he felt towards me; he had been a big part of my healing journey, and we had shared a creative, imaginative and intellectual life together. We were close, but we had never talked about feelings, at least none that I could name and act on. Nor did I know how vulnerable I felt. But he was a mature young man. It wasn't difficult for him to hear the truth.

'I've often worried about your mental health, especially when you had those irrational outbursts. I remember once you became so distressed, you left the house and went off in your car. You wouldn't answer Mum's or my calls. I really feared for your life that day. We were all beside ourselves.'

I felt deeply ashamed that I had caused him so much grief, and devastated that he thought he had lost me. I went to sleep that night immersed in sadness. He had named the terror I had felt as I desperately tried to find a safe place to hide and rest from the war. From this day, though, a larger seed sprouted and it would take some years before I could allow myself to name it: he loved me. I had lost connection with that language. Now I could let in love even though I was yet to understand its lexicon.

***

Counselling with James was drawing to a close. He was to move to another section inside the department. I was aware that I still had an unsureness with this man, and a part of me continued to hold back, but as the end approached, I understood the huge debt I owed him. He had embraced my intellect as he had guided me to those buried feelings, easing these disparate entities away from their securely guarded cache in my physical body. He had taken me to where the traumas had been interred and had guided them into the light of day, releasing their adhesions.

We wished each other well on the last day, knowing we may not see each other again. I walked out into the street exhilarated, fully alive for the first time in my adult life. I imagined I would feel like this for the rest of my days, joyfully free of anxiety.

But when the rages still erupted, seemingly irrationally and easily triggered, I was scared I had lost that feeling of aliveness. I struggled to accept that my anger may be legitimate. The force to negate it, instilled by my parents' prohibitions, was still active. The more I took ownership though, the more the blame could be laid squarely on the shoulders of Leunig. And though I knew that what I needed and wanted was justice, for now, that voice was still silent.

***

Since 2009, newspapers had begun to regularly report shocking stories of abuse within the Catholic Church, and in 2012, a Parliamentary Commission of Inquiry was established in Victoria. Harry, now living in Melbourne, emailed, texted or rang each time there were new revelations of abuse, making sure I was coping with what was surfacing in the stories of so many other peoples' lives. Over time, he revealed more of his anxieties, and for the first time in my life I did not react defensively. How remarkable to feel ashamed and not deny it. I was deeply saddened though, that my distress and anguish had not only isolated me from fully knowing him, but it had also sown anxiety and distress in his life.

I still hadn't told Tash. Apart from the nearly six-year gap in their ages, my relationship with both children had been necessarily compartmentalised, another coping strategy. If it had been hard telling Harry, how could I reveal such an intimate violation to her? She was nineteen when I had told him. I'd rationalised at the time that she was too young and so a year had gone by. Every day I wondered, *Is this the right moment?* Then another year. My gut-wrenching fear neutered me every time I thought the opportunity had arrived.

Now she was twenty-two. Sitting across the table from me one day, she was telling me how shocked she was to read about the extent and severity of a litany of sexual abuse cases that had taken place in a government hostel in Western Australia. She seemed comfortable talking about it.

'This is probably a good time to tell you. I was abused when I was a young boy by our local Catholic priest.'

'Oh, Dad, I'm so, so sorry. That's terrible! That's awful. You must have felt so betrayed. Why didn't you tell me? Who was it?' She was comfortable with her feelings and not afraid of the bad stuff. She would have understood years ago; I was the arrested one. 'Can you tell me what happened?'

I candidly described the minutiae of the sacristy, the beach, the presbytery bed in Quairading. My voice still trembled describing those nights Leunig lay on top of me, easing my thirteen-year-old legs apart, simulating sex, the rape of my innocence. She listened so intently, I was both proud of her maturity and ashamed of my mistrust.

I had rediscovered how feeling loved felt after telling Harry. And now Tash. It was extraordinary – such faint and raw sensations of openness, of trust, of being loved – but so vulnerable, the sense they would evaporate as soon as I turned away. As the year progressed, she frequently showed me articles on cases in court and issues being presented to the Commissions. She talked openly with me about them.

'You know I'll support you if you want to go to the police or the Church again.'

I was touched by her solidarity but, as with Harry, deeply saddened that I had not been able to trust. But I was grateful that my difficulties as a parent had not prevented her from trusting and voicing her own feelings. I had Louise to thank for filling those voids.

I felt loved by my children, despite the collateral damage of my internal and ongoing war. Louise, central to my survival, was yet to be granted access under this new softening of my shell. Unfairly, in the tough moments, she was still a potential enemy. I loved her, even when I didn't know that that was what I was feeling, but it had become perverted by the eruptions of rage while the truth stayed buried. Now, when I tentatively prised myself open and she was admitted, it was another joyous reunion.

I had lived my life surrounded by friends, family and colleagues, able to function admirably to all accounts, but doing so sitting on the fence. Since the age of nine, I had been a loner who had learned a script that ensured I was liked and my secret was safe. But my heart was isolated and unsafe, and vulnerable to forgotten or unwritten lines, to others' lines, to war scenes. As I experienced their love seeping in and felt its warmth, I reciprocated. To love again was so warming but fleeting, so unknown.

Is it fraudulent? How can you trust that this is what love is?

Around this same time, another measure of optimism emerged. An old acquaintance, Pete Monger, asked if I wanted to join him on a camping trip into the desert. He used to be a livestock buyer and agent in the Kimberleys and the central pastoral regions of Western Australia, and was experienced and well-equipped to live in the outback. His family were anxious about his age and wanted someone to accompany him. Over the next six or seven years, two or three times a year, Pete and I travelled all over the state, the Northern Territory and South Australia, camping in deserts, under rocky outcrops, on stations and on riverbanks. We travelled slow, slept in swags on the ground, rose before dawn, stoked the fire, put on the coffee, boiled up water to wash. He knew the names of all the birds, the animals, the trees, the bushes, and all the gossip of the station owners and their families. He laughed at the follies of humankind, and we talked of how we would change the world to be a better place if we were in charge. He approached life pragmatically from a farmer's point of view, acutely aware of the waste in our society; I approached from a soft-socialist one, aware of its hypocrisies and inequalities. He quietly mocked the left-leaning press but also laughed at 'Murdoch's lies', as he called the conservative press. We laughed at the failings of all systems and all media. They were memorable journeys, immersed in the wisdom of the natural world, embroidered with humour and trust in each other. In this sense, Pete embodied the philosophies of both Uncle Paddy and John Stewart Collis.

In 2011, inspired to remove architecture as the backbone of my identity, I decided to close my practice. For thirty-five years it had variously enthused, frustrated and angered me, but it had also very modestly supported my family and had maintained the backbone of a professional life. Its course had run though and it was time to wander again. I gave my two remaining staff twelve months' notice. Louise and I planned a six-month sabbatical, freewheeling in Europe again. Setting off early in 2012, I experienced the liberation unencumbered by responsibility, and soon started writing another lengthy travel journal.

Part Three

34

'Church Holds Sex Dossiers', *The Age*

November 2012

The Parliamentary Inquiry into Child Sexual Abuse within the Religious and Other Non-Government Institutions in Victoria was announced in April 2012, and hearings began in October of that year. Hardly a day went by that there wasn't a front-page article of another revelation of appalling abuse and cover-up, with the Catholic Church and its bishops 'mishandling' reports. In Western Australia there had been less press coverage of these events, but in Melbourne, it was front-page news.

It was 17 November 2012. Louise and I were staying with friends David and Glenda in Melbourne. Louise and her colleague Mary were attending a professional conference and I had arranged to meet them at a café in the city. At the tram stop, a gentle wind ruffled the magazine and newspaper posters clustered outside the door of the newsagency. I bought a copy of the *Saturday Age*. A banner headline on the front page caught my eye: 'Church Holds Sex Dossiers'.

Sitting at one end of the tram, apart from the few passengers, I started reading. The article reported that from 1997 until 2008 the Catholic Church ran an extremely secretive program 'to assess and treat male clergy for psycho-sexual disorders' at the Wesley Private Hospital in suburban Sydney. The program had treated 'about 1,100 people, including hundreds of clergy from Australia and nearby countries.' The article stated that it was a world-class treatment program, 'highly expensive and highly effective', and that the organisation that ran the centre for the Church, Encompass Australasia, was linked to Catholic Church

Insurance Limited. They had kept dossiers on the offenders, including assessments of the likelihood of their re-offending. The dossiers were apparently made available to senior Church leaders and the Church's lawyers. None of the offenders had been reported to the police, as they would not have submitted to the program if a police report was a possible outcome. After treatment, 'offending clergy were quietly "transitioned" out of the Church, receiving generous payouts, accommodation and a university education.' (2)

Rage spread through me like a virus. The Church had challenged and diminished the victims, but it had assiduously looked after its 'psycho-sexually disordered' clergy, a euphemism for this group of paedophiles.

I tried to imagine the cost to the Catholic Church to run a world-class treatment program for eleven years and treat over a thousand clergy, followed by generous payouts, accommodation and a university education. I estimated perhaps hundreds of millions of dollars. And this in the climate of the Church apparently offering only tens of thousands of dollars to victims in exchange for their silence, not treatment. The voice inside my head hurtled into a formidable, full-blown righteous rage. I writhed in my seat, pushing against the sidewall of the tram.

The bastards! The bastards! What about the victims? And the police? These men are criminals, and the Church is concealing their crimes, spiriting them away from being named and even paying them on the way out. What about the victims? Why haven't you stood up for yourself and reported Leunig to the police?

The whole matrix of my shame and guilt and fear metamorphosed into a tempestuous loathing of the morality of the Catholic Church. The Church's action in supporting the paedophile priests and other clergy was an appalling affront to the thousands of victims – whom the Church continued to vigorously challenge in the courts – and a complete betrayal of their families, and the faithful, unknowing worshippers.

I got off the tram in the city and walked into the café where I was to meet Louise and Mary. Mary looked up with cheer and warmth, then her brow furrowed, even though I was across the room. As I reached the women, she said, 'What's wrong?' She knew it was something big.

I couldn't answer. I sat down and, fighting tears, showed them the front page. Mary knew about my abuse but not in any detail. She was one of the women I trusted and with whom I had begun to talk openly in recent years. My body was pulsing as my heart stopped and started, trying for oxygen. The women leaned in and read the article together. They gently touched my arms and held my hands.

My phone rang. It was Uncle Paddy's daughter Margie, ringing from Perth. The report had also appeared in Perth's newspaper. She and I had often talked about my abuse and, as her father would have done, she railed at the Catholic Church when I wasn't able to. I went outside the café and walked aimlessly along an arcade. My voice choked for long moments. I could only sob.

'I'm sorry,' I kept muttering. 'I'm sorry.'

She was crying. It was humbling knowing I was not alone, no longer completely imprisoned by my shame, and that I was loved by these women.

That night, talking with our friends David and Glenda, I showed them the article and told them my story. David said, 'You should write it down, tell your story.'

I had a strong bond with them and took heart from their compassion and their 'permission' for me to have a voice. With David's support, I began to document the episodes and watched as the pages revealed layer upon layer of feelings and memories unfurling from the anaesthetised foundations. Whole conversations resurfaced with disturbing clarity. Long-buried nuances reappeared, in particular the inner conversations of my trips to and from Quairading, of the moral implications of being in the car with Leunig, of sitting on the tree branch at Kwolyin. The anxiety and terror that gripped me as I wrote underpinned the veracity of the recall. It was another shade of the rawness I'd felt with James in therapy, the memories charged with an electric intensity. The more I wrote, the more the minutiae revealed itself. I stopped when the sobbing became too overwhelming. I became more fragile and vulnerable until one night, Louise rang the Sexual Assault Resource Centre. 'Come back immediately,' they said.

Coincidentally, James had returned to SARC and so, in parallel with the writing, counselling recommenced. This time I did not feel fraudulent. I sat on the mustard-yellow couch and honoured the squirming. My anger was legitimate.

35

Reporting the Abuse to the Police

April 2013

I reported my sexual abuse to the police fifty-two years after it had begun. The phone directory now listed the Sexual Assault Task Force. As the distant burring sounds of the ringing phone purred down the line, that extraordinary aloneness swept over me again; the nine-year-old boy's bewildered panic adrift in a moral wilderness with no-one to tell. Anxiety and sweat beaded on my upper lip, and I felt my heart crashing around trying to find solid ground.

Despite all the years of therapy, and now the feeling of the legitimacy of my complaint, I still felt shame as my call was answered. The constable was sympathetic, but his section only dealt with recent assaults. I would have to report my abuse to detectives within the jurisdiction that it occurred, Claremont–Cottesloe. They would also handle the assaults in Quairading given that the town was rural. He gave me the number to call at the Claremont station. He was sensitive and skilled and kept me talking, remembering my name even though I had only mentioned it once. He asked me quietly and cautiously if I could name the priest.

'Leo Leunig.' The words caught in my throat. 'I saw a report in the paper and on the internet of his other assaults, his conviction and imprisonment eighteen years ago.'

He cautioned me. 'You should document your allegations independent of any publicly available information. Be careful to describe specific details.'

'I can do that.'

I carefully wrote down the detective's number. I folded the slip of paper and watched myself put it in my wallet. This time I would not lose it. This time I would ask for an appointment to lodge a formal complaint, rather than talk over the phone. I wanted my report to be physical, not electronic.

I rang the office the following day. This time my crashing heart dislodged and spiralled up into my throat. My voice forced itself past it as a curt voice answered. I described the process that had been suggested in reporting a historical case of abuse. I briefly summarised the story.

'The priest's name?' The question was sharp.

'Leo Leunig.'

'I'll make some enquiries and call you back.'

He was abrupt, the business-like attitude of someone hardened by crime. He hung up. I couldn't help but feel adrift. It seemed impossible to nail someone down so I could report the abuse.

That afternoon, he called back. I was impressed and my hopes rose. Finally, justice had arrived.

'The person is deceased.'

Seconds passed in silence. The telephone suddenly seemed lifeless, as though the electricity had shorted out. I heard my voice, an echo, muttering. 'Of course. Thank you.'

'You understand there is now no case for the police to investigate, so the matter is closed.'

'I understand.'

'I'm sorry,' he said.

The detective kept talking but I wasn't listening. My mind drifted, lost in a remote desert somewhere. I heard his voice come back from the wilderness. 'Do you want to pursue the matter?'

'Yes. I understand it's too late, but it feels important to formally register the abuse, to put it on the public record, if only for my own satisfaction.'

'You'll need to go to a police station and make a statement. You'll get a report number.' We talked for a few moments longer. I thanked him and stared out into the garden.

Leunig had escaped me. Why had I imagined he would still be alive? He would have been well into his eighties, and he had been a heavy smoker. What had I expected?

I expected he would still be alive so that when I finally summoned the courage to go to the police – after all the years of fear and hiding, dodging bullets and leaping into craters – he would be answerable. After all, he was still alive in me. Why wouldn't he live as long as I would? I felt cheated. I could no longer hunt him down, confront him and have my day in court, stare him in the face and not flinch or flee as I had that day in the Fremantle Arts Centre gallery.

He was dead. The bastard. I walked around the garden in disbelief. Now I really was on my own. The part of me that sought justice, that part I had dragged unknowingly all my life, dithering and recoiling, had been excised, ripped out and tossed aside.

When I was thirteen, with no parent or uncle to advocate in my defence, I had had the courage to refuse him in his car, and at fifteen, face him down on the steps of my childhood home. Now, years too late, when I called the police as I had threatened to do in 1967, he had left me empty-handed. What right did I have to expect justice now?

But I wanted justice. I wanted a wrong to be righted, the aggrieved to be honoured and the separated child reunited with his lost self. I paced up and down the garden, circling the beds, tracking the lawn like a man possessed. Picturing him – short and fat with his pudgy hands and face, his snub nose under his deep-set, beady eyes – I tried to imagine him on his deathbed, but he was still coming towards me in the gallery, the life sucked out of him, no spark as his head swivelled from side to side, disinterested. Did he die that day, or did he live on for years?

How did he die?

Was he alone?

Was he sick?

Was it slow?

Did he commit suicide? From shame?

Did his peers and his archbishop support him as he died, comfort him and forgive him his sins?

Did they perform Extreme Unction?

Did anyone weep?

Was the Order of Melchisedech renounced?

Did he ask his Redeemer that his soul to be guided to Heaven?

Or did he stare at the ceiling as he was dying and fear where his soul's destination might be?

Did he pray for a happy and a holy death?

Did he slip away in silence, buried in an avalanche of shame from his abuses?

Did he turn his head and look at the curtains, stare at the sliver of dark in the gap and wonder whether God was on the other side staring in at him, judging him, condemning him?

Did his brothers and sisters come and sit by his side and love him despite all his wrongs?

Or did he too live an alienated life, estranged and apart from them?

Did he remember his mother as he lay dying and wonder whether she had ever noticed he'd changed?

Did the wind blow and scatter dead leaves on the ground under the pallbearers, eddies of death descending into the ground ahead of him?

Did they bury him in a grave with a headstone? Or was it unmarked?

Was it on the manicured lawn at Karrakatta Cemetery where they bury the Catholic priests?

Was he cremated?

Did his coffin slide quietly away through the chink in those curtains, swallowed up by fire?

Did his fat, pudgy hands and nicotine-stained fingers curl in protest in the flames?

Did they scatter his ashes in the wheatfields where I drove at sixty miles per hour, or did they put them under a rosebush somewhere where they could be reborn as thorns and flowers?

Did the smell of scorched cotton on his over-ironed cassock and his aftershave burn too, or did they still linger in the funeral home?

My mind, terrier-like, pursued him beyond the grave. I wandered around the garden, lost. A demon had been resurrected and then immediately torn from my grasp.

I had told the detective when I had last seen him. 'I bumped into him in a gallery around 1999.'

'Well, you won't bump into him again.'

I think he was trying to say the evil might finally be over. But my mind bumped into him all the time. I was not free of him. He was in me, intrinsically set in every fibre, had always been and would always be. Days went by where I would forget him, but then he was back, unsmiling, reigniting my anxiety with a small twist of his knife.

I was angry that he had never owned up to his crimes against me. Would he ever have had the courage to confess these sins to judge and jury, to his God and to me, and tell the courtroom that there were more than four children defiled and destroyed with his hands? He'd pleaded guilty only to those for which he'd been charged and nothing more. The Church and his archbishop knew at his 1994 trial that I was also a victim. What had Leunig felt, standing in the dock in silence, pleading guilty to those crimes yet knowing there were more? What did that say about his Christian ministry, about his sacred duty as a priest?

***

Tash was curled up on the sofa, typing an assignment. I slumped down beside her.

'I rang the police today. They said Leunig's dead.'

Her face clouded as she realised the implications. 'Oh, Dad. I'm so sorry. Do you know any details?'

I shook my head. Tears of deep sadness seeped out. Sitting with her, I was grateful I'd been given a second chance to love and be loved, to feel the flood of her caring.

A few nights later, she called me into the sitting room.

'I've been doing some research. I've found out the date of his death. And where he's buried. There's not much information available, but he died in 2011. He was eighty-five. They didn't bury him among the priests in the Catholic clergy section of the cemetery. He's buried in the lawn area for civilians, in an older brother's grave. His grave's next to the children's memorial garden. How ironic. That's cruel.' She paused. 'There were eleven priests concelebrating at his Requiem Mass.'

I sat in silence for a while, letting her presence wash over me. She continued. 'I feel so angry! I want to go and deface his grave. If he was alive, I'd want to hit him. Smash his windows. I feel so sad for you.'

Then, after another silence, she said the most remarkable thing.

'After you told me, I wanted to protect you. To fight for you, to vindicate who you were.'

She told me that in her teenage years, when I had those irrational outbursts after she had 'pressed my buttons' and I'd driven off into the night and ignored her calls, she'd sat on the edge of her bed waiting for the phone call, or the police at the door, telling her they'd found my body. And it would be her fault.

This was the cruellest moment, realising what I had put her through, and Harry and Louise as well.

'I'm so sorry,' I whispered. 'I'm so sorry I blamed you. I was the problem.'

'Dad, it's okay now. When you told me about your abuse, it all made sense. I understood. I am so grateful that you could tell me. It has explained all the little oddities; why I never spent much time with my cousins like other kids, why our family seemed to be the black sheep, why Nanna and Pop were close to the other cousins but not me and Harry. And all our family friends were Mum's.'

She recited the list, so astutely observed, of how she had seen our family existing in a bubble.

'I just wanted to be a white sheep.' She paused, lingering in this moment.

'But you and Mum were amazing parents. You did everything for us. You created the most amazing house and garden. You always welcomed my friends and fed them and listened to them. You both came to all my concerts. You managed my netball team and Harry's cricket team. Other parents didn't do that. You were always there.'

Once again, I was grateful to Louise for imparting to Tash and Harry the ability to talk openly about feelings and not be afraid to express them. If only I had had the tools and courage to stop reacting and listen.

***

In the ensuing weeks, small parts of Leunig were set to one side in my mind and, as the weeks melted into months, he faded from centre stage to become a ghost in the wings.

For the first time, I wondered how many more victims there might be, other than the boys in the court cases. Those who would never be able to have their moment in court, who had stood transfixed by the hopelessness under their metaphorical honeysuckle vines, unable to imagine a future and deciding to suicide then, or in a year or two, or maybe ten or twenty years later? Or had they struggled on, dragging or pushing their shame with them, their lives unfulfilled, their buried feelings, unrealised relationships and half-lived lives spewing rage or silence from the unknowable depths?

36

A Formal Police Report

April 2013

The waiting area at the Fremantle Police Station was small for an urban office. Two grey, plastic chairs lingered like lost souls in a corner. Faded posters of past crime prevention initiatives drooped on a pin-up board. Three men in workmen's clothes were deep in conversation at the counter. I waited until they moved, then squeezed past them. The counter was a short, vinyl-clad barrier with bulletproof glass panels to the ceiling. I leaned in towards the tiny holes in the glass, trying to create a connection with the officer on the other side.

'I'd like to report an offence,' I said, my voice getting louder.

'The nature of the offence, sir?'

'It's a case of sexual abuse. On me. A long time ago'. I was shouting now, embarrassed but relieved that the waiting area was deserted, now that the men had left.

'Your name, please?'

I responded and she replied, 'Please have a seat.' She nodded towards the chairs in the corner; I chose the least dirty one. Scuff marks and boot prints on the depressing, blue-and-grey-flecked vinyl of the walls and doors of the waiting area hinted at years of anger, frustration and resistance.

Your issue is trivial, said the voice. *How presumptuous of you. Drop it. He's dead.*

My name was called, and I went back to the counter. A young constable introduced herself, then said, 'I'll find an interview room we can use. Please wait a moment.'

The security lock clicked on a side door, and I followed her down a narrow corridor into a small room. We sat at a free desk, and she turned on a computer.

'Can you briefly describe your complaint?'

I summarised the events and named the priest. I had an oblique view of the computer screen. In a top corner an image appeared, seeming so normal but the hairs on the back of my neck prickled. Leunig, neatly dressed in civilian clothes, stared out from the screen. He looked ageless and benign, the same unsmiling, expressionless face giving nothing away. I wouldn't have been surprised if his arm had arced slowly up to his mouth with a cigarette, like that late afternoon in Quairading in 1965 when I had climbed out of the plane. Across his belly, electronic letters showed his name, a date and some numbers. I couldn't read them. The white wall behind him was innocent and bare, with no imprint of the grotesque acts he had committed. There should have been signs and banners describing the terror of the nights I was given up to him by unknowing, trusting parents. But there were none, just whiteness and loneliness. I couldn't look for long and turned away. The constable stopped, her fingers poised on the keyboard, and looked at me.

'I've never handled a complaint like this. Perhaps we should start with where and when these events occurred, then we can look at the specific abuse.'

I methodically described the events, the approximate dates and the number of instances. It was a curious conversation. This stranger, well-used to the depravities of life, listened, clarifying and questioning, unemotional but focused, asking exactly how and what happened.

'Was there penetration or just fondling? When he masturbated onto your stomach, what else did he do?'

Each time she queried a point, she looked directly at me. She was a good listener, her tone free of judgement or inference of complicity. The old patterns of guilt and shame, so embedded within me, all surfaced and tried for air but simply vaporised in the atmosphere. I was surprised that it felt so empowering and thanked James for this new consciousness. I was unused to it.

She went through her notes and checked their accuracy. She tried to put words to how I must have felt living with this burden, perhaps trying to comfort me. I gave her some phrases: 'unacknowledged rage', 'blame', 'fear of intimacy'. But I didn't need comforting, and she didn't pursue it. I thanked her for her sensitivity. The young constable, on her first historical sexual assault complaint, had made my encounter as painless as possible, and I was grateful.

37

The Professional Standards Office

May 2013

Even though filing a complaint with the police was an important, symbolic handing-over of the facts of the abuse to those charged with administering the law, I was surprised that it did not bring a feeling of achieving justice. Had Leunig's death precluded that? But as the weeks passed, I realised that justice must now come from the source of my unease.

My anger towards the Church as an institution had not abated since reading about the secret psychiatric clinic. I had become even more incensed that the Church had not openly acknowledged the thousands of victims, and offered them real, impartial and unconditional resolution. Where were the full-page advertisements in newspapers, listing the priests and the parishes and the dates? Instead, the Catholic Church had continued to challenge, or threaten to challenge, every survivor of abuse presenting in the courts. I needed to go back to the Church again. To not do so felt like a tacit approval of their stance.

I rang the Archbishop's office. This time his secretary seemed sensitive. As she spoke, and I registered my relief, I was surprised that I was still primed to feel judged, even after all the work I had done with James.

'Do you mind me asking what your enquiry is about?'

I told her the bones of the story. Her next question alerted me to how often she must now field these calls.

'Is it related to the Christian Brothers or is it about a priest from the diocese?'

'The diocese.'

'In that case, it is a matter for the Archbishop. He'll be away from tomorrow, but I'll discuss it with him before he goes.' She promised to get back to me. Half an hour later she called and described three courses of action.

'You can wait until he returns and discuss the abuse directly with him, or you can discuss it immediately with the Vicar General of the diocese, or you can take it to the Church's Professional Standards Office.'

Given the lack of resolve from my original reporting to Archbishop Foley, I did not trust that route, nor via another priest, even if he was called a Vicar General. I smelled the taint of self-interest and quiet cover-up. A 'Professional Standards Office' seemed an appropriately independent route, even though the use of the word 'professional' suggested a business career. When did the conveyance of spirituality become a 'business profession' rather than a vocation? I had to let go of this inner conversation.

'I'll take the last one as a first step.'

'I will ring their office and give them your details. They can then take responsibility for contacting you.' She sounded genuinely caring. It was my first experience of a woman within the Church who was empathic and sensitive.

The following day Moira called from the Professional Standards Office. After some preamble, she said, 'I'm sorry, but I'm new in the job and still finding my feet.'

Her message seemed to be to go easy and not expect too much at this stage. I registered this first note of unprofessionalism. She asked me to outline my complaint. I gave her the years, the parishes, the priest and the details as much as I knew them. I told her I had reported the abuse in detail to Foley in 1989. She promised to search the diocesan records to find my report.

'If the Archbishop has registered any of your information, you won't have to go through it all again unnecessarily. Once I've done that, I'll contact you.'

I told her I had been writing a detailed account of my abuse. She asked me to email her a copy, and I agreed.

A few days later, she emailed to say they couldn't find any record of my report or my visit to the Archbishop, but that wasn't an obstacle to continuing my current report to the Church. The email also mentioned access to immediate counselling should I desire it. Mentioning the word 'obstacle' seemed to suggest the possibility of one, even though it was a reference to there being none. A bell jangled quietly in the dark recesses of my mind. I was put in touch with a contact person and a meeting at their office was arranged for the following week. The email described the process. It was called Towards Healing and was designed to 'promote reconciliation and forgiveness'. I took the email at face value, not attributing much import to its contents.

Over the following days, my uneasiness increased. What did they mean they couldn't find any record of my visit to the Archbishop Foley? I understood it was challenging if I couldn't give them a definitive date, but the meeting would certainly have been recorded in his diary, which would be in the Church archives. The unease became paranoia. I went back to the email and analysed its terminology, especially the phrase 'the promotion of reconciliation and forgiveness'.

The word 'promotion' suggested the Church would try, but only up to a point. As the Church had spent eleven years paying for a psychiatric clinic and rehabilitation for paedophile priests, why would they not also offer me the same generous support and a similar retirement package? The Church would not seem to be fully participating if reconciliation and forgiveness were the only outcomes a survivor could expect in this process.

And who was forgiving who? The Church? God? Me? Their approach seemed to suggest that I had merely lost my faith because of the clerical sexual abuse, and the reconciliation and forgiveness were to allow me to be non-judgmentally welcomed back into the fold. With God's goodness, everything would be alright again. Was it being suggested that it had been my fault after all?

Furthermore, why was the word 'forgiveness' being used? Reconciliation and God's forgiveness were Church-based resolutions had I suffered self-inflicted moral and spiritual transgressions. What I was reporting was not self-inflicted.

The Professional Standards Office was in an old building in North Perth, adjacent to a church and a primary school. Three gates subdivided an imposing, red-brick pillared fence. All the gates seemed to have the same number. I chose the first gate, but it led to the primary school. Etched in large letters on the gable wall were the words: 'Suffer the little children to come unto me.'

The next gate led to the church. The third had no indication of what business was there, and the anonymity made me anxious. I went into a garden courtyard surrounded on three sides by an imposing, nineteenth-century, cream-and-red-brick building. The architecture labelled it heavily religious, institutional and foreboding; of the style of the convent and boarding-house buildings of my childhood. I couldn't help but feel a lingering, historical malevolence harboured in the building. The entry gable high up had a bold inscription: 'Monastery of Our Lady of the Sacred Heart.' It made sense that this building had once been a convent.

The path to the front door was bisected by a life-sized statue of Jesus standing on a pedestal. One hand was opened out showing the bloodied nail hole, while the other was pointing to his Sacred Heart with its exposed flame in his chest. I thought of James asking me to put my hand over my heart, where the panic was resided.

On the pedestal base, under Jesus' nail-punctured feet, was inscribed: 'Sacred Heart of Jesus, I Place My Trust in Thee.'

I had to go around his statue to get to the entry portico. I pushed open the solid timber door and stepped into the foyer. An older woman sat in a room off to one side, barely visible behind an imposing reception counter. She didn't move or stand up. Clearly I was expected, as she merely pointed to a room on the other side of the foyer. She was abrupt, telling me to wait in there, then settled back down behind the counter. She emanated the same ill-concealed hostility as Archbishop Foley's secretary years before. Her demeanor told me, *You've kept your mouth shut like you were supposed to for fifty years, so why are you opening it now?*

The waiting room was small with naive paintings arranged haphazardly on the walls. A bookcase stood in one corner and in an adjacent corner, an elaborately tiled Victorian fireplace. On its empty, tiled hearth, where once coals would have burned, leaned a large-framed photograph of a severe-looking nun in full habit. This building must have been her convent, but now there was no place for her photo except in the fireplace. Her face, barely visible, was pinched under her white wimple and tucked inside the taut cloth framing of her black habit. Heavy, black-rimmed glasses hid what little was left of her face, magnifying her penetrating eyes to give her a ferocious air. The picture was disturbing and in a perverse way, I couldn't take my eyes off her. She carried a remnant of the Catholicism of my childhood, invoking the fear instilled by the nuns, as well as an awe and subservience to the medieval culture of the Church. Having had to deviate around Jesus to get to the entrance, if I was at all unresolved or unsure about reporting my abuse to the Church again, this foreboding image of the nun may well have triggered a final, passive retreat. I would have liked to think I was immune to her aura, but still I kept looking at her. Why was she in the fireplace in this waiting room, this once powerful Mother Superior in her convent?

My reverie was broken by a figure appearing at the door. He was tall and older than me. His clothes were casual-looking and slightly unkempt, and he was wearing a sweater that was too short and too small. He seemed misplaced, as though he was the gardener and had gotten lost. Perhaps it was intended to invoke a relaxed atmosphere? It wasn't the professional look I'd expected given the title of the office, and it was off-putting. Jim introduced himself.

If this is the Professional Standards Office, then the bar is pretty low. Clearly the Church is not directing many resources into this office.

However, Jim was genuinely warm. He smiled as he shook my hand.

'My office is on the top floor. Would you like to take the lift or the stairs?' As an afterthought, he added, 'The lift is slow.'

'The stairs are fine.'

We climbed the flights of timber stairs, curling our way creakily upwards, the exotic newel posts on the handrails pointing to a past era of opulence in the Church. Panting slightly, I followed him into a small, light-filled cubicle. It was so small I had to stand to one side and shift a chair so he could squeeze past me to his desk. I moved the chair and shut the door behind me. I immediately felt uneasy. I was expected to declare past wrongs in what might once have been a nun's bedroom. I understood that discretion might be necessary for the business of dealing with the abuses, but it seemed inappropriate that this convent building had been recycled for the 'Professional Standards' offices. The room evoked a feeling too religious and too remote, the single window giving only a slender connection to the world. I looked up at the high ceiling and thought of a prison cell. It started to appear intentional, this tiny room as an office for the impoverished-looking Jim.

I tried to steel myself against the age-old impulse to be likable and compliant, a fleeting sense that if I weren't, I'd be swallowed up and never emerge from this building. But already I could feel myself becoming more malleable.

Jim leaned towards me, saying, 'I'm new in this role and not entirely familiar with the processes. But your case will be treated seriously.'

Am I at risk of not being treated seriously?

Now my lingering paranoia ratcheted up. Why had both he and Moira apologised for being new and inexperienced. Perhaps, I surmised, it was such a difficult business that staff moved on frequently.

'I've read your email account of the abuse.' He seemed genuinely concerned and understanding. 'So I presume from its content that you are not here to pursue the Church's program of reconciliation and forgiveness?'

I nodded and described the *Age* article. 'I want to tell the Church, again, what happened to me. But also my disgust at the Church investing millions of dollars rehabilitating and compensating the paedophile priests and other clergy.

'I deserve at least the same treatment. Can I, as a victim, expect an appropriate justice, at least equal to what the perpetrators received?' My question was not rhetorical.

He stared at me across the desk, clasping and unclasping his fingers, not knowing what they should be doing. He half-laughed, perhaps his way of responding, that I was surely joking.

Our conversation quickly turned to compensation, to the tangible rather than the rhetorical.

'You can pursue this through the Church's process of facilitation, but also through civil action.' His tone, the turn of his head and lowered voice pointed to the Church's preference to keep the process 'in-house'. 'Civil action might be more expensive but possibly more rewarding for you. But the Church's process will be simpler, less traumatic and perhaps quicker.'

What does he mean 'less traumatic'? Is he suggesting a quiet in-house settlement so I would avoid being crucified in a courtroom cross-examination?

A perfunctory knock at the door fractured our conversation and the door swung open. A solid, middle-aged woman stepped into the room, uninvited. She was dressed conservatively, in the manner of an elderly aunt. She faced me squarely, her feet apart in an intimidating stance. She looked me up and down. She turned and acknowledged Jim, and then nodded towards me. I stood up out of courtesy and Jim introduced me.

'This is Moira.'

She didn't say hello or shake my hand. It seemed a pointless intrusion, even subtly abusive. Panic now fed my paranoia. This was not reconciliation. It pointed towards capitulation, to let the Church quietly sweep the whole sorry story under the carpet. My parents had a measure of the approach twenty-five years before.

Jim gave me a formal declarations document, which he quickly explained I didn't have to sign at that point. It contained three sections. The first was titled Consent to Obtain Information, to authorise the Church to pursue information and enquiries to substantiate my complaint. The second section was their Privacy Statement, the sort that was on most documents these days. It seemed harmless, except that it suggested any information may be given to the police, 'if required by law'.

Then, the third section: Police or Civil Authorities Statement.

> 'The Catholic Church has strongly urged me to take my complaint to the police or other civil authority.

> It has been carefully explained to me that any process the Church establishes cannot compel witnesses, subpoena documents or insist on cross-examination of witnesses. It cannot impose the same penalties as a criminal court. Aware of these limitations I still state that I do not wish to take my complaint to the police or other civil authority at this time and I ask that a Church process be established. I undertake that if I change my mind and decide to have my complaint referred to the police or other civil authority at any subsequent time, I will give written notice of this decision to the Professional Standards Office.'[3]

While not denying a route towards a police report, the document indicated that the Church explicitly preferred to maintain the secret, to keep the exposure of my sexual abuse hidden away from the public eye, no doubt to uphold the stature of the Church. It seemed they were counting on, even inculcating, a lingering fear of the Church so that I might acquiesce and not report my abuse. It was the eerie feeling that my victim status was being perpetuated to keep me disempowered. I should accept what morsels were on offer and crawl away in silence.

I had come to understand three distinct strands to the abuse trauma – physical and psychological damage, shame, and the secret. The power of secrets infiltrated and silenced one's personal authority. It was an insidious and paralysing force, and not until it was defused by public disclosure (with friends, the police and in therapy) and acknowledged could there be any adequate resolution of the shame and the physical and psychological abuse. And here it was in print. The Church was not only wanting to maintain my silence, it was promoting it as a preferred method of resolution. I would forfeit my authority and my voice if I signed the secrecy agreement.

A barely concealed hostility seemed to underpin this process. The secretary downstairs had already flagged that sentiment. In not keeping silent, I was the problem, to be spirited away as quietly and submissively as possible.

Jim's voice seeped back through my disgust.

'The Church will of course fund ten free counselling sessions as part of a resolution.'

'Ten?' I looked at him, incredulous. 'I've already had a lifetime of therapy and counselling.' I didn't think to add that what was missing was a sense of justice. The abuses by their priests on children had lifelong consequences for them and their families. In protecting their public image over the mental health of the victims, the Church was not just trivialising the damage, they were trying to white-out a generational catastrophe.

'A Contact Report will require formal statements from other sources. Can you get a copy of your police report and a report from the Sexual Abuse Resource Centre? I'd also like you to draft an impact statement on how the abuse has affected your adult life,' Jim said.

'What about how it affected my childhood? My schooling?'

He looked sheepish. Again, his fingers entwined and unravelled, clawing for answers to the unanswerable.

'Well, no. That can't be part of it.'

I stared at him, my mouth agape. How could anyone with a conscience, having read my story, tell me this?

I sat for a moment in silence. It seemed our meeting had come to an end. I stood up and we shook hands. He wished me well. I went back down the flights of stairs, our conversation crashing around with the other voices: keeping the process in-house to deal with the matter away from the civil courts; maintaining my silence to uphold the 'good' name of the Church; concealing and trivialising the traumas. It was my father talking.

Back in the entry courtyard, I again skirted Jesus, standing tall and unmoving, His Sacred Heart cast in concrete, as mine had been. The footpath felt like jelly. If I missed my footing, I would be swallowed up in a black hole that was wobbling up through the cracks. For many minutes, I sat in the car and stared at a brick wall across the street. The unwelcoming receptionist and unkempt Jim were a cacophony of belligerent images scrambling to make sense. And then Moira, the intruding, solid aunt. She just wanted to see me in person, to get my measure, to see who she was up against. I struggled with the feeling that I'd just been mauled.

I'd misunderstood and misjudged my vulnerability. I had no solid foundation yet for the idea of a personal authority and the Church's position seemed to exploit this. Again, I had had no-one accompany me to advocate on my behalf, and neither Jim nor Moira suggested it might be helpful. They hadn't provided me with contacts for an independent support service, given that revisiting the abuse might trigger suicidal feelings. The ten counselling sessions would only become available once I'd signed their secrecy contract. Their process was unprofessional and dangerous. Despite my best resolve to be strong and stand up for myself, I went home traumatised, a feeling that lasted for days.

38

The Professional Standards Office Report

29 May 2013

In our meeting, I'd asked Jim if he could supply the dates and parishes in which Leunig had served. I wanted to establish an exact timeline for the events of my abuses. A week later he rang to discuss his report.

'I have some dates for you. Father Leunig was in the Cottesloe parish from 1964 to 1968.'

Anger snaked up from my belly, visceral and venomous. I wanted to shout at him.

'He was abusing me in Cottesloe long before 1964. The Honour Board in the Cottesloe church itself states he was curate there from 1961 to 1964. I want exact dates. The months! The abuse in Quairading occurred after he started visiting us at my grandfather's house, which was early 1965 onwards.'

Jim apologised, lamely muttering, 'This is a work in progress.'

I gave him the benefit of the doubt. But soon the inner voice arced up, trawling through our conversation, dissecting its message. He probably did not mean it to be, but it felt contemptuous.

Jim emailed a draft of his Contact Report for me to sign. Every aspect of my abuse and the aftermath was noted – with one exception. There was no mention of the appointment and visit to Archbishop Foley in 1989, even though it was a key element of the statement I'd given his office. They believed every word I'd said about Leunig. After all, he was a convicted paedophile, so it was more than likely my story was true. I presumed that for their report to state that I'd been to see Archbishop Foley and nothing had been done might be seen as an admission of failure of process, or even an admission of culpability in concealing a crime. For whatever reason, it was clearly a deliberate omission.

The rage I'd felt on the Melbourne tram erupted again. But now it was fuelled by a loathing of the might of the Church as an institution that would stop at nothing to subvert me, obfuscating under the smokescreen of warm words like 'reconciliation' and 'forgiveness' and 'healing'. The age-old nausea, the knot in my chest, twisted again with the sensation of being manipulated and controlled. I had a voice now, however meek, and I feared the pull to silence it.

I had approached the Church on my own in the belief that, based on my detailed written account, there would be an open acknowledgement and accountability for what had happened. I expected, as the lawyers would say, the administration of a just remedy, an acknowledgement of the trauma and the pain and suffering. Jim and Moira may have felt they were acting in good faith but, as the process unfolded, it was clear they were following a script in which everything was on the Church's terms.

I could not do this on my own. I emailed the Professional Standards Office, advising them I was going to seek a legal opinion before I would consider their report any further.

I still needed to establish accurate dates of Leunig's parishes, so I bypassed Jim and rang the Church's Archives Office in Perth and spoke to Stefanie. She was friendly and helpful, but when I stated my business, she was lost for words.

Recovering somewhat she said, 'I'll need to get a direction on this from the administration. I'll phone you back within the week.'

'I've been in contact with the Professional Standards Office, and in particular Moira.'

'Yes. I know her. We have quite a bit to do with each other,' she remarked.

She never called back. Several months later, a letter arrived marked 'Confidential', the acronym WAPSO above a return address. It was from the West Australian Professional Standards Office. I opened it and quickly read the contents. Though the letter was signed by Moira, it assiduously avoided any overt connection with the Catholic Church, the word 'catholic' with a lowercase 'c' appearing only in the email address.

She acknowledged that four months had passed since I'd notified them that I would seek a legal opinion on their draft report, and she wrote that the Archbishop had decreed I be given the dates of Leunig's parishes, cross-referencing with my request to the Archives Office. The dates of Leunig's relevant tenures were now specific and appeared correct (Cottesloe: (March) 1961 – (February) 1964; Quairading: 1965–1970). To affirm the official position, as an afterword, she confirmed no record could be found of my complaint to Archbishop Foley. It was the third denial.

The letter referred to receiving 'an apology and being eligible for counselling and some compensation.' The original offer of reconciliation and forgiveness had matured to an apology. The voice lapsed into a cynical anger.

An apology? If victims had not already committed suicide, the Church imagined it could simply apologise? And who will apologise, an email address? Or the Archbishop, having just finished his breakfast, cleaned his teeth and neatly arranged himself in his magenta robes? Archbishop Foley already apologised to me in 1989 and, in the end, that was meaningless and brought no resolve.

The letter also asked if I wished to pursue the process through their office. I felt defeated and isolated, as I had outside their office in North Perth. It was the difficult realisation that a just resolution could not be had dealing directly with the Catholic Church.

I wrote and officially notified them I was withdrawing from contact. Within days, a letter came back: 'It is regrettable that in spite of the support provided by this Office and other Church resources, we were not able to meet your needs regarding this claim … If at any point you decide to revisit your Towards Healing claim, our door will always be open.'

My inner voice began to rant: *It IS regrettable that one of your priests was able to betray my parents' trust to sexually abuse me, among others, and that you kept moving him around parishes for years. It IS regrettable you cannot see your way to now meet me humbly and generously, and unconditionally offer support for my physical and mental wellbeing without obfuscation and denials. Whatever was good enough for your paedophile priests in Sydney will do for me, too.*

There was a churlish tone to the letter's expression of regret, 'in spite of the support provided'. Regret was the language of feeling and it betrayed the subtext. The letter was about the Church's position, not mine. It implied 'hurt', that I didn't want to keep my abuse a secret. It seemed like a last-ditched effort to invoke guilt and appeared purposefully manipulative.

***

My reactions to the arm's-length response of the Standards Office brought to consciousness what it was I sought. I wanted something that might fill the intangible but remembered void of childhood innocence, the restoration of the loss from a life half-lived 'in a state of perpetual defeat'. I wanted a methodology that would restore wholeness. I wanted a physical justice. I wanted a voice.

In therapy, James had set me on this path towards living a wholesome life. I was yet to understand that it needed to go to a new level, and yet to understand what this justice might look like.

I made an appointment with Phil, a lawyer who specialised in personal injury cases. This time, Louise insisted she accompany me. At our first meeting, he explained how a just resolution, or the remedy of a wrong, was never considered to be fully transacted unless there was a tangible offering of something of material value in the process, usually money.

'There are three components to a remedy. Firstly, there is the measure of pain and suffering incurred, and this is based on what happened, over what period, and the effect it may have had on your wellbeing. Secondly, there is the assessment of medical costs – past, present and future. In your case that would be the cost of all your therapy, counselling and psychology sessions from the very beginning into the future. Thirdly, there is the calculation of an economic loss, the effect the abuse might have had on, say, your capacity to earn a living.

'This is just a start to filling that void. But this process rarely delivers the sense that justice has been served.' Then, bluntly, he stated the legalities of the Church and its position.

'In terms of compensation, they are very difficult to sue. They have established a structure that puts their wealth – and believe me it's vast – in trusts outside the reach of the secular legal process. As well, they have claimed their priests were volunteers, not employees, and so the Church could not be held responsible for their actions. This has become known as the "Ellis Defence". That doesn't mean there isn't a terrible moral responsibility on their part to resolve claims unconditionally and in the best interests of the victims and their mental health. But legally, in this country, that's all it is, a moral responsibility. And that is dependent on the Church stepping up and generously offering you something. What do you consider would be fair compensation?'

'Three months full-time residence in a psychologically supportive clinic with a professionally trained counsellor like

James, then a university education, accommodation for life and a generous payout to support me until the end of my days. In other words, exactly what the sexually deviant clergy received following their treatment in the Sydney psychiatric clinic when they were transitioned out of the Church.'

Phil winced, wordlessly demonstrating the apparent absurdity of my statement. Nevertheless, he agreed to be my advocate. We would pursue the Church for a just remedy, as comprehensive as was received by those clergy. Even as we spoke, I was challenged by my lack of trust. I was handing over the complexities of my abuse, and the debris it had left littered along the way, to this man I hardly knew.

He instructed me to compile a list of the many psychologists, counsellors, psychiatrists and therapists I'd seen since 1976. I contacted the ones who were still practising, asking for dates of sessions and for reports or commentaries on what had transpired.

39

A Return to Quairading

July 2013

The simultaneous process of transformative, long-term counselling and writing my story had helped externalise the facts of the abuse trauma, and provided a framework with which to view and understand the patterns of negative behaviour. The positive outcome had been an empowerment to act and talk openly and freely. The not-so-positive one had been an increased vulnerability to events which retriggered the trauma.

The Church's repeated and emphatic refusal to acknowledge my meeting with Foley kept raising a red flag. I saw Foley five years before Leunig was convicted in 1994 and, despite Foley's response that my story 'explained a lot', the crimes for which Leunig had been charged, and his abuse of me, had occurred twenty-seven years prior. It seemed a reasonable premise that there were other victims before, in between and after those mentioned in the trials in 1994 and 1995. Like the irritation of an oat seed in my shoe, this idea began to demand attention. Who was this paedophile who had strafed my childhood? Who else had fallen victim? I weathered the resistance from the *Let it go!* of my inner voice.

The Church being a reluctant source of information, I decided to drive out to Quairading to see if anyone remembered him. Small wheatbelt towns that still existed often had a stable older population. It seemed like a good place to start.

What will you find? Who will remember a priest after all these years? Who will care? What authority have you got to pursue this? The critical voice ramped up its taunting.

The name 'Quairading' had remained a toxic construction in my memory, conjuring up images of Leunig's naked body, the freezing presbytery, the gap in the curtains, the imploding petrol drums, the judgmental eyes of the farmers out at Kwolyin. Therapy had diminished the terror, but the memories had not been excised. Nevertheless, I felt impelled to make the trip. Louise offered to accompany me, but it was a journey I needed to do alone.

Leaving the city in the early morning, I drove east into the dawn. A weak winter sun flashed through the trees along the Great Eastern Highway. This was the same road I had travelled in 1965, when my thirteen-year-old mind was analysing the practical and moral implications of my presence in the car with Leunig. I turned off the highway at The Lakes and onto the road to York. Silken strands of a ghostly mist were strewn across the valleys. Crossing the river in York, the road to Quairading climbed uphill and east into open farmland. The crops were low and sparse, but there was water in the creeks.

Why are you doing this? Let sleeping dogs lie.

That inner voice chattered for the remaining hour to Quairading. I caught snippets of the monologue: *presumptuous, futile, arrogant, none-of-your-business.* I heard no voice of encouragement.

The sky had turned grey and ominous, and low-slung clouds hugged the fields. I turned into the main street. The town seemed far too small as I oriented myself to the general store. It was still there, in between newer shops. I could see where we parked that day after the driving lesson, where Leunig stood on the footpath and talked with the men while I'd cringed and hunkered down low in the front seat.

You'll find nothing here.

Turning left from the main street, I drove up a side street. On the next corner stood the white-painted, Spanish mission–style church, encircled by hard, bare sand. I parked beside the kerb. A bitter, cutting wind hassled up from the south and I put on an anorak. Walking across the sea of sand, I read on a painted sign screwed to the side wall that the parish now operated from Bruce Rock, sixty-odd kilometres away. The timetable with its alternating weeks and times of the Mass indicated this church was now an outstation in the diocese. The church seemed lost, standing alone on the corner of the deserted streets. A couple of garden beds hinted at spasmodic attention but lacked love. Around the back of the church, there was a single-car fibro garage with a tiled roof. I had no recollection of it and the first hint of doubt crept in. Behind the garage was the presbytery, small – tiny even – no more than a few rooms, with high, red-brick walls and a tiled roof. The image I'd carried from 1965, picked out in the headlights that first night, was of a low, grey building. Was this the same building?

It appeared to have been recently altered. A fibrocement panelled addition was crudely attached to the back. I tried to imagine the brick building without it, reminded of the disparities in memory by my encounter with Leunig in the gallery. I was pre-adolescent when I was here, so the memory recall of it being big seemed reasonable. I wandered around the outside, imagining which windows belonged to the bedroom. I peered through a corner of the curtained windows but could see nothing. Were these the same curtains? Where had the petrol drums stood?

Up the hill, away from the presbytery, the next building, built of the same brick-and-tile construction and of a similar era to the presbytery, was a private home judging from the washing billowing on the line and the paraphernalia of family life stored on the verandahs. I huddled against the wind, walked up to the front door and knocked. No-one answered. The letters 'PC' were etched in an ornate font in the glass of the sidelights at the front door. I remembered the same letters in the leadlight above the door to the Presentation Convent in Mosman Park. This must have once been a convent, but I had no memory of it.

The rasping barks of dogs echoed down from a derelict-looking, red-brick building still further up the hill. Two enormous dogs, ranging back and forth in a pendulum of agitated fury, snarled and frothed behind a steel mesh caging of the verandah. It was the old school building. I looked at the foundation stone. The small, two-roomed school, identical in style and materials to the presbytery and convent, had been built in 1956.

The classrooms were sadly neglected, evident from the fretting brickwork, the peeling paint and the corroded gutters. It looked like it was inhabited by squatters: washing hanging from a make-shift line; older model cars sinking in a sea of weeds; a discarded air-cooler rusting away in a corner. It had not been a school for many, many years.

A wide, semi-cleared area sloped away from the school, down towards the convent and the church. It was dotted with tall, spindly gum trees. It did not look like an oval as I wandered across its dry ground, through the stands of trees and the knee-high weeds waving helplessly in the southerly. The grey, embattled remnant of a concrete cricket pitch appeared then disappeared among the weeds. I went over to it and saw the ancient pitch, cracked and pitted, being smothered and consumed by the elements. It would have been in the centre of the oval, so I scanned a circle around it, from the school and the convent and the presbytery on my left to the road on the far-right side. The gum trees scattered across it would have sprouted after the school closed. They looked like they were at least thirty or forty years old.

I positioned myself for that memory picture, in the bottom corner of the oval. I had stopped hitting golf balls and looked up at the church and imagined the parishioners inside at Mass, assured that the dispensation from Leunig to skip Mass was watertight. The church seemed closer, which was reasonable given that my memory had been formed through the eyes of a child.

I was troubled that I had no knowledge of the convent building barely twenty metres away from the presbytery. It would have had nuns living there, running the school and preparing the church for Mass on Sundays among other things. Had any Sisters known I was inside the presbytery? Had I been shielded from them and told not to come to Mass so as not to raise suspicion?

I imagined them crossing between the convent and the church, with voluminous, black habits swaying and swelling under their long, clacking rosary beads and their institutional, black shoes crunching on the gravelly sand. They would have had to walk past the presbytery to get to the sacristy door. I hadn't heard them.

Fossicking around the outside of the presbytery, I searched for signs, triggers on which images might be hung, but there were none. It looked little used now. Going to every window again, I peered in through the slits in the curtains as once I'd feared the men doing. I tried to recreate the interior – the kitchen and the sink with the oozing Lux detergent, the bedrooms, that window, that doorway. I had nothing in my memory that could help me recreate the building from the outside apart from that one single image of where we'd pulled up in the headlights that first night.

I drove down to the shire office in the main street and asked for contacts in the Catholic community and whether there were other churches in nearby towns, or out at old sidings. The staff were friendly and helpful without being at all curious. They described two churches, one at the old townsite of Kwolyin, and one at Mount Stirling. The name 'Kwolyin', those two syllables long dormant, brought a rush of recognition. They looked up the town directory and gave me the names and phone numbers of three women who were active running the Catholic out-parish.

One of the women, Penny, worked in a business nearby. I walked up the street and found the office to one side of the main road. I peered through the windows. It seemed deserted. As I pushed open the door, a middle-aged woman came out of an office. She was friendly, but also country-shy and reserved. I told her I'd come to Quairading curious about when Father Leunig was the parish priest, particularly from 1965 onwards. She was matter-of-fact and said she had only been a child then, but her mother would remember him. 'Perhaps you should talk with her.'

Unashamedly, I told her why I was there. She listened quietly and did not seem surprised. I asked if she would call her mother. From her office, I heard the muffled strains of their conversation and after some time, she came back.

'My mother wouldn't feel comfortable talking about him and that topic, but she said to let you know there were rumours at the time about that priest. There was talk in the town, in the years after Father Leunig left, about several boys from the school having been abused. Unfortunately, the woman who could have told you everything has since died.'

Thoughtfully and slowly, Penny began to open up. She mentioned several families she knew who had had boys that were abused by Leunig.

'I still keep in touch with one of them. Alan.' She gave me his number and told me he would be a good person to contact. 'He also stays in contact with other women in the parish. He's had a troubled life.'

I thanked her for her generosity, grateful she had been forthcoming and non-judgmental. She could so easily have retreated, like my father, to the burial ground of secrets. Outside, the wind still blew, my anorak feeble against the gusts of chilling news. So, there had been other boys. I had counted myself, the four boys in the court cases and the boy Leunig bragged about when we were in Quairading – six in all. Penny mentioned at least six other families, some with several boys in each family. That she could have had that conversation with me and name those boys so easily after so many years led me to wonder how many conversations had been whispered in the town and, if they had been whispered here, had they also been whispered to the Archbishop?

An uneasy feeling tempered my curiosity. Penny's description of Leunig was that of a serial paedophile, yet I was still reluctant to embrace the evil that that term connoted.

I rang the next number on the list from the shire office. Denise answered and I briefly explained my purpose. Almost immediately, she responded.

'When you said why you were here, I knew the priest's name you were going to say. I can meet you down at the church later in the afternoon if you'd like.'

With several hours to wait, I set off to find those other places that had reverberated in my memory. The cemetery, down a narrow bitumen track buried in the low scrub, seemed depressingly drab under the dull, cloud-burdened sky. I pulled up beside some large gum trees in the centre of the car park. The layout had changed. My recollection was of a flat, gravel area with some shrubs in a median strip against which I had learned to park. Different coloured areas of bitumen surfacing described the car park's expansion over the years. I tried to find a feeling but there was nothing, as if the past had been extinguished and could not be rekindled.

The Quairading airfield was on the opposite side of the main road to the cemetery. I parked at a gate that opened onto a wide, gravel apron. Beyond it, the gravel airstrip stretched out towards farmland. Along one side of the apron were several old, rusted farm sheds, hangars in better times. The wind moaned softly as it bustled through gaps in their unused doors and around the fringes, where weeds pressed insistently. A sudden gust rattled loose sheets and doors, and the noisy grating echoed in the emptiness. I walked out onto the strip and tried to imagine where the lengthy negotiation took place between Leunig and the pilot, but I could not picture it here. This airstrip was only just outside the town limits and, in 1965, the drive back to the presbytery after the flight was a long journey with the shadows of the trees stretched across the road. I vividly recalled the moist bite of the cool, evening air coming into the car. There were no hangars on that narrow apron where Leunig had stood, nonchalantly smoking. This could not have been the airstrip.

I looked at the mud map the shire staff had given me. Turning onto the road to Bruce Rock, I drove the thirty kilometres to the old siding at Kwolyin. The rusting tracks of the abandoned railway crisscrossed the road here and there, exposing the faded bitumen of the old road surface parallel to it. The 'Kwolyin' sign pointed down a dirt track off the main road. There, amid a scattering of rough-barked York gums, stranded high and dry in the bare earth like a beached ship, stood a solitary red-brick building. The Catholic church. There was no townsite here in 1965, so it seems it had always been the only building at the siding. A driveway ran up the right-hand side of the church and I pulled up where Leunig had parked. I got out and walked around, pulling my anorak in tightly. The surrounding bushland, low and unremarkable as I remembered it, had proliferated since the main road had been relocated and no longer passed by. The scrappily barked gums were now tall and ranging, creeping right up to the edge of the church, dwarfing it, with long finger-like branches threatening to envelop it. The building emanated a forlorn face, its consumption by the elements imminent.

The inner voice kept repeating, *What's the point of being here?*

The church was as I remembered it. The low fence joining the brick pillars was still in front, marking a division between the churchyard and the old roadway where the farmers had once parked their cars. The fence, now dividing bushland from bushland, looked faintly ridiculous. I walked over to the back corner, picturing myself carrying the vessels and implements for the Mass. The sacristy door was there, exactly as I remembered.

A crucifix was still mounted at the apex of the roof over the little entry porch, the roof tiles entirely covered in grey-green lichen. Inside the porch enclosure, ancient cobwebs drooped with dust and debris, and bird and lizard droppings sprinkled the concrete floor in a salt and pepper desecration. I peered through a crack in the doors. The church had long been stripped out, locked and abandoned.

Looking back towards where he'd parked his car, I saw a sideways leaning York gum with a long, thick branch just a few centimetres off the ground. I walked over to it, sat down and looked back to where the farmers had gotten out of their cars. This was the branch I had sat on for the hour of Mass, contemplating the moral dilemma I'd found myself in. It was now three times as thick. How remarkable that it was still here, after nearly fifty years. In my imagination I watched the men filing into the church. What had they thought, here in the middle of nowhere, as they looked across the yard at a solitary young boy not inside at Mass? It had been a bizarre experience for me as a thirteen-year-old. It was even more bizarre now.

I was troubled. Everything seemed in its place – the shape, the cross, the windows high up along the side walls, the sacristy door in the back corner, the old roadway, the trees, the driveway, the low fence and the car park. But the colour? I remembered a pale-green building. This was red brick. Was this a trick of memory?

Doubt crept in again. I went back to the car to escape the chilly wind and think. Staring at the building and its surrounds, this was definitely the church. What had my memory done to the colour over the intervening years?

I drove out the road to Kellerberrin towards Mount Stirling, a massive cluster of rocky outcrops that sculpted the farmland quite beautifully into protected valleys. The little church there was unfamiliar. Soon the clouds parted, drawn back like a curtain, and the afternoon sun glowed, restoring the green wheatfields with a golden promise. Cheered by the show of warmth, I drove slowly back to Quairading, all the while puzzling about the red-brick church. Was it possible that, as I sat on that branch all those years ago and stared at the lichen-covered roof over the top of Leunig's car, I had internalised that colour? This realisation made me cautious about the other images burned so indelibly in my memory. If I had expected anything from this visit, it would have been certainty.

***

Denise was waiting at the church. She was warm and welcoming, if somewhat cautious. We stood outside the presbytery while I shared more of my story. She was generous, like Penny, about wanting to help in whatever way she could, and I was surprised that she was so forthright, hearing about my abuse. I started to sense there was more to this story and it was not far below the surface. Otherwise, why were these women not shocked?

Pointing at the presbytery, she said, 'I don't suppose you want to go into that place with its terrible memories?'

'I would.' I wanted to see something of substance that might stir feelings, but in truth, I felt nothing. The memories were just that, images generating no effect. She opened the front door that led into a lounge room set up for parish meetings. It was not large but would comfortably seat a dozen or so around a collection of small tables covered in white cloths with old-fashioned lace edging. She lit the gas heater.

She talked openly about the parish and its priests, the town's dwindling community and the school that eventually closed. The nuns had left in 1975, after only twenty years in the town. The priest too had left and was stationed at Bruce Rock. She talked affectionately about the generous, caring priests before and after Leunig, the ones who had embraced the town and joined in social functions.

'Father R. was the best of them. He played golf and drank whisky with the men down at the club afterwards. The priest at Bruce Rock now is wonderful. And the others, they were caring men. They knew how to comfort. They became part of the social and spiritual fabric of the town. But Father Leunig wasn't like that. He was unapproachable. He didn't join in.'

She described his eyes, deep-set and unsmiling, and his roundish face, bringing her hands up and holding them out from her cheeks in a mime of his appearance, painting him perfectly. Though careful not to speak ill of the dead, there was a hint of unpleasantness in her description. She was watching me intently.

'There was one occasion when some men of the parish had come for a scheduled 'Parents and Friends' meeting that was to be held up at the school in the evening. They had waited and waited for Father to come. When he still hadn't appeared, one of the men went down to the presbytery and knocked on the door. After quite some time Father opened it and, in an abrupt tone, asked him what he wanted. When the meeting was mentioned and that he was late, Father Leunig replied angrily, "I'm the one who calls meetings and there'll be one when I call it." He slammed the door in the man's face.'

Her voice rose with more than a ripple of remembered resentment, then she fell silent. That story would have raced around the town, galvanising hostility towards their incumbent priest.

We walked around the house, cavernous in my memory but now tiny as I squeezed down its corridor and into its few rooms. I re-imagined that first night in the presbytery. Bathed in terror, I was looking at him standing ahead of me down the narrow, blurry-edged tunnel. The walls now seemed so benign; I could not picture where I had stood. The kitchen, where I don't ever remember him cooking, was not wide and farmhouse-like as in my memory, but the sink was where I remembered it opposite the door. I opened the cupboard underneath. The Lux was gone.

Across the hallway, in a bedroom, a single bed huddled in a corner. Did the big bed I'd climbed onto only seem big because of my age? A window was on the right, but this room had two identical windows on the outside walls. One was onto the entry porch and the other faced the oval. Which was the one I'd looked at in terror on those nights? The image of this room has lingered in my memory as an empty stage with a bed and door and window floating in a haze. This actual room was tiny.

There was an even smaller bedroom to the back of the kitchen. The single window was the same size and height as in the other bedroom and it was to the right of where a bed would have been, next to the open space outside the garage where the empty drums may have stood. Was this the room? The sound of the imploding drums in the still night air was so cacophonous, and the presbytery so small, it would have made no difference where the drums had stood. Parting the folds of the stiff curtains, I peered out the window. The convent was in full view, barely twenty metres away. How had the nuns reconciled their trust in their parish priest during the six years Leunig was there, the priest Denise was describing as unapproachable? Had they heard the gossip? Had they tried to keep the children away from him?

Or were they, like my parents, so embedded in the fabric of the Church and implicitly trusting of their priest, they were only able to imagine him as venerable?

I tried again to conjure up a feeling, but there was nothing. I didn't tremble with terror as I had in the therapy sessions when I'd revisited the moments in these rooms. Why was there no fear, no anxiety, no rage?

We sat in the lounge room and Denise talked more about the years Leunig was her parish priest, thinly veiled contempt again lacing her description of him. She hinted that those were the years her faith had lapsed. It made me think about his priestliness. It occurred to me he had never displayed or expressed any signs of personal spirituality. The priest's 'Office', a long prayer of commitment to the priesthood, was required to be read daily. I had been with him every minute over two weekends in 1965, sleeping in his bed, accompanying him on the trips. He never said his 'Office'. We never said the rosary. We never said any prayers.

'He went to Embleton after he left here,' she said. 'The school remained open just five years after he left.' Had he been the trigger for its demise?

'Would you like to look in the church?'

She opened the sacristy door and we walked into the cold nave.

'I have no memory of this. Leunig gave me dispensation not to go to Mass. I played golf on the oval instead.'

'That must have been a real calamity for you as a young boy.' She was wide-eyed in disbelief.

'No. At first, I felt liberated. The guilt didn't come until after my second visit.'

Leunig's flagrant disregard for my spiritual welfare seemed embodied in this empty, lifeless, freezing church. The thought spawned an uneasy feeling. Giving me dispensation from Mass would have been easy for someone who only paid lip service to his faith and his priesthood. A corollary, to which I was still resistant, suggested his spiritual laxity denoted that his priesthood was a front; priest enough only to allow him access to young boys. Did that mean that in upholding our pact, I had been protecting him and his craft? I struggled to accept this notion.

It was getting dark. I thanked Denise and we embraced. She had been generous sharing her stories, and her sensitivity and understanding had made it easier than I had anticipated. I noted again that it was the women who presented the face of a more empathic Church.

Driving home, the low sun slanted its yellowness across the road. I wound down the window and let the lush-smelling, damp evening air swirl into the car, as I had breathed that evening after the plane flight in 1965. But there was a nagging anxiety. The day with Penny and Denise had been comfortable and revelatory, and I'd been curious, with my intellect engaged but not my feelings. This was a familiar pattern, and it left me unsettled.

40

The Aftermath

July 2013

As Phil the lawyer had asked, I'd approached many of the psychologists I had seen over the previous thirty years, asking for clinical reports. Several insisted on a consultation to assess the reason for my request, no doubt regarding my current mental health. One such consultation, with the clinical psychologist Bridie, whom Louise and I had seen together in 2003, was scheduled for the day after the visit to Quairading. Bridie was the first clinician to identify and articulate my suppressed rage, insisting I work independently of her and Louise. In our session the next day, I told her of my sexual abuse. It was a revelation, she said, but she was not surprised. Our discussion ranged wide but when I began to talk about my recent therapy with James at SARC, a savage lump swelled in my throat, and it became dry and choking. I tried to speak but nothing came out. Then the trembling started. It had taken twenty-four hours, and this session of revisiting the abuse, for the 'nothing' feelings in the bedroom of the presbytery to reach the surface. I was feeling the foreshocks of a pending earthquake, but I did not have the instinct to crawl away to a safe place.

By evening I was introverted and vulnerable. At a long-planned dinner engagement with friends, I put on a brave face and endured the night. The next morning, my mood began swinging uncontrollably, chaotic feelings cascading around an acute sense of aloneness. I was inconsolable and untouchable, unable to put words to the maelstrom. I couldn't let anyone near me and recoiled when Louise tried to comfort me. I wandered around the house, lost and twitching. In the evening, it gave way. I fled in my car and drove aimlessly around the city, my eyes blurred with tears.

Louise, Tash and Harry rang or texted every hour, desperate to tell me they loved me, but I couldn't hear them. Nothing could stem the tide of despair or diffuse the alienation and the sense of a lost life, of a sabotaged childhood. I parked the car and made myself write down what was happening, trying to fix the feelings, to give them form so I could hold them. Denise's expressionist picture of the priest, her hands held up to her face mimicking his pudgy cheeks, had instilled a concrete form to the images and memories of the place and the man. I had been thrust unwittingly into a new place relative to my abuse. No longer was I inside it as just *my* story, but party to one peopled by those women and a legion of boys both named and alluded to. Naming those other boys formed a conduit to what I was experiencing, and a prison door was thrown open. The abuse I had endured as a child was in full view, unfiltered. Picturing those boys in the presbytery, I saw myself, from the outside looking in. My body vibrated and shook, my shirt saturated with tears.

I drifted home towards midnight, barely able to drive. I crawled onto a sofa and slept the sleep of the dead. In the morning, Louise sat and held my hand as I described the terrible aloneness and sense of loss. Tears welled and I turned away, sobbing. On the plane, after that similar episode, I had felt empty. Now I felt the abandonment I'd experienced that first night in Quairading – being given over to the priest, having to endure and deal with the abuse on my own. It brought on a profound sadness.

Despite traversing the territory of these traumas over and over with James in therapy, it seemed like I had never been able to fully go to this terrible place. I saw that the consequences of abandonment had led to my life in isolation, unable to trust.

Sometime later, I described the events of these few days in a counselling session with James. At the end of the session, he gave me a copy of an article entitled 'The Abandonment Depression' and pointed to a paragraph.

'... Abandonment is a catastrophic experience, different "... from other forms of separation in which sadness, pining, and grief are experienced." On the one hand, the abandoned one suffers a consummate betrayal, the loss of a loved and needed person. On the other hand, persecution by that same person is experienced. As a result, one's sense of reality is totally threatened: the good has become bad, the nurturing has become persecutory. From a seeming state of well-being a chaotic state of panic becomes imminent because the entire fabric of one's perception of reality has come into question.'[4]

In my imagination I was on the beach again at Cottesloe. Leunig was trespassing onto my only safe place. I felt betrayed. He was talking with my mother. She was pointing me out. She was now on his side. She was no longer my mother. She was just another woman on the beach.

41

The Other Victims

July 2013

It was a cathartic day. The next morning, I felt renewed. In trepidation, I called the number Penny in Quairading had given me for Alan. Expecting to hear a boy's voice, I was taken aback when a man answered the phone. Naively, I asked for Alan.

'Yes, that's me.'

I explained how I had come by his name and carefully asked if he might be able to talk to me about what had happened to him in Quairading.

'Yes. I was abused by Leunig.' A pause. 'And so was my brother. Pretty bad.' Another pause. Then, as though I had removed the lid from a lifetime of grief, he launched into his story.

'I was an altar boy. Leunig used take me back to the presbytery after Mass. There was always a pretext, something had to be carried back, or a gift had to be picked up. My parents were waiting in the car to go back to the farm. He had to be quick. There was not much time. He'd tell me to put my hand down his trousers and hang onto his penis. He'd say, "Further down".'

I could hear Alan's breath expelled in sharp gusts.

'At other times, he came out to our farm and lent a hand at seeding or harvesting, befriending my parents. He used to bring older boys as well, and they'd all go out stump-picking in the paddocks. That was when he convinced my parents to let my brother or I stay overnight at the presbytery.'

Alan described the bed he slept in with Leunig. He was reluctant to say more. I didn't press him.

'My brother got it much worse than I did.'

In a roundabout way, he finally got to the word 'penetration'.

'We used to talk about it to comfort each other. It made him so angry. The boys at school all talked about it too. They called it "being done" by Father.

'My brother told my parents soon after it happened, but it seems they were so deeply ashamed they were unable to report the abuse to the Church or the police. Leunig was the priest, after all. A priest was holy. How could he be involved in something so evil? It was a contradiction. Nobody could imagine what was happening. As well, sexuality at that time was taboo and if anyone did know, they'd have found it hard to talk about.

'After being told of our abuse, our mother said, "What have we done wrong?" I talked about it with her recently. She said that because Leunig had still been in Quairading, she and my father discussed confronting him and going to the police, as it might stop other boys being abused. They must have realised Leunig was a serial abuser. In the end, they did nothing, choosing not to "make a fuss". She said they wanted to protect my brother and me from further trauma, which would follow if the abuse was made public.'

Alan's voice hovered between a vital energy and a sense of defeat. He paused, as though summoning the courage to go on.

'Leunig did bad things after he was finished with us. There was another family. They had three boys. When the father found out that they had all had "bad things" done to them, he was horrified.'

Another pause. 'Leunig destroyed that family.'

He named another family whose two boys had been abused. They had both been on Penny's list.

'And then there was Gordon. His family had been having a difficult time with him. His elder brother had been moved away to a Catholic children's home in Perth after having difficulties at home. As it happened, he was abused by someone at the children's home as well. Leunig abused Gordon really badly. He later died when his car hit a tree. He was twenty.'

Alan was talking so fast, my notes had become a scrawl. I struggled to stay focused.

'My brother was three years older than me and had been sent to boarding school in Perth. His abuse had been very bad and, although he was a strong personality, he had become very vulnerable and was severely bullied. I know that affected my mother. My sister had also gone to Perth, so I was alone on the farm with my parents.

'One incident still pains me. It was just after my brother had left for Perth. I was about ten. I was practising the piano. I had just finished my scales and my prescribed piece and started playing something else for fun. My mother came rushing in, screaming at me, and started hitting me around the head from both sides, really violently. It was so unprovoked and uncalled for.

'She was very sick. She should have had counselling to deal with the abuse my brother had endured, but counselling didn't exist in country towns then.'

He edged around the words before conceding her condition was mental illness.

'My father would be out on the farm all day and there was just my mother and me home together. My grandmother, my mum's mother, had been a venomous woman, emotionally and physically abusive to her when she was a child, so my mother felt particularly alone. The way she was with me that day mirrored Grandma's behaviour.

'I used to sit with her for hours while she off-loaded all this hatred and anger and regret. I was her counsellor. It was exhausting.

'One day, while I was sitting in my room alone, doing nothing, she burst in and started shouting at me. "You can get the hell out of here and never come back! Go! Never come back! Pack your bags and go!" I was about ten or eleven. I put some things in a bag and started walking down the road. I was crying. I'd gone about a mile when my father came past in the car. He asked me what I was doing. He started laughing when I told him, and he told me to get in. From that day on, all I wanted to do was leave. I wanted to run away.'

He lapsed back into silence. Overwhelmed by his story, my mind wandered to my grandfather's house and the subsequent years of my mother's violent outbursts, of her hospitalisation, and my counselling by her bedside. I pondered this coincidence.

Alan's voice broke back into my thoughts.

'I became really angry. It's shameful to think about it now, but when things weren't right, I became very aggressive and took my aggression out on the farm animals. I was violent with the sheepdogs, abusing them if they hadn't done something correctly. I was ultra-violent with the sheep. Once I was crutching a young sheep and it started kicking me. It made me so angry, I started kicking it back. It kicked more violently. I started using greater and greater force on it, pushing it harder and harder until I crushed its diaphragm and killed it in a violent rage.'

The pain in his voice was unbearable. In the depth of similar rages, I'd kicked furniture with such ferocity it had terrified me. Louise had talked about her fear in my worst rages. The psychologist Bridie had had an insight into that bubbling volcano.

'Strange as it may sound, I felt I was more affected by my mother's uncontrolled violence than by what the priest did. My mother was supposed to be my protector, my advocate, but she took her anger out on me.

'I was sent to a Christian Brothers boarding school in Perth a year earlier than usual, Year Seven instead of Year Eight. Maybe it was to get me away from my mother, or the priest, or from both of them. Anyway, it didn't deter Father Leunig. He visited my school during term time and twice came to my classroom with permission to take me out of class. I remember being told, "Father Leunig is here to see you" and thinking, "That's odd. Why would he want to see me?" He told me, "Your Mum and Dad asked me to call in and see you". I was suspicious because, quite apart from what he'd done to me, I knew what he'd done to my brother was so much more hideous. He took me down to his car and sat me in the front and tried to get me to sit close to him on the seat. I said I wouldn't do it. I knew he was friends with the principal. I suppose that allowed him to do what he liked in the school.

'Some time later, back at our farm, Leunig flew a plane in and landed in our paddock. I don't know if he had any affiliation with an aero club, but it seemed he had a pilot's licence. We all went out to see him and the plane. There was a boy in it with him. It was a real shock seeing him because I knew him from school. He was someone everyone looked up to. I felt so ashamed.'

Alan described and named the boy. He was the one Leunig had told me about in his nonchalant, boasting manner on my last night in Quairading, the boy who was 'experienced and knew what to do.' The intersection of our stories lent credibility to my recollections, but simultaneously fuelled my growing anxiety of the dimensions and complexity of the web that had entrapped us all. It seemed not just about sexual gratification, but about power. Leunig was showing off his 'trophy', the school hero, perhaps to normalise his culture of abuse and demonstrate the scope of his control. It demonstrated the lengths he would go to in his carefully calculated methodology to create opportunities and protect his sources.

'My older brother was "aggressively promiscuous" as an

adolescent and a young man. This did a lot of damage to him, and the girls involved.'

Again, he paused. These painful words. My mind drifted outside to the garden, imagining what he was inferring by his choice of words. A wind had come up and was wildly thrashing the shrubbery outside the window.

Alan's voice corralled my escaping mind. He talked of his own life journey and the internal struggles that accompanied his sexuality as he grew up.

'Only those who've been sexually abused can understand this inner turmoil and loss of innocence.'

I could hear him breathing as he summoned the courage to continue.

'It was my wife who helped me survive. She helped me conquer my violent rages and raise our family. My brother was not so lucky. Even though he raised a family, he struggled all his life with alcohol. He died quite young.'

Our conversation was coming to a natural end. We both knew it was enough for this one day. He confessed that he had been crying as he'd talked. I reassured him as best I could that I understood his pain.

I put the phone down and stared out at the garden again. The wind was gusting more strongly now, and the trees leaned heavily over the bushes being buffeted below them. I had been talking to Alan for an hour and a half. I had struggled just listening, and was exhausted. I grappled with his stories, of the three Quairading families Leunig had systematically infiltrated to access and abuse all of the boys, and the boys at the school talking about 'being done by Father'. And Gordon.

It seemed Leunig had abused nearly every boy he'd had contact with, and he engineered situations where he could promote and maintain those abuses. The picture being painted was of a priest so calculating and indiscriminate in his exploitation, so devoid of a moral consciousness that the word 'psychopath' came to mind.

The previous week in Quairading I had begun to get an insight into the truth about Leunig, but had resisted the implications that he was a paedophile who had *disguised* himself as a priest. This would explain why he had not said any prayers, nor his 'Office', nor the rosary, or why giving me a dispensation to skip Mass was easy. He had no spiritual conscience and cared not at all about mine. I remembered the time he had laughed heartily, telling me how the farmers gave him free petrol. He was taking their boys for free too, under the clever ruse of his priesthood.

I saw my own abuse in a new light. It had nothing to do with being a compliant, sensitive boy, the myth I had subscribed to all my life. I had been in the grip of a serial paedophile. There had been no attempt to establish a relationship or partake in grooming that first day in the sacristy in Cottesloe. The new priest, he had pulled me aside and went straight for my genitals. What hope had I, or anyone, to escape him? Curiously, I felt a new sadness for my parents, for the betrayal of their trust in the Church and its priests. Their total subservience to their Church meant there was no possibility they could intervene in his very clever grooming of the family.

But I could not dismiss their lack of vigilance at the time, nor their blind obedience to the Church, nor indeed any decision they may have made, consciously or subconsciously handing me over to the priest, nor their subsequent abdication in favour of the Church.

My mind was set loose like a terrier on the scent. The Quairading parish school and the altar boys were clearly not his only source of victims. He'd created opportunities, driving to Perth to collect me and the other boy who he'd said 'knew what to do'. He'd sought out Alan and his brother at their school. Why then wouldn't there be others, from Cottesloe and his parishes prior to Cottesloe, and the parishes after he left Quairading?

Would he have spared my brothers? It would have been impossible for him to abuse Joe, the wilful one who was in control of his life. But what about Terry, Paddy and Dom? Terry had told me twenty-four years prior that nothing had happened, and I believed that my threat to report Leunig to the police had prevented him from being abused. But how had Leunig actually behaved? I rang Terry and we agreed to meet.

42

Terry's Story

August 2013

It seemed necessary to have this conversation on neutral territory. We chose a small bistro near his house. It wasn't busy, so we ordered some beers then found a quiet corner. We had grown closer in recent years, not back to the boyish, trusting camaraderie of the Jabber Club, but a 'blokey' sort of mute understanding. Before I had a chance to say anything, he started.

'I know you are writing your story of being abused. When you rang, it made me want to tell you what happened to me.'

That familiar wave of nausea surged up and stuck in my throat. 'That's what I wanted to ask you.'

Tears welled up in the corners of his eyes, as though a lifetime of dammed up feeling was released.

'He stood there naked and asked me if I knew what a stiffy was.'

The moment was too big for both of us. He stopped and wiped his eyes.

'Jesus.' I heard my voice coming from somewhere else. My body was swaying but I wasn't moving.

Unexpectedly, his teenage daughter came into the bistro and, seeing us, came over to join us. He motioned she didn't know and with that one gesture, the story stopped. With his daughter beside us, we both reverted to our default personas of cheerful, competent men. Later, as we were winding up, I signalled that I would call that evening and arrange a more private meeting. It was a troubled night, my mind in a whirl, pained and guilty and sad and angry all at once. Leunig's contempt for my threat, and his abuse of Terry, beggared belief. We met for lunch the next day at the café in Kings Park. The sun was shining in a seamless blue sky, and we had the afternoon to talk uninterrupted. Once seated in a sunny corner, I opened my notebook. I was back in 1967. Terry was thirteen.

'Tell me from the start.'

'Leunig was learning to fly, to get his private pilot's licence. He used to tell us about it when he came to our house for dinner. I remember him coming often. He kept promising to take me flying. I loved planes and he promised if I came up to Quairading, he would take me flying. "At our air show," he'd said, "Then you can fly in lots of different planes." I went up with him one weekend. When we got to Quairading, there was no air show and there was no plane. He made some excuse about the pilot not being able to fly.'

'Where did you stay?'

'In the presbytery.'

'What sort of car did he have?'

'It was a pale blue Falcon. On the way up he had wanted me to sit close to him on the bench seat. I didn't think it was unusual. We used to do that at home when Dad let us help him steer the car. When we got to Quairading, he showed me to my bedroom. It was at the back on the right. I was getting into my pyjamas and about to get into bed when he said he wanted me to go into his bed. He said it was "More comfortable and bigger" and "there's nothing wrong with it". I was completely naive. Priests never did anything wrong, so it couldn't be bad. But I sensed what he was asking me to do wasn't quite right and I didn't want to do it.

'That's when I noticed his hands. They were quivering. When I remember that image, I've always assumed he was excited and trembling with lust. He took me into his bedroom and we both sat on the bed. He talked about what some men do, that it was fine. His fingers were pudgy and stubby, covered in nicotine. They were shaking the whole time. His face was flushed red. The veins in his cheeks stood out purple.

'He asked me if I knew what a stiffy was and did I want to see one? He dropped his pants and took his pyjama top off. He was stark naked. He had a fat belly and a stubby, stiff, little cock. I had no idea what size a cock was supposed to be. I thought it looked funny, never having seen one like that before. He got me to feel it. I touched it reluctantly, feeling how hard it was. It had a red bit like a rash under the tip. He was quivering all over. I wasn't cold so I couldn't understand why he was trembling. He said, "Let's just lie on the bed." I didn't want to do that, so he said, "What if we turn out the light?" He got up and turned off the light. That's when he got me to take my pyjamas off. He said, "This is normal. Men do this all the time. It's much better when you don't have any clothes on."

'He made me lie on top of him and simulate sex. He was under me and rocking his body. He made me rock mine back and forth. After a while, he said I wasn't doing it properly. He made me push harder against his cock. I knew I had to be good to the priest, to do as I was told. Eventually he told me, "That's right, that's the way to do it." I didn't feel any pain and there was no hurting, so I wasn't frightened. He was holding onto me tightly, keeping me on top of him. Afterwards I was all sticky and he wiped me clean. I put my pyjamas back on and went back to my room and slept in my own bed. I never held his cock, and he didn't hold mine.'

He stopped and wiped away his tears. Our food had arrived but neither of us had an appetite to eat it. We both teased the edges of the dishes, playing with the salads, rearranging the tousled heaps, separating the ingredients, establishing order.

'The next morning, I remember going out of the presbytery and across to the church. I sat in a pew in the front. I can't remember if there were any people there. I can't remember if it was Mass.

I can't remember if we ate anything. He certainly didn't cook anything.'

I asked him about the relationship of the rooms in the presbytery. He drew a mud map on a napkin. The layout was exactly as I had seen in the presbytery a week or so prior, the room sizes, the door and window locations. Everything was correct. Unlike me, he had a very clear memory of the floor plan.

'I think I was only there one night. We went up on a Saturday and came back on the Sunday. I felt cheated because I'd missed out on the flight in a plane. On the way home, we drove past Fremantle Prison. He pulled into the garage that was on the corner of High and Ord streets. From there you could see the prison. I can still see it now – the limestone walls, the guard towers, the afternoon sun shining on the bonnet of the Falcon. We went past some wool stores to get there, so it wasn't the normal way home. He must have gone out of his way to go past it.

'Pointing at the prison, he'd said, "We have to keep our secret, because if anyone finds out they'll put me inside there. You don't want me to go in there, do you? I'm a friend of your mum and dad. Your parents will be really upset, and you don't want to upset them?" I had said, "No". It would've been my fault if he was sent to prison.'

The impossibly heavy years of silence filled the air between us.

'I never said anything. I just blotted it out. I was completely naive. Besides, he hadn't hurt me.'

I became aware of the clatter of dishes, the scraping of chairs and the conversations in the café. The sounds broke a spell. I was numb. A kookaburra landed on the awning outside the café and pecked aggressively at its reflection in the glass of a highlight window. The *peck, peck, peck* punctuated the space. We watched its persistence in silence, granted a moment to stop talking and take in the world outside, still sunny and beautiful.

I was deeply saddened that my confrontation with Leunig on

the backsteps had not deterred him. Rather, it had emboldened him to press on and abuse Terry as he'd done to me, worse in some ways, if degrees of depravity could be attributed to sexual abuse. Then he'd contrived the pre-meditated, out-of-the-way return journey past the prison to put the onus of the crime onto Terry's shoulders. This was not opportunistic or succumbing to a weakness. It was systematic paedophilia, and he was fully conscious of its criminality. What chance had Terry, or any boy, at the hands of this cunning, ruthless criminal?

With an inrush of chagrin, I had the peculiar sensation of having been deceived by Leunig, that he hadn't heeded my threat to go to the police.

Terry and I compared our memories: the priest and his fat belly; his pudgy, nicotine-stained fingers; the curled-up snub nose. We laughed as our images intersected, our laughter a release of the tension.

'The bastard,' he said finally.

'Why did you deny you'd been abused when I asked you twenty-four years ago?'

'I was about twelve or thirteen when it happened. I just got on with my life. When you asked me, the memory surfaced again. I felt too ashamed to admit to it, especially with our parents standing nearby. I didn't think about what constituted sexual abuse when you asked. I thought abuse was penetration. He hadn't done that to me, so I assumed I hadn't been abused. I suppose I took our parents' side, feeling the shame of it, and kept it hidden. It's different now. I'm sorry I didn't support you.'

What would I have done with the information had he admitted it at the time? I couldn't go to the police for myself. I doubt I would have reported Leunig had he told me.

I told him more of my story, the years after Mass in the sacristy, the beach at Cottesloe and the four nights in Quairading. When

I mentioned the beach, his face creased and he looked at me with a quizzical openness. I could see a question in his soft, brown eyes as something long-buried and unused to the light was slowly surfacing.

'He used to take me for swims to the beach, too. It was down at Leighton Beach. He took me right up to that section where there were no people, miles from anywhere. We were the only ones there. I can't remember what happened. We always went in his car, and he wanted me to sit close to him on the way. He promised me an ice-cream afterwards. It was when we lived on the highway near the church. I must have been really small.'

The northern end of what is now Leighton Beach was very remote in the 1960s, a strip of deserted coastline bordered by a rubbish dump. There was no road and public access was difficult; a safe place for the clandestine.

Leunig was in Cottesloe from March 1961 to February 1964. The oldest Terry could have been was nine years old, the youngest six. He would have been taken to Leighton Beach the same years I was being abused in the sacristy.

The implications slowly sank in. I do not remember Leunig in our house on the highway, but I must have seen him there on the occasions he collected Terry, because on the beach that day in 1964, I'd registered that the beach was the *only* place where I was safe from him. Our home, like the church, must have also been an unsafe place. It affirmed my feeling of having scant memory of my home life in those three years.

After Leunig had abused me in the water that day in 1964, Terry had come over and lain down beside me on the sand. Why had Leunig chosen to abuse me that day, and not him?

Terry's voice chased my grasping thoughts.

'I thought all my life I was the only one he'd had a go at. It didn't seem right to make a big deal of it.'

I pondered again this mechanism of the uniquely solitary nature inherent in the secret that, for us as children, ensured we could not imagine this trauma happening to anyone else. What power of silence was embedded in those secrets that they would survive unscathed inside our family for decades, and so unassailably alienate Terry and me to keep us apart all these years? And the other families I had come across in the previous weeks; the disintegration of the ties between those boys and their parents and siblings; the destruction of their lives; and their deaths. I thought about Matty, our fellow altar boy and comrade from the Jabbers Club, committing suicide in his twenties. Matty had struggled with a terrible drug addiction after he left school. Terry and I had survived and could sit here and talk about the traumas. I felt blessed in the saddest way possible.

The afternoon sun slid in low from the opposite side of the café. Hours had passed. Over coffee, our conversation drifted to our mother. I described my adolescence; the poems written after the crash of cups and plates hitting the kitchen wall, the tinkling of the shards spraying across the floor, her anguished tirades against my father and Joe, her cheeks tear-stained, her eyes red-raw, her fingers clawing my arm as I sat on her bed holding her hand, listening to her distress, nursing her out of one day into the next. When I mentioned the night the back door had slammed and I had heard the car crash outside, his face softened in an empathic, knowing way. I had always thought I had been the only witness until Terry told me his version of that night.

'She rushed out the back door, screaming she wanted to kill herself. I ran out to the car after her. I pulled open the passenger door and jumped onto the front seat beside her as she started up the car. I begged her not to kill herself. She drove up over the verge and the car crashed across the kerb. She was sobbing, saying, "I want to kill myself." She stopped up the road and told me to get out. She kept screaming at me, "Get out of the car! Get out of the car!" But I wouldn't. She tried to push me out. I clung onto her and wouldn't let go. Then she became limp, like a ragdoll. She gave up trying to push me out. She said, "I can't do this anymore. I just can't do it." I slowly talked her into coming back home.'

Safely in my bedroom that night, in detached, unempathic language, I'd written a poem:

What an odd day
Mother ran away
And it rained.

A silence, pregnant with pain, seeped in with the yellowing light. We both stared out at the gardens. While I was writing poetry, Terry had been clinging to her to stop her from killing herself.

Our conversation turned to the tension in our grandfather's house soon after we'd moved there.

'I remember painting the walls inside the house when she was in hospital. We got rid of the blue kalsomine paint in Grandad's kitchen. She hated that blue. We were all excited when she was coming home.' He looked at me for affirmation.

'Yes. Those outbursts, her screaming, "I hate this place. I hate everything in it!".'

I described my odyssey into the garden, hacking down the overgrown and decaying plants and the bonfire I'd lit, hoping in my purging of the garden, I would wipe the slate. We were voicing these stories of anger and sadness that, in all probability, had separated the whole family, not just the two of us.

A memory surfaced and snapped me back to the café and Terry. It was in 1967. I was fifteen, so he would have been thirteen.

It was after he went to Quairading with Leunig. I was standing with Mum and Dad in the kitchen. We were discussing his behaviour. He had changed from his usually cheerful, happy-go-lucky, intelligent self, and become angry and 'difficult', and was doing poorly at school. For some time, I'd watched him walking around the house dispirited and lost, defeated and purposeless. I'd noted the dramatic change and was upset and genuinely concerned for him. I suggested Dad should take us both on a holiday road trip. We all agreed it would cheer him up. I offered a solution to his apparent purposelessness, one that might give him more responsibility – I would give up the elder's right to be navigator. This would be a meaningful new role for him in the family.

Dad borrowed a camper trailer and we set off on the week-long trip. First stop was Aunty Grace and Uncle Paddy's in Goomalling. Then, staying in caravan parks, we travelled east to Kalgoorlie, south to Esperance, west to Albany, then back through the fruit-growing country towns to Perth. Terry showed no interest in the maps or where we were going. After two days, I took over the navigating, disappointed my plan to give purpose to his life had failed. I questioned myself at the time, worried I'd too readily stepped in when he'd shown no interest. He seemed as forlorn at the end of the trip as he had at the beginning.

Just as Mum had noticed my 'change' in 1961 and had not acted, she did not ask Terry what had happened to him. Had she thought there might be a correlation between the dispiritedness, depression and failure that followed both her sons' trips to Quairading?

Looking into Terry's tired eyes now, I remembered his sorrow and my well-meaning plan for him to find purpose and direction. What 'honeysuckle moment' had been happening for him at that time? What I'd observed in his purposeless air and the collapse of his school marks were the same markers of my experience, very likely universal consequences of sexual abuse of young boys. I mentioned the well-meaning road trip.

'I remember that. I really enjoyed it.'

At first, I didn't believe him. I had decided that the trip was a failure. But of course he had enjoyed it, anything to take his mind off his depression. He couldn't have cared less where we went or what the maps were showing us. Maybe he had simply enjoyed leaving our home, the stage of so much trauma.

There was a long pause. These stories were shy.

'I used to love school. I did well and was in the popular group and near the top of the class. In my final years, I hated it. I was failing and coming last in the class in some subjects. I started going late to school, skipping chapel and stopped doing my homework. I didn't care anymore. When I saw the reports that Mum had kept for all those years, I wasn't shocked. I knew my school marks had collapsed. I came last in the class in Year Eleven, thirty-eighth out of thirty-eight and had to repeat the year. "Given up hope and not really trying hard" was on one report. I was demoralised. That's when I used to get off the bus at the Ocean Beach Hotel on my way home from school, and go in have a few beers.'

The air in the café seemed suddenly thin. Terry was telling this story of absolute despair for the first time in his life. It flickered in his eyes, as alive now as it had ever been, the hopelessness and resignation.

Leunig had destroyed his education as well. I understood why I hadn't known about it at the time. His two years in Year Eleven, and his Year Twelve, were my university years – when I was in that home physically but absent in every other respect. In abandoning the household, I had abandoned him.

'I'm really, really sorry.'

'It's not your fault.'

'I know, but this is awful. I can't believe I didn't know this was happening to you.'

'After I left school, I enrolled in engineering at the WA Institute of Technology. I'd more or less become an alcoholic. For the next four years, I drank. I was struggling trying to study. When I failed, I couldn't stand that I was a loser, so I shot through and worked on farms and on stations for five years. When I finally had a girlfriend for twelve months, she told Mum she'd never known me not to either be drunk or to have been drinking. Mum promised me a plane fare to England if I stopped drinking, so I did.'

Dad's emotional absence in dealing with family issues meant Terry's and my respective unhappinesses had been addressed solely by our mother. But why had it taken her so long to intervene with Terry, especially given her own father's alcoholism? Despite their best intention to be good parents, their blind spots had far-reaching consequences.

But I had to honour what else they and our schooling had imparted that had kept us alive, and not succumbing to suicide in our respective moments of despair. We had obviously absorbed the positive aspects of our parents' loyalties and their aim to live moral lives, the positives of their kindness, selflessness and generosity, their commitment to our education, and their love as best they were able. We had also received an uncomplicated love from Uncle Paddy and Aunty Grace, and their influence in our lives seemed to have been a significant contributor to our survival.

I was grateful that the threads had at last come together. We had survived, but not at the rosy end of the spectrum that had been the promise of our childhood and our mother's hopes. An air of betrayal and sadness hung around us.

'The bastard. The bastard,' he kept whispering.

43

The Royal Commission Private Hearing

August 2013

The Royal Commission into Institutional Responses to Child Sexual Abuse was announced by the Commonwealth Government in November 2012, with formal establishment in January 2013 and private hearings commencing in May 2013. I contacted the Commission and immediately received a contact and reporting protocol. The email impressed the availability of a twenty-four-hour counselling line and contact numbers for counsellors and clinical psychologists in all states. The alacrity and comprehensiveness of their response was reassuring, as was the support infrastructure behind the protocols. I completed a statement of the history of my abuse, including my reporting of it to Archbishop Foley in 1989, and the dialogue I had had recently with the Church. I emailed the submission one evening. At eight-thirty the next morning, I received a call from an officer of the Commission. She had read my statement and confirmed its contents fell within the Commission's mandate.

'Would you like to attend a private session of the Commission to present your story?' She reiterated the availability of immediate counselling.

'Are you at risk of self-harm? A counsellor is on stand-by if you need to talk.' The contrast between this response and the Catholic Church's limited and conditional care for my mental health was alarming. A private session with the Commission was arranged. At the end of each phone conversation leading up to the private session, the officer again asked whether I needed immediate counselling.

I was now able to embrace having Louise by my side as I embarked on the next stage of this journey towards resolution and some form of justice, and she accompanied me to the hearing in a suite in a city hotel. I'd also invited Terry. Since our momentous day in the café, we had talked often. Even so, I was unsure. Considering how long and over what terrain he had travelled to get to this point, his relatively recent acceptance of his trauma might make the experience risky. Nevertheless, he was keen to be an observer.

Waiting in an anteroom, I was not conscious of my anxiety until Louise touched the back of my hand and I instinctively jerked my arm away. I couldn't see that she was squeezing through one of the cracks in the carapace to say she loved me.

We were ushered into a simple suite and introduced to the commissioner, Andrew Murray, and an assistant. Murray was very careful with his language. My story was important, he said, and they were there to both witness and honour my experience. I hurtled into the saga of the abuse and its aftermath, my anxiety barely letting me take a breath. He stopped me often to clarify a point, with an ear for a truth disguised by what was not said as much as what was – and what hung in the air in half-finished sentences. He was interested in the minutiae of my experience. Abuse memories, held as traumatised fragments in our bodies, seemed to surface in disordered and incoherent packets of language and affect. He wasn't deflected. He asked questions from different angles, pursuing a fuller, three-dimensional picture of the abuse, cognisant no doubt of the irrational way shame released such intimate information.

The terms of reference of the Commission were to investigate the institutional responses to the reporting of sexual abuse. He was particularly interested in my appointment with the Archbishop in 1989, and more recently, the Professional Standards Office. He wanted to know the details, the letters, the dealings.

He probed me for an opinion on the most recent process. Reflecting on my observations of not just its failure, but the perverse way it managed to reverse the roles so I was made to feel I was the problem, he asked what the Church could have done that would have been better. I was still reeling from the distress of that process, so the best I could offer was that the Church was, perhaps deliberately, muddying the waters. The Catholic Church, as the perpetrator's organisation, in attempting to deal with the abuse away from the public gaze, was maintaining the secrets and, in this collective silence, perpetuating the victim status of the survivors. While a survivor had no voice, he or she could have no lasting resolution. It demonstrated the Church was acting in its own interests and not those of the survivors.

The session lasted one and a half hours. I was exhausted. The usher led us to another suite adjacent where we were met by a clinical psychologist.

'You have as much time as you need to talk about the hearing. How are you feeling? What's happened for you as you were cross-examined? Has it triggered thoughts of self-harm or suicide?'

She was warm but careful in a professional way. Although I felt shaken, I had not been immediately traumatised by the session. Terry, on the other hand, was visibly distressed. Both he and Louise had cried through my interview. I offered for him to engage with the psychologist. He talked for an hour. Occasionally I interjected, to help him articulate his feelings as he scrabbled around trying to put words to the tumult being unleashed. As the session came to a natural end, the psychologist turned to me and gave me her number and the number of the twenty-four-hour counselling service.

'You're to call immediately if you become distressed. I'll call in two weeks to follow up with a phone counselling session. Your welfare is of the utmost importance.'

44

More Boys

August 2013

'Yes, I've known some boys who were abused by Leunig.'

It was a statement I was still not able to get used to hearing. It took my breath away. I'd been referred to Laura by a mutual friend who knew about my abuse. I'd called her and she agreed to meet.

Her house was tucked down a long laneway and in the dull, evening light, I found my way to the concealed gate. It opened onto a courtyard garden awash with autumn leaves. In its seclusion, it seemed safely sheltered from the world, appropriate for what I feared would be more stories of Leunig's abuses.

We talked for several hours about her advocacy for her friend, Richard, who, after many years thinking he was the only one who had been abused, told his parents. When his three younger brothers were asked, they all admitted to having been abused, the youngest from the age of six. Their father tracked down and confronted Leunig, threatening to go to the police. Leunig apparently fled to the Eastern States at this point, purportedly to access psychiatric help. Her story confirmed Archbishop Foley's statement of Leunig's reluctance to return to Western Australia. When the brothers heard that the priest had returned to Perth and was living in the presbytery next to a primary school in South Perth, they were incensed. Laura said she supported Richard and his brothers in reporting their abuses to the Church. When nothing came of their approaches, they went to the police. They were the ones who brought Leunig to court in 1994.

'Richard lives interstate. He might be willing to talk to you.'

She also confided that a friend of hers had grown up in Claremont and knew Leunig's family. The press coverage of the Royal Commission had reignited their interest in the Church and the two had talked about Leunig recently in the context of the widespread incidence of abuse. The priest's younger brother was still alive. Would it be useful to try to meet him?

My visit to Quairading had triggered terrible grief. I did not want a repeat of that, especially if the brother looked like the priest. That familiar panic spiralled up into my throat and, even as it entangled itself, I nodded. Laura said she would see if she could organise it.

What I had uncovered in the previous months seemed to have taken on a life of its own, and something was drawing me down that road. I sensed I had become the messenger, and I owed it to those other boys to pursue whatever opportunities arose to affirm their stories and seek some sort of collective justice, however abstract or ephemeral.

I walked back down the dark laneway from Laura's house. Pale streetlights cast eerie shadows in the deserted street. The world felt suddenly empty of humanity, yet I sensed an optimism. Laura described Richard as a survivor who'd advocated for his brothers and demanded justice, and however belated and spasmodic my own pursuit of justice, I identified with his story.

A few weeks later she rang to say Richard was in Perth on holiday and they had spoken about my writing. He wanted to meet me. I seized the moment and called him, and we agreed to meet later in the day at a small bar near where he was staying.

Apart from Terry, it was the first time I had met another of Leunig's victims face to face. Richard had a determinedness in his manner and greeted me with a smile and a warmth that immediately fostered trust. It was humbling, finding a stranger who shared my terrible past. There was no need for platitudes or incidentals, and we immediately started telling our stories.

His family had lived not far from St John of God Hospital in Subiaco, and we conjectured it must have been when he was stationed there that Leunig started calling in frequently. As I'd learned in Quairading, Leunig was attracted to families of boys, and systematically and indiscriminately abused all of them, oldest to youngest. None of his brothers knew the others were also being abused, affirming the profound anaesthetisation that sexual abuse and its secret triggered in the collective family life.

'When one of my younger brothers found out that all of us had been abused, he was really angry. It dispelled his belief that he was the special one, Father Leunig's favourite.'

Leunig knew how to foster 'specialness'. I had felt special driving at sixty miles per hour on a country road and having a ride in a plane. It sounded like a playbook.

Richard's abuse started when he was eight, before he became an altar boy, and continued until he was sixteen. He went to Quairading many times, during the school holidays he thought. He described sexual encounters Leunig had been alluding to when he'd said 'knowing what to do' and 'being experienced'.

'I was never physically hurt, so I grew to accept what happened when I was taken there.'

Hearing his story, I couldn't help feeling that I had been spared Yet still I was shivering. Thinking it was the cold, I went back to my car to get a jacket. When I came back though, I continued to shiver.

'All of my brothers went to Quairading at some time. One of them said he and Leunig used to walk around the presbytery naked. They kept a pair of shorts folded neatly by the door so if anyone came, they could quickly put them on.'

I remembered I'd seen a dresser by the front door of the presbytery. I imagined the man from the Parents and Friends Association, that Denise in Quairading had spoken of, knocking to remind Father he was late for the meeting. Leunig had taken some time to answer the door, and when he had, he'd angrily rebuffed the man, slamming the door in his face. I pictured a naked boy huddled in the bedroom, perhaps feeling the terror of discovery. Had he too worried about being marched off to prison as the guilty one?

Our conversation turned to the years of therapy we had both had, and our luck discovering therapists who could reignite ownership of our lives. Despite, or perhaps because of, our shared story, we were able look at each other and not cringe in shame, feeling the camaraderie that survivors often described in the aftermath of a catastrophe. Stepping out into the street four hours later, it was as though we were emerging from a shared dream landscape, where in a distant time we had travelled together, unknown to each other. We had only scratched the surface of our common tragedy.

We arranged to meet later in the week, this time at a café at Leighton Beach. When Leunig had brought Terry there, it was a remote, largely inaccessible, deserted coastline. It was now a popular and safe stretch of calm water with wide swathes of soft, white sand, well used by families and dog owners. The café overlooking the beach was friendly and bustling and, after ordering, we sat and looked out over the sand dunes at the low swells undulating in from the west under the endless blue sky.

We talked again for hours, sometimes with tears in our eyes and sometimes laughing, that strange reaction one has to the absurd and its attendant terror. As the trust between us grew, Richard opened up and became more explicit about his experiences.

'Leunig took me to Quairading first when I was nine. That first night I was in the small bedroom out the back of the presbytery, a sleep-out with louvred windows. He came in and asked me if I was afraid. I said I was scared. He took me into his bed and asked me to rub his stomach. When I'd done that, he asked me to rub further down. I felt his erect penis. He asked me if I knew what I'd touched.

"Yes."

"Do you know why it's like that?"

"It's because it's erect."

'I wasn't ashamed of my own erection because Dad told me it was nothing to be ashamed of. By the third night in bed with him, he'd taught me how to masturbate him. I was curious to see what happened when there was ejaculation. I was shocked and revolted.'

He paused, perhaps for breath, but more likely summoning the energy to placate the tremors emerging with the memory.

'He told me, "Don't tell your parents about this. This is our little secret." Once the pattern of the abuse was established, it became more and more difficult to disclose what was happening. If it ever came out, I would have appeared complicit. By the time I was ten or eleven, the sex had become more explicit and more deviant.'

We both lapsed into a long silence, drifting off into our own worlds. I was staring out over the dunes to the rhythmic wallow and slap of the waves at the water's edge. The depravity of Richard's abuse triggered a panic, drawing me back into the therapy room and James's voice encouraging me to breathe through it. After a minute, Richard's voice snapped me back to the table.

'He used to lie in bed with me and get me to recite all the words for penis. It was like the litany we used to say when my family said the rosary. He was obsessed with penises.'

It was so bizarre we could only laugh. Richard's eyes danced with relief.

'That was about as spiritual as he got. I was surprised he never prayed, ever. All he did was say Mass a few times a week. I felt sorry for him because other religious people prayed a lot, and he didn't. It was as though his priesthood was just mechanical.'

I told him that, since my conversation with Denise in Quairading, I had come to this same realisation, that his priesthood was a front to allow him unfettered access to boys.

'Yes. How fucking bizarre. And supported by the Church.'

I asked him about the nuns. Since hearing Alan's stories of life at the school, and after my trip a few months ago, I was surprised at the proximity of the convent to the presbytery.

'Did you ever have any contact with them?'

'No. I never saw one. I knew there was a convent there, but I never saw one.'

He too must have been taken there during the school holidays, as I reckoned I had been as well.

'Leunig used to take me to the pool. There was a boy there, Geoff, who Leunig said was very attractive. He wouldn't let me go into the change rooms, but he went in, and when he came back he said Geoff had "a real beauty". I asked him if he'd "done it" with him and he said he hadn't yet, but that he hoped to.'

Richard stopped and stared out at the sea. I followed his gaze. I'd heard this story before. A fleeting memory surfaced from a distant article or conversation, but I couldn't place it. Afforded a moment to muse on his story, I thought about Alan and his brother being followed to their school in Perth. Leunig must have spent every waking moment planning and effecting the next abuse encounter, his sole purpose as he traversed the countryside. I felt the taint of having been touched by him, just another conquest in his modus operandi. The comfort of sitting with Richard challenged my age-old impulse to succumb to the powerlessness of my childhood impulse to flee.

'Talking of "real beauties",' Richard suddenly said, 'Mum had a second cousin who studied for the priesthood in St Charles

Seminary in Guildford at the same time as Leunig. Leunig told me this guy "had a real beauty" too. He was bragging about the real beauties he'd known.'

So it seemed Leunig was already deviant when he was training for the priesthood. It was another observation suggesting he had become a priest solely to enable his paedophilia.

We started to talk about our emergent sexuality. Richard seemed more comfortable than I was and talked openly. I noticed myself squirming in embarrassment.

'When Leunig picked me up to go to Quairading, we would take out our penises in the car on the way. He always had an erection. I asked him once if he thought mine had grown. I was always scared on these trips, but also fascinated as to what would happen next. I was intensely curious about sexuality.'

Encouraged, I talked about my own curiosity on my last weekend in Quairading, my initiation into 'shooting' and ejaculation. It was a natural preadolescent state, but for me it heralded a personal moral crisis, enough to make me withdraw from the abuse. At the same age, it had also troubled Richard.

'I was thirteen. I became really confused about what we were doing, whether it was right. Leunig used to say it was alright and he was the priest, after all. But I was afraid what we were doing was "homosexuality". Mum had told me homosexuality was a "terrible thing men did". I asked Leunig if this is what was happening, and he said it was "a form of it". When he was moved to Embleton in the city, I was fourteen.'

Richard's story had become unendurable. I found myself splitting off, staring out at the ocean again, at the sunlight glinting and dancing on the water as the afternoon breeze ruffled the swells, at the seagulls drifting unhurriedly in the uplift over the sand dunes.

'There was a boy called Ollie who used to hang about the

presbytery at Embleton. Leunig told me he'd "done it" with him, but Ollie just wanted to wank. Leunig said he wanted to teach him some other things, bragging how he did this with all the other boys. Leunig said he'd introduce me to him, but the day it was arranged, he rang and told me the boy had gotten drunk and vomited in the bed. He said he'd had to shower him and change the sheets. I was shocked and made up some excuse about changing my mind.'

He paused. I waited.

'When he moved to Embleton, I thought Leunig could easily have access to all my brothers in the city. I made him promise that he'd never touch any of them. Years later, when I found out that he'd been abusing my three younger brothers as well, I was angry. I felt deceived.'

We laughed. It broke the tension. We had both held onto the expectation of a high moral standard from Leunig as a priest. How could we have possibly understood the depravity of his life? But of course, we were still children.

Our conversation drifted to our parents and particularly our mothers. I described my mother's years of distress and my role sitting with her in her anguish. Richard nodded.

'I never sat with my mother like that. But she was hospitalised once for six weeks with some sort of breakdown. It was blamed on the stress of renovating our house. She was in St John's in Subiaco. My brothers and I used to visit her there on our way home from school. We were all looking forward to her coming home. But when she walked back into the house, she burst into tears and had to go back to hospital again.'

Curiously, my mother's breakdown was attributed to our move into her father's house, with its depressing interior and garden. She too had burst into tears when she came back from hospital.

His mother's nervous breakdown lasted six weeks, twice my

mother's three-week sojourn. Alan had said his mother should have been treated for her mental illness. There seemed to be a compelling correlation between our mothers' mental states and the abuse of their boys. It did not seem such a tenuous thread.

I mentioned that Laura had told me about him and his brothers confronting the Church and he hardly hesitated before launching into that part of his story.

'After we told our parents about the abuses, I think it was around 1980, Dad tracked down Leunig and confronted him, threatening him with the police. Leunig then disappeared to the Eastern States. Dad said he'd also had a meeting with Bishop Healy at Cottesloe, so the Church had been told of the abuses. Years later, when we heard Leunig had returned and was stationed in the presbytery that was in the middle of the playground at St Columba's Catholic Primary School in South Perth, we were incensed. We went and saw Archbishop Hickey.'

'What was the timeline?'

'We had several meetings over a year or so. It was in the early 1990s. At one of them, Hickey told us we were being vindictive pursuing Leunig the way we were. We knew Leunig's abuses involved many other boys. He'd told us himself. Hickey denied it. He said Leunig was no longer abusing children. We asked him how he knew, and he said, "Because [Leunig] told me so". There must have been a file on him, because when Dad originally met Healy, Healy told him Leunig had not absconded east but that Archbishop Goody [Archbishop Foley's predecessor], had sent him for psychiatric treatment. Healy told Dad that Leunig had been removed from Embleton because of his sexual offences with children. Healy was at one of our meetings with Hickey. He said he had actively discouraged, in fact had tried to stop, Archbishop Foley from repatriating Leunig in the mid-1980s. Healy may not have put it in writing, but they all knew. We found out Leunig didn't undergo the psychiatric treatment he was supposed to have in New South Wales, instead fleeing further afield to Queensland where he hid for several years.'

Richard's version of the story dovetailed somewhat with Foley's explanation. Foley must have known about Leunig's abuses but, giving him the benefit of the doubt, my story perhaps did 'explain a lot', at least about the extent of Leunig's abuses. He must have known there were other victims and now he'd met one of them.

'My brothers and I knew there were many other victims, so we pushed for the Church to find and help them, to offer them support and counselling. They brought Leunig along to one of our meetings to find out the truth. That was confronting, to sit at a table with him. Hickey made Leunig write down a list of the boys he'd abused. When we asked him what he did in the year he was chaplain at St John's in Subiaco, where there was no congregation or altar boys or school, Leunig said he found families or drove around the city picking up boys to molest. He said it unashamedly, like he was contemptuous of us all.'

'Was my name on the list? Or my brothers'?

'There was one name from each of the early parishes where he'd been assistant priest – Palmyra, Scarborough, Northam and Cottesloe. There were a few from Quairading and a few from Embleton, twenty or so names in all. If there was just one name from Cottesloe, then he was obviously lying.'

Penny in Quairading, and Alan, had listed around twenty boys in total that they knew were abused in Quairading. If there had been dozens of boys there, it was reasonable to assume there had been dozens in all the other parishes. I thought again of the first day of my abuse in Cottesloe. There had been no grooming. Leunig's abuse was immediate and direct.

'When Hickey asked Leunig whether he was continuing to abuse, Leunig said, "I no longer abuse children as you get nothing back from them and masturbating them is a waste of time".'

I was squirming on my chair. Richard paused, took a breath, leaned back then forward, rocking on his chair, the angst of those encounters still imprinted and lined on his face.

'After one of those meetings, we got a letter from Leunig apologising for the "hurt caused". We learned later that the Church had done nothing about contacting the victims on the list, so we decided to go to the police. Hickey wrote to us saying Leunig was being sent over East again for psychiatric help, and that was when he was arrested and extradited back here.'

'Tell me about the court case,' I said.

'What was extraordinary was that Leunig pleaded guilty to the charges so there was no need for a defence. The Church retained lawyer Brian Singleton QC to keep Leunig's name and that of the Catholic Church out of the press. My brothers and I told the judge that we had no wish for a suppression order to be made. We wanted Leunig's abuses to be public so the other victims we knew might be encouraged to come forward, so when the judge ruled in our favour and lifted the suppression order, Singleton launched into a stinging and personal cross-examination to denigrate me and diminish the veracity of my evidence. It was abuse all over again. It would have cost the Church a fortune to retain him. How much better would it have been had they spent the money finding and helping the victims like a true Christian organisation?'

The irony was not lost. When I'd seen those stories in the papers, I had seriously contemplated going to the Court. I regretted that I had not had the courage to advocate for myself.

We lapsed back into a long silence. The sea shimmered silver in the late afternoon glare as the clatter of staff cleaning up suggested it was time to leave. Outside the café, the sea breeze eddied around us. I felt its cleansing wash, sluicing me of the sordidness I had heard. We embraced. We knew we would stay in touch.

His story impelled me to revisit everything I had uncovered or remembered. When he described the backroom of the presbytery in Quairading, he said it had louvred windows. Louvred windows were typically used in the 1950s to enclose back verandahs that were usually clad in grey asbestos-cement sheets and had roofs pitching down to just above the windows. The building I saw in the glare of the headlights on my first night in Quairading in 1965 had been L-shaped, low slung and grey. Acknowledging the faultiness of memory, I conjectured Leunig must have pulled up behind the presbytery, not beside it. I had stood, frozen and afraid, and watched as he walked over and unlocked the back door onto the enclosed back verandah.

Over the coming months, Richard and I phoned or texted each other often and, as my legal challenge of the Catholic Church took its various twists and turns, with corresponding ebbs and flows in my own mental health, Richard's voice was a constant one, affirming the courage and resilience required to undertake that journey towards justice. We exchanged emails of our dealings with our respective lawyers, as my case had proceeded to the point where my lawyer Phil had initiated dealings with the Church's appointed lawyers.

45

Terry's Police Report

September 2013

Whenever I met up with Terry now, the rawness of his trauma was forefront and he reverted to his mantra, 'The bastard. The bastard'. I did my best to help soften the pain, offering that the guilt and anger were not his to carry. He was not to blame.

'That belongs with the priest and the Church. I thought there might be a resolution dealing with the Church, but I found out the hard way that justice must come from elsewhere. Their only focus is on protecting their image and keeping us silent. In their Towards Healing program, I had the distinct experience I was the problem, induced to feel guilty for breaking my silence. The Church "regretted" that I did not want to engage in their process of a backroom acquiescence.'

He looked at me for what seemed minutes. He had cast himself adrift with his disclosures, and with no firm base with which to integrate them, I could see him struggling to understand what I was talking about. He could not think of justice for himself. Nevertheless, I planted the seed that his process of healing should start with a report to the police.

'It wasn't easy,' I continued. 'I struggled for almost twenty years in an on-again off-again attempt to contact the police. It didn't happen until I had the courage to act for myself. I never trusted anyone to advocate for me. Not even Louise. I always seemed to have to do things on my own. It did help, though, to externalise the guilt and the shame, and remove some of the burden off my shoulders and onto the justice system. Think about it for your mental health. And think about counselling too.'

I told him I would accompany him on the journey and advocate for him, but he could not yet see what that would lead to. And yet, a few weeks later, he called.

'I want to make a report to the police.'

The police station had moved since my reporting, to a newer and more clinical building. We went into the foyer and this time there was a more discrete counter, and a neater row of clean chairs in the waiting area. We stated our business, and a constable came to collect us and accompany us to an interview room. He was thoughtful and sensitive. I discussed my previous report and statement, and he reviewed it on his computer. He then turned to Terry and invited him to start at the beginning.

Terry cried his way through every detail, at times stopping, choking with anger, as the image of the priest emerged as a scheming, calculating and malevolent criminal. Tears trickled down my cheeks as I sat quietly to one side.

Later, outside on the pavement, we stood mutely for a while. He kept muttering, 'The bastard.'

'The next step, if you feel that you might want to pursue justice, is to engage a lawyer to approach the Church for a resolution. That is the only language to which they will respond. It's incomprehensible they did not know about Leunig, and we're the collateral damage. They need to be held accountable.'

He looked at me blankly. I held his elbow gently. 'Only when you're ready. It's a huge step. It takes the telling of the story to a whole new level. In your own time. Justice is an incredibly slow process.'

I became more and more unsettled in the ensuing weeks. In spite of what I'd uncovered, I still struggled to fully admit to myself the nature of Leunig's compulsive paedophilia, this criminal who'd relentlessly crisscrossed the city and the countryside for his quarry. I could not integrate the dissonance that I'd been in the grip of a man who, underneath his priest's cassock, was the aspiritual and amoral side of his Jekyll-and-Hyde persona.

'That's the definition of a psychopath,' my psychiatrist said a few years later.

The unsettled feeling morphed into a crippling sense of helplessness in the face of his deceptions, the realisation that Terry and I were just two out of perhaps hundreds of his conquests. It reframed my experience in the Fremantle Arts Centre gallery, the feeling of being the prey as the predator approached. Paradoxically, as I came to understand the small part my abuse had been in the wide-ranging psychopathy of his paedophilia, I was grateful that the moment under the honeysuckle vine had not proven to be the end of my life.

My thoughts now turned to my other brothers, Paddy and Dom. And Joe. The months slipped by. Paddy and Dom would have only been four and six years old when Leunig was at Cottesloe, but I asked all the same. Neither could remember him, or anything peculiar having happened.

It was difficult thinking how to approach Joe, the resilient one, the rule maker and the rule breaker. We had been close when we were young, but then he'd become unhappy. He seemed to retreat from us, and I felt intimidated by him. We became close again as young adults when I was sympathetic to his battles with my parents, even though they caused terrible angst in the family. We'd sat together many nights back then with a bottle of red wine, talking into the early hours as I listened to his side of the story, his guilt at the grief he was causing. I cared about what was happening to him and tried to balance both points of view in the family stand-off.

It was never the same after I left home. We drifted apart and I watched from the sidelines as his life took a very different trajectory. In the few, brief moments that we were together over the next decades, our conversations were perfunctory. To ask him if he'd been abused seemed like an insult. Even as I reminded myself that Leunig had abused every boy he could lay his hands on, not just the sensitive or the easily manipulated, I still didn't ask him.

46

The Royal Commission Public Hearings in Perth

April 2014

The full bench of the Royal Commission convened in Perth in April 2014. In its first week, the Commission heard horrendous stories of the sexual, physical and psychological abuse of orphan boys at Christian Brothers homes in Western Australia, particularly at Keaney College, a farm school at Bindoon. The newspaper was full of the men's stories, especially those who had been kept as sex pets by the Brothers. These men reported being used as slave labour, forced to work barefoot constructing the buildings in which they were later housed and where they would be sexually abused. They described beatings and rape so severe some were hospitalised, blood from their anuses soiling the sheets.

In one account, the matron of the hospital in Moora, who happened to also be the sister of a Monsignor, did not report the violence to the police, but sent the boy back to Keaney College, where he was beaten again for telling the truth. There were stories of boys running away and reporting the abuse to the police only to be threatened with charges for lying, and sent back to be beaten again. The men described how, during all those years, they received no education and that they left Bindoon with no hope of a future.

The reports correlated with stories Uncle Paddy and Aunty Grace's daughter Jess had told me. Boys from Keaney College had sometimes turned up on their doorstep in Goomalling. She remembered it was in the late 1950s and early 1960s. Their house on the edge of town was opposite the road to Bolgart that led in from Bindoon. She did not know how the boys knew that theirs was a safe house, but there would be a knock on the door in the night. She particularly remembered one boy who had arrived in tears, having walked the ninety kilometres from Bindoon.

'Dad drove the boy back to Bindoon. I was about seven or eight and was in the car with Mum. We were on our way to have a picnic in New Norcia. The boy cried the entire way and when we arrived at the college, he refused to get out of the car. We waited for ages as Dad went inside. He must have negotiated a safe passage for him, as Dad was able to reassure the boy he would not be mistreated. The boy, still in tears, went back in with him. Dad came back with a face like thunder. I was scared and remember him gripping the steering wheel. We drove across to New Norcia for the picnic and Dad said he had to report it to the abbot.

'If the boys who came were older, Dad used to find work for them on the farms. I remember one boy lived with us for quite a while.'

***

Reading the daily bulletins from the Commission triggered the same feelings of vulnerability and helplessness I had experienced after my trip to Quairading. Nevertheless, I took a day off work to go to a public hearing. Given the effect that each of my ventures to uncover the history of my abuses had had on me, Tash said she'd accompany me as a support. We caught the train into the city and walked to the hearing. As we entered the waiting area, two women approached and introduced themselves as counsellors assisting the Commission.

'If you're a survivor of clerical sexual abuse, we're available for support anytime during the day. Don't hesitate to come and talk to us if you feel the need or become upset.'

It was reassuring. Inside the courtroom, I scanned the milling clusters of officials, lawyers, survivors, supporters and counsellors. Out of the sea of people, a familiar face appeared. It was John D., an old school acquaintance. He'd been in the Star of the Sea youth group with me. I hadn't seen him for many years.

In that knowing way, eyebrows raised, we each asked, 'Who did you?'

'Leunig. And you?'

'Bert Adderley.'

Seconds passed as I felt the air sucked out of my throat and the past burst back in. I struggled to hear John's voice in the flood of memories crashing through my mind.

'Along with dozens of other boys, too. At all his schools – Scotch College, Aquinas College and his country parishes. He was a housemaster at Scotch before he became a priest, and used to take groups of boys nude swimming at Swanbourne Beach back when it was a wilderness on Commonwealth land.

'Adderley had been close friends with my parents. He'd married them. I'd known him my whole life. His friendship seemed normal, and what would turn out to be grooming was just part of the family friendship.'

John described some of his and his friends' stories of Adderley's grooming and shocking abuses. Sadly, he told of one boy he knew of who had committed suicide.

As these images piled onto those cascading through my memory, I wondered if Adderley had joined the priesthood solely to have access to boys, as I suspected of Leunig. I felt another pang of sorrow for my parents, remembering the times Adderley had arrogantly strutted through our house, calling my mother by her first name, mesmerising us with his wit as the preamble to bundling the chosen boy into his sports car and taking off for the beach. He was a constant visitor in the same years Leunig was abusing me and taking Terry for swims down at the Leighton coast. Adderley took me to the remote beach at South Cottesloe, just north of Leighton. Did he and Leunig each have their own turf? Had either of them ever been in our house at the same time? Had they decided between themselves which boy each would take? I pictured my mother welcoming and fawning over these two paedophiles, Leunig laconic and sour, Adderley jovial and flirtatiously arrogant.

The pennies were dropping audibly. If Adderley had displayed paedophilic tendencies as a lay teacher, as John was reporting, why had he gone to Rome for his theology doctorate in the 1940s? Would there have been less scrutiny of his predispositions there? It would seem he knew becoming a priest was a good strategy to enshrine and legitimise access to young and adolescent boys.

Adderley's arrogant sense of entitlement underpinned his style, that boys were part of the priest's deal. His paedophilia must have been blatant though, and reported to the bishops, because he had been moved continuously to ever more remote and smaller country towns. It dispelled the family myth that it was his outspokenness on issues of Church theology and practice that lost him his editorship of the Bunbury Catholic newspaper.

Yet he never lost his wit or that cheerful air of entitlement. Every year, my mother displayed his Christmas card among the many others clustered on their mantelpiece. Occasionally, I'd read them when I was at their house. Something perverse attracted me to his card, in which there was always a long letter sharing his year's achievements and activities. Adderley called it his annual 'Epistle', an appalling allusion to St Paul. That was his unrepentant style. His final posting had been as chaplain to a 'gaggle of nuns' in a small convent in Fremantle, adjacent to a local primary school.

***

The Commission convened and proceedings had a disciplined and determined air. The Counsel assisting the Commissioners quietly posed questions as the current principals of the Christian Brothers nodded or agreed with facts being presented. Screens around the courtroom displayed a myriad of documents, the evidence trail written in ecclesiastical euphemisms, of suspicions and affirmations of abusive behaviour. There were letters from principals to the Head of the Order in Ireland describing a Brother as 'unsuitable to be housed with boys', with the subsequent documentation outlining the relocation and 'retraining' of the offending Brother. But the same name would reappear several years later, accused of abuse, again in coded language, in other institutions in other states. The list of Christian Brothers offenders went on, page after page after page, from the 1920s onwards, seeming to peak between the 1950s and the 1970s. If the Brother Principal hedged around the cross-examination, the Commissioner cut through the obfuscation and stated the facts. A small murmur of, 'Hear, hear' rippled along the rows of elderly survivors as they nodded in unison, muttering between themselves, not always sotto voce, about this Brother or that.

'He was a bastard, that one. He was the worst.'

These were old men, with satchels and backpacks full of papers, in well-worn clothes that hinted at hardship and poverty. They were not holding back with niceties. The Commission counsellors sat with them or stood discreetly nearby.

During adjournments in the hearings, Tash and I walked around the CBD to get some relief. Each time I returned, the counsellors approached and checked that I was coping. I nodded, but as the day drew on, I was unravelling. In the ensuing days, the helplessness and panic resurfaced. I awoke one morning in a deep depression. What was it that kept dragging me down into that dark place? I was scheduled for a therapy session the next day and it was as gruelling as any session had ever been. I thought my abuse had been 'well dealt with', so why was it still the source of such grief? James looked at me in his intense, gentle way.

'Remember the days after your trip to Quairading? It's the same. You knew Adderley well. He ingratiated himself in your family. He was grooming you. You were close to him. That's enough to connect you with his and your own abuses. These events are still there in your body, a physical presence, remembered and felt, and they lie dormant until you shine a torch on them and bring them into the light of day. Then you re-experience your traumas. They're still alive in you, but you've learned to live with them.'

'Why don't I just give up, bury them and pretend they never happened?'

'You can't,' he said. 'If you deny the physical feelings, the rage and unfulfilment that you've described in your life will resurface.'

He held my gaze, and I took comfort from his sureness.

'You can do it,' he said. 'Don't deny the feelings when they emerge.'

I winced at their ferocity when the torch illuminated them. Such was their intensity it was impossible to work. I took the rest of that day off, besieged by feelings of rage, betrayal, loss and grief. Previously, days and weeks elapsed before I could restore the semblance of calm after such trigger events. Now the time between the onset of the grief and the calm lessened until it became just hours or days.

Musing on James's certainty, of not denying the feelings when they emerged, I had an insight into the amount of psychological effort required in 'blotting it out', as Terry had put it. If exposing 'it', the trauma, caused such intense feelings of grief and desolation, would a similar amount of energy be required every day to keep it down and blot it out? Presumably so, and such energy would be a negative effort. That was what my unvoiced rage had felt like, blaming everyone and everything else with no possibility of resolution, the unrelenting lack of fulfilment, living a half-life in a 'perpetual state of defeat'.

***

A week or so later, Louise, our friend Mary and I were discussing the Royal Commission hearing. In passing, I mentioned meeting John and told his story about Adderley.

'I knew Adderley,' Mary said. 'He was chaplain at my convent boarding school in Narrogin in the 1960s. He was everyone's friend. All the boarders had gone to the pool one day. I was shocked to see him there in his Speedos. I'd only ever seen him in his priest's clothes. It was as if he was naked. He was playing in the water with the kids, then he'd stand on the edge, pick them up and toss them into the water.'

I winced as I heard the word 'Speedos', remembering so vividly Adderley standing with me on the edge of the reef at Cottesloe. And then Richard's story of Leunig at the Quairading pool. It was like there'd been a handbook on the methodologies of sexual abuse of children.

'Years later, I was talking with D.G. He'd been in primary school with us. His Dad had told him and his brothers that if Father Adderley ever tried anything with them, they were to kick him in the balls and run like hell.'

She spat it out, half laughing, but with that latent anger that former Catholics invariably produced when disclosing the injustices and hypocrisies of the convent and school walls that had harboured them. Obviously, some of the parents knew about Adderley and had attempted to give their children protective strategies. Even so, they still seemed impotent in reporting, or attempting to prohibit, his paedophilia, relying instead on the children to look after themselves.

***

Every week, the Royal Commission was exposing countless more horror stories, and the Catholic Church was appearing to diminish the gravity of the tragedy, abdicating from full responsibility for the abuses within its ranks. Cardinal George Pell railed at the community's indignation focusing so acutely on the Catholic Church, intimating that sexual abuse was also widespread in the community: '... We object to being described as the only cab on the rank',(5) as though that somehow condoned the rampant abuses by its priests and diminished their criminality. He also likened the Church to a trucking company, whose employees were not the responsibility of the company.(6) Was his Church merely a taxi service to God and Heaven, the actions of its drivers not the responsibility of the company?

47

My Brother Joe

June 2014

I still hadn't asked Joe about his experience in our family in those early years. The time had come, not because I believed he might have been abused, but because he would have another perspective on our parents' disputes, our mother's mental state and the paedophiles who had infiltrated our home. I'd reflected deeply on the complex web the Church had woven in and around our childhoods, and even incidental observations from that time brought new colours and layers to the story. I was still too shy to broach the subject with him, even though there had been markers in his life suggesting a pathway sometimes followed by those who had been sexually abused as children.

His second wife, Connie, once asked Louise and I why our children hadn't gone to Catholic schools like the other cousins. I'd simply answered I was no longer Catholic. Years later, she'd asked Louise why I seemed unhappy and not part of the wider family. Louise broached the subject of my abuse and its effect on my relationship with my parents. In a roundabout way, I assumed Joe knew. I'd talked about the breakdown of my 'belonging' in the family with him once, particularly in relation to our mother, without ever specifying the trigger.

One afternoon, he and I were talking on the phone about our mother and her progressing dementia. I told him directly about my abuse, that I was writing my story and I had some questions about our home life. Could we meet? He agreed and we scheduled a time. I was surprised at his willingness, but not at his detached air. In our day-to-day lives, we'd had no reason to be close.

We met at a small bistro, the seemingly requisite neutral territory for these conversations. We ordered drinks and found a quiet corner. He didn't wait for an invitation to share his thoughts.

'I wanted to tell you I have contacted the Royal Commission. To add my name to the list. If it needed one more name to bring the story out, I didn't want it to fail because I hadn't spoken up.'

I stared at him. 'Leunig?'

'Yes. In the sacristy after Mass.' He paused. 'I used to hate changing from our gowns in the altar boys room and going back across into the priest's sacristy. I had no choice but to go past him. I eventually organised it so I only served on Sundays when there were more people around, coming into the sacristy after Mass to ask something of him, so he couldn't do it.'

'Do what?'

'Groping around in my shorts, grabbing my dick. Or feeling for pubic hairs. When he felt some, he used to say, "Hmm. What have we here?".'

'So, it was when you were alone? On a weekday?' I was already shaking.

'Yes.' Silence. 'It used to make me so angry, I hated having to serve on weekdays. I got out of it as often as I could.'

The implications dislodged in my rattling mind. I finally found the words.

'You and I were in a rostered group together, and I've never been able to work out why I served alone so much of the time. Every time I was alone on a weekday, he abused me. If there was a boy from another family there, Leunig used to make me stand aside and wait until he'd gone.'

He winced, his eyes creasing and his cheeks puckering. He didn't say anything. I waited.

He then described the excuses he'd come up with to get out of serving, mostly about an excessive amount of homework. Why had I never tried to get out of serving? I had been paralysed by the abuse whereas he'd become angry and empowered to act. Had our mother noticed he too had changed? Perhaps his determined, wilful and self-possessed nature concealed his anger so that all she saw was what was familiar. I had always believed I was vulnerable to the abuse because of my sensitivity, and he immune because of his determined nature. Yet even after discovering Leunig abused every boy he could reach in every other family, sensitive and determined alike, I was still shocked to hear he had abused Joe.

'What made me so angry was that I couldn't avoid him,' he continued. 'He could do that to me, and I couldn't stop him. I coped by putting all my effort into my schoolwork. I did my homework diligently, focusing on getting the best marks I could and being the best in the class so I could bring home the prizes from the Speech Night at the end of the year.'

As though to underscore the gravity of his reaction, he added. 'When I was young, I saw myself as the priest in the family. Leunig put paid to that idea when I was twelve.'

Hang on! shouted my indignant inner voice. *I was going to be the priest! I was the spiritual one! How could you see yourself as the spiritual one when you got out of serving so often?*

Then I remembered our play acting of Mass when our Goomalling cousins came to stay. He was always the priest. I was the altar boy. Long before the abuses began.

We lapsed into the silence that inevitably followed the unearthing of such long-held secrets. There was too much to integrate. I looked away, towards the evening hubbub as the bistro came to life. It allowed me a moment to sift through the scattered cuttings of our childhood together. It had always been exciting, my brothers and I willingly following Joe in his adventures. Being abused by Leunig would have been disastrous for his self-esteem, and it gave me an insight into his resultant anger and withdrawal from the abuse.

I plucked up the courage to meet his gaze again. 'Did anything else ever happen?'

'Much later, he invited me up to Quairading on the pretext he could organise a flight in a plane. It was after I'd left school. I'd withdrawn from engineering at university and was studying at night to try to get into another course. I had a job, so I'd bought myself a new Ford Cortina. It must have been some time in 1967, when I was eighteen. I drove up to Quairading on my own. On the Saturday afternoon, I met three girls, I think in a milk bar. They were underage so it wasn't at the pub. Leunig gave me his car to drive, a pale blue Falcon, so I invited the girls out. They wanted to visit a friend in the next town, so we all drove there in the Falcon. I remember there was a long, straight stretch of road and I went really fast. We went to the pub when we got there, and because they weren't recognised, we could get away with underage drinking. The girls were impressed. They asked me if the car was mine. When I said it belonged to the priest in Quairading, they were disapproving. They couldn't figure out why the priest would lend his car to a boy so they could all go to the pub in the next town.

'That night, as I was getting ready to go to bed, Leunig appeared at the door to the bedroom. He was holding a Polaroid camera. He asked me to take off my clothes. I told him to fuck off. That was all. He didn't try anything on.

'He'd arranged a flight for me the next day. The pilot and I flew around over the countryside. That evening, I drove back to Perth. I just got on with my life. I didn't think much more about it.

'When the stories of abuse started surfacing recently, I saw how the Catholic Church challenged the victims, often the weak and vulnerable who'd put their hands up. It made me angry.

I could see how those vulnerable people would have felt abused all over again as the Church adopted its adversarial position, its aggressive defence and often blatantly hostile attack on them.'

He looked directly at me with an openness I'd long forgotten.

'I had no idea of the significance of what happened between you and our parents. I can see how you might get over a functional failure, like a poor performance at school, and repair your life afterwards. But a rift between you and them is really sad.'

It wasn't just a rift. It would have been impossible for him to know that it was an excising from the family, with the decisive moment traceable back to the beach at Cottesloe. We had never talked among ourselves about the abuses as Alan and his brother had done. During and after university, I'd cut myself adrift from home and the family in such a way that these conversations could no longer happen, even in the early hours of the morning when I'd sat with Joe, nursing him through a red-wine haze, discussing the angst he was causing in the family.

'When I learned of your story and realised Leunig's predation in our family had been sequential and deliberate, I saw I had a responsibility to put my hand up, and I contacted the Royal Commission.'

He stopped. I didn't fill the silence. Even though I understood the paralysing stranglehold that shame had on our capacity for feeling and telling, I couldn't understand why it hadn't made him want to contact me. It nevertheless showed the importance of the Royal Commission as an enabling conduit for the stories to be released. Joe could embrace this method to bring his abuse safely out into the open.

Again, I saw his sensitive side. His incisive intelligence understanding my story and his concern for the other victims displayed an empathy and fearlessness that took me by surprise. It shouldn't have. This was the relationship we'd had as young, adventurous children. But I worried. He'd contacted the Royal Commission because of the patterns he'd seen in Leunig's predatory infiltration into our family and the Catholic Church's intimidatory stance to victims. What about him? Where had the anger he'd experienced gone?

He was eleven when Leunig first began abusing boys in the Cottesloe sacristy. Becoming aware of his disempowerment, his subsequent anger enabled him to remove himself around the time he turned twelve. Was this an age-related awareness? Or personality? Or a combination of both? My abuse started in 1961 when I was nine. The Royal Commission had reported that ten years old was the average age that the abuse by Catholic priests started. At that age, I endured the abuse submissively with no memory of anger, just the terror of discovery. Three years later however, at twelve, Leunig's intrusion into my safe world at the beach triggered the same feelings of rage Joe was describing. Importantly, it was my first consciousness of the abuse and its effects on my life. Perhaps then, one's immediate response to abuse was age-related, twelve being the defining age where one could recognise the intrusion of the abuse and register anger and betrayal, then perhaps remove oneself. Yet at twelve, after my brief explosion of rage on the beach, I could only comprehend how trapped I was and unable to escape. I'd felt defeated. As predicted by the midwife nun at my birth, Joe and I were very different boys.

We talked on for several hours. I was heartened by what we'd shared. But it would be a few years before we discussed it again. Nevertheless, a non-verbal understanding now existed, an acknowledgement of what had happened. Perhaps we didn't need to keep dredging up the details, shining the torch on them. I was open to it though, and suggested we could talk anytime.

48

The Forensic Psychiatrist

June 2014

My lawyer Phil had emailed to say that a forensic psychiatric report was the necessary next step to accompany my complaint to the Church. He'd commissioned a psychiatrist to prepare the report and the appointment was for the following week. His message instantly triggered a panic.

Perhaps from experience, or perhaps from fearing the unknown, a lump had spiraled up and gripped my throat as I walked into the psychiatrist's reception room. The receptionist pointed to a waiting area. I had just sat down when the psychiatrist stepped out and invited me into his office. He pointed to a chair next to a window and sat at his desk some distance from me. Directly behind him and in my line of sight, positioned just above his head, was a statue of Jesus on the cross. Seized by an instant, irrational paranoia, it took every fibre of self-control to pull my eyes down from the statue and focus on the psychiatrist. Any trust I may have been prepared to imbue him with vanished. Taking in his detached air, his averted eyes, his casual introduction and the hint of condescension as he'd pointed to that chair, I understood my anxiety. This stranger's mandate was to cross-examine me, to prod and tease in a non-therapeutic manner to exhume the intimate details of my abuse, and, for reasons of impartiality, not to be empathic.

My intuition about the clinical absence of empathy was correct. For nearly two hours, with rapid-fire questioning, he traversed every corner of my life, incising with cool, surgical precision every vulnerable and raw crevice. He pressed every trigger of the abuse until I was shaking, yet still he pressed on relentlessly in his quasi-legal, dispassionate manner. He challenged all my perceptions.

'How do you know?' 'Why do you think you ...?' 'What made you feel like that?' He breathed mistrust, but it was his job. In between questions, as he wrote his notes, I became aware that I'd been splitting off, escaping out the window into the jacaranda canopies lining the street outside his upper-floor room. They were so blue, or was it mauve? They swayed in the breeze, waves of melancholic clusters of bells. Suddenly, he stood up and thanked me. 'I'll be in touch with my report in due course.'

He ushered me out into the foyer with no mention of how I might be feeling, or what I might expect in the next hours or days, or who to call should I need support.

I desperately needed the toilet. His receptionist directed me down the corridor. Inside the cubicle, I stood for what seemed minutes, my hand shaking so much the pee went everywhere. I squatted down beside the bowl, tearing off toilet paper to mop it up. Outside, I stood in the shade of the jacaranda trees. The footpath had gone to jelly. I felt scared. All my life I had raged and blamed, desperately keeping up appearances whenever I'd been challenged or cornered in this way. Now I recognised what was happening, even though I was powerless to change it. I stood for perhaps five minutes, then made my way to the car where I sat and listened to music.

I rang Phil and reported my experience.

He was understanding, but I sensed he didn't get it. Using the Royal Commission private hearings as the benchmark, I suggested that in future, when commissioning such reports for people who had suffered abuse with psychological implications, he should also arrange counselling with a qualified person immediately following the cross-examination.

When the psychiatric assessment arrived, the envelope lay unopened for days. Summoning courage, I finally pulled out the thick sheaf of papers to read the psychiatric dissection of my life. Of the traumas of my childhood and the subsequent behaviours as an adult, the psychiatrist labelled me as most probably suffering from Post-Traumatic Stress Disorder. As a diagnosis, it was both reassuring and troubling. I still wanted to think of myself as normal, but he suggested that the unpredictable mood swings, the irrational rages, the long and unacknowledged depressions, the continuous and severe feelings of disempowerment, and lack of fulfilment were real attributions of a disorder traceable back to childhood trauma. The trauma had not just been the sexual abuse, or the resultant shame, or the guilt at feeling complicit, or the disembodiment inherent in maintaining the secret, or my mother's and Leunig's betrayals. It had also been the permanent separation from my family after the abuse. I'd been skived off from that sometimes-troubled life of love and acceptance, and had been on my own for the remainder of my childhood. And I had continued to feel cast adrift until my late fifties when I had started my therapy with James.

49

Mediation Begins

9 February 2015

Phil emailed that he had invited the Church to attend a mediation hearing to initiate a claim for compensation. The Church had responded, proposing it be with a representative from WAPSO at the Church's offices in the city. Despite several years of negative publicity at the Royal Commission, the Church was still holding the sexual abuses at arm's length through this quasi-autonomous body. I was furious. I had clearly stated that I no longer wished to deal with that organisation. I wanted to confront the Catholic Church itself. Any mediation, I responded, must at least be at an independent venue. Later he rang to say they had agreed to meet at his office.

As the day approached, the inner conversations ran amok on an anxious mental loop. Phil asked me to prepare a Victim Impact Statement documenting the effect of the abuse on my adult life.

'Why not an Impact Statement on my childhood?'

'That won't be considered in any settlement, as it's not quantifiable.'

'The direction of my early adult life and tertiary education was largely determined by my school results, which reflected significant failure, directly correlated with the episodes of abuse. Not to mention my sudden lack of ambition. As an adolescent, I could not see I had a future,' I argued.

Undaunted by his scepticism, I collated my school reports, diligently archived by my mother in her determination that her sons' pathways to university be documented. I analysed the marks and comments and drew up a graph correlating episodes of abuse with school performance. It made for sobering viewing, what the financial analysts might describe as a negative trajectory to bankruptcy.

Four days before the planned mediation, I awoke tensed, like a frightened animal, reactionary to any negative or critical comment. I spent the day writing, chasing the flashes of angry thoughts and memories, the tension humming in my chest. I rang SARC and spoke to a counsellor.

'Could I see James? It's urgent.'

The counsellor said they would call me back when they'd had a chance to see what could be arranged at short notice but, in the meantime, was I at risk of self-harm? Or suicide? What thoughts was I having? The conversation went on for ten minutes and she skillfully talked me down to a calm state. It was like a sea breeze on a hot day. It took three days to return to a level of equanimity. The night before the mediation, I had the following dream:

'A meeting had been arranged with a businessman. I went into a large hall, like the central chamber of a library, and walked towards him as he came from the opposite end. I took up a defiant stance, stating my name, loudly and clearly. Confronted by this, he ran away to hide behind rows of bookcases. I left the building and consulted with a number of friends waiting outside as to how best to handle the situation. We discussed options. I went back inside to find him, but he was nowhere to be seen. As I was walking along the rows of books looking for him, he suddenly jumped out from behind a bookcase. I was surprised when he pulled out a gun. *Where did he get that from?* I asked myself. He lunged forward and shot me in the stomach. I had an initial shock registering this, but then went back outside to my friends. I lifted my shirt. We all looked to see where the bullet had gone in but there was no sign of injury. My skin was intact. I was not particularly worried or upset.'

It was early morning. Faint grey light seeped around the

corners of the blinds into the bedroom. I could feel the tremor in my larynx and upper chest. I understand dreams as personal metaphors, the poetry of my psyche as it were, overlaid on a matrix of archetypes. I value them as cryptic and seemingly one-sided conversations with my unconscious. Apart from the dream representing some aspects of my traumatised inner world, in the imagery the Church was portrayed as it seemed to be, or at least how it behaved, as a business. The Church's representative was a businessman and, unable to deal with me confronting and naming myself, he had run away to hide. This time I was not alone in the war, and I had a voice. I had friends and support, and I knew how to consult them. When I had the courage to go back and find the businessman, the fearful, abstract shooting nightmares of the past had become specific: the businessman leaping out to fire a single shot into my belly – as Leunig had done, four times. But now, even as he and the Church would try to harm me again, with the support of these friends, I was not injured. My innocence in the dream worried me though, the expectation of fair dealings. I took comfort in understanding that at least my psyche was immune if what was coming was an assault.

***

Louise came to the mediation. We had decided, after my experience with Archbishop Foley, and then with WAPSO, that I should have a witness in all dealings with the Church. We arrived early as instructed and met Phil in his office. He briefed us on what we might expect and said he couldn't be certain of any resolution. He asked me if I would be happy for him to firstly meet Peter, the mediator from WAPSO, to establish some structure for the mediation. At first, I was reluctant, but I had to trust him. He had been one of the friends I was consulting outside the library.

I tried to take reassurance from the dream, that I would not be harmed by anything that the Church might try to do, even though I was primed with an impulse to flee, similar to what I'd experienced in the art gallery.

Phil went out to an adjoining meeting room. After some time, he returned.

'Peter has no authority to enter into a mediation leading to a remedy. He has come with regrets that your past experience of the Towards Healing program through his office was not satisfactory, and wished that you would re-engage with them so that you might be able to be offered an apology for the hurt caused, and some counselling. He also stated that you could be welcomed back into the fold in a process of reconciliation and forgiveness. His message was all warm and fuzzy. Do you want to engage in this?'

'An apology for the hurt caused? Hurt! Jesus!'

This was worse than before. Apologies were meaningless. What were they thinking? How could a just reconciliation be achieved, or a just remedy, or even a just expression of failed duty of care, when the WAPSO organisation did not even acknowledge itself as the perpetrator's Church. And forgiveness again! Of whom and by whom? On offer was an invitation from the lion back into his den, to be mauled again? I'd felt diminished by Jim and Moira at WAPSO the first time. I'd sworn I would never re-engage in that process. Now they'd sent an emissary to lure me back into their process.

'It's still all about the Church. On their terms. What about the abuse? I refused their offer of forgiveness and reconciliation before. They're meaningless words, empty of empathy and justice. Please come back into the fold? They just don't get it. As if I'm the unreasonable one!' I was ranting, squirming mercilessly on my chair. Louise touched my arm.

'I'll take that as a "No".' Phil gave a wry smile and returned to the meeting room.

Any dialogue the Church was offering was meaningless if it was inside the secret process of their Towards Healing program. The Church was not taking responsibility for Leunig's crimes. While that remained their position, the burden of the abuse would always be mine to carry. There could be no resolution for me, the removal of that yoke, until a process leading to a just outcome was initiated. I needed the Church to publicly say: 'We believe you and also that you told Archbishop Foley. You are not to blame. We accept full responsibility. How can we help?'

I had to come to terms with the fact that my notion of a just remedy might never come, either in the form of a tangible program to enable some economic independence or meaningful independent support into the future, like the paedophile priests had received. Again, I took heart from the dream. I had to stand up to the Church. They were still trying to shoot me down, but now I wasn't alone and I would not be harmed.

When he returned a while later, Phil spat out the response. 'Peter was so patronising and belittling, I felt like leaning over the table and punching him.'

My jaw loosened with relief. I could trust him to stand up to them.

This seemed to be the end of the road. The Church was not going to meet me with any tangible and meaningful acknowledgement of the abuses without me subscribing to their hideously demeaning and secretive program.

In the evening, Louise and I went down to the river in East Fremantle and walked in silence along the shore path. Finding a quiet alcove in the tidal wall, we sat while the still, evening air settled around us. The incoming tide rustled a shoal of mussel shells at our feet. Four ducks and a pelican swam by, the pelican fishing in the shallows, nuzzling underwater then leaning back and wobbling its gullet with floppy, gulping swallows. In the calm, I felt released. Watching the pelican swallowing the fish, I had a sudden thought.

'By maintaining my silence all these years, I've let the Church keep its hands on my genitals. Most of my life I've felt unsafe, in one way or another. My psyche has been running and hiding to dodge the bullets in my nightmare. The Church refuses to be public about the extent of the abuses. It wants to maintain the secrets. If I don't declare my abuse publicly, I support them in the silencing. I allow them to still have their hands on my genitals. With my genitals back, I regain personal authority and I have a voice. The Church does not want that.'

After some time, Louise added. 'And the Church had its hands on your parents' genitals as well. And their minds. There were three parties to that marriage. It stands to reason you missed out when the chips were down.'

Her comment gave birth to the idea that in the 1950s – in an age before the social unrests and upheavals of 1968 onwards – my parents had themselves been like children, obedient inside the authoritarian, parental structure of the Church. As a result, they were vigilant of their own children in every way *except* within the orbit of the Church. The Church had directed everything in their lives, including their sex life. They were not independent-thinking adults. In this parenting vacuum relative to the Church, priests found themselves, or positioned themselves, in the de facto role of the parent without ever having experienced a mature, adult sexual or parental relationship for themselves. Perhaps it explained why paedophile priests, acting purely in self-interest with helpless and obedient children, so easily crossed the line a psychologically healthy and mature parent would not.

Leunig and Adderley were both grown men when they joined

the seminary. Looking back at their respective pathways to the priesthood, it seemed a not unreasonable assumption that their 'vocations' were a smokescreen for their already deviant sexual pursuits, and that they already knew their Church turned a blind eye to those blurred boundaries between the children in their charge and paedophilia. Their motivations, however, appeared to be different. Adderley, already alleged to have acted deviantly as a lay teacher, was smilingly arrogant as he groomed and abused, his paedophilia seemingly predicated on entitlement with no sense of its criminality. Leunig, on the other hand, never smiled. He was angry. This train of thought suggested that his abuses were getting back at something or someone, a type of revenge. Yet Richard's account suggested a narcissistic obsession with his own sexual fulfilment via children. In this he ultimately saw its futility, or lack of fulfilment, saying in Richard's hearing that he'd stopped abusing children because 'You got nothing back from them and masturbating them was a waste of time'. Apart from revealing his appalling lack of empathy, it suggested an extraordinarily arrested, infantile mind.

Part Four

50

Sister Carol's Years in Quairading

1969 & 1971

Standing behind the presbytery in Quairading the previous year, I had looked up at the convent and tried to imagine black-garbed Sisters walking over to the church, passing close enough to the presbytery that anyone inside would have heard the crunch of their stiff, black shoes on the gravel. It seemed logical to question what they had seen or known about Leunig's unabashed 'sleep-overs' with boys. Were any of those Sisters still alive, and if so, had they suspected anything of their priest?

I phoned my cousin Peter for a current contact at the convent in Mosman Park and rang and made an appointment. The foreboding convent building, where as a child, I had sat in the dark and muted loneliness of its rooms, had long been demolished. The newish convent building had an anonymous, modern appearance, rather lacking in spiritual gravitas. I went up the steps and pressed the bell. I was expected and a Sister showed me into a reception room. Gone also were the voluminous black habits, replaced by skirt, blouse and cardigan, all in soft blues.

'Sister Noella will be with you shortly.'

My eyes roamed the walls and furniture in the reception room, all arrayed with the usual holy pictures and small icons of the Holy Family looking happy and safe. The slow shuffle of slippers on the passage carpet heralded an elderly Sister. We shook hands. I'd met Sister Noella several times on family occasions, the last being at the vigil after my father's death. She remembered me and welcomed me warmly.

She sat quietly as I told my story, listening and commenting with an open-hearted empathy that once more made me think the Church might have been better served had it been run by women. I didn't expect to get an answer, but posed the question nevertheless.

Were any of the Presentation Sisters stationed in Quairading in those years still alive? Had there been whispers that they suspected, or reported, what their parish priest was doing in the presbytery just metres away from their convent? She promised to find out.

A day later she phoned. 'Yes, there is one of the Sisters here who was stationed in Quairading with Father Leunig.' She gave me the name and number for Sister Carol. When I called, Sister Carol said she'd been briefed and knew why I wanted to meet.

Driving to our meeting in Mosman Park, I felt a long-familiar anxiety. I thought at first it was an age-old reaction to the pervasive authority of the Church, but quickly realised it was because I was about to speak to a Sister who had taught at the school while boys in her care were being abused by their parish priest. I was anticipating it being a difficult, even evasive, discussion, considering my previous dealings with the Professional Standards Office. I was about to get out of the car when a sudden storm released a cloudburst. Raindrops the size of grapes crashed onto the car roof and the deluge flooded the street. The cacophony silenced all thought, and I had no choice but to sit with my anxiety and wait. My imagination, set adrift in an Old Testament moment, could not help but think this was a Catholic God's wrath in anticipation of the questions I was about to ask. I shook myself and quickly moved to a more empathic thought, of the release of the tears of the many abused boys from all over Australia who had suicided. I ran from the car as the last drops spattered down and dived under the awning over the entrance to her office.

Sister Carol was younger looking than I'd imagined. She welcomed me with a warm smile, and indicated two chairs against the wall opposite her desk. She then moved to sit down beside me, on the same side of her desk. I noticed this and appreciated that we would both be facing the same direction. My 1989 meeting with Archbishop Foley was in the forefront of my mind, sitting opposite, separated from one another, his hands clasped neatly on his desk.

'Are you likely to get into trouble with the Archbishop if you share any sensitive information with me?' I was remembering Stefanie at the Catholic Church Archives office.

'Good heavens. No!' she exclaimed, scoffing at the notion. 'I have my own mind.'

I was disarmed by her frankness and generosity of spirit, particularly her willingness to revisit her years in Quairading. We quickly pieced together dates, places and people. She'd been there as a very young Sister in 1962, newly out from Ireland, and then again for two separate years, 1969 and 1971. Since she'd been alerted to the reason for my visit, she had been thinking about her time there while Leunig was the parish priest.

She leaned over to her desk and picked up a small, spiral-bound notepad. It was already open, and pencilled down the left-hand side of the page was a list of names, maybe a dozen or so.

'These are the boys I had concerns about after I heard about Father Leunig.'

I leaned in close to look at the notepad. Her handwriting was neat, considered and deliberate.

'Some are family names,' she said, 'so there could have been two or more brothers who might have been abused.'

We went through the list, pointing out the names together, particularly those Alan had mentioned when I interviewed him after my trip to Quairading. Sister specifically mentioned the boy

Gordon, whose death had really shaken Alan. He had asserted that Gordon was definitely being abused by Leunig.

'Gordon was a gentle lad, but also very troubled and always in strife. I was anxious about him and used to give him jobs to do. That cheered him up. After he got his driver's licence, he was killed when his car hit a tree.'

Looking up and down the page, as Sister's finger hovered over each name and she mused on the outcomes, I understood I was reading a list of the ill-fated. Over one family name, almost under her breath, she said, 'I wonder if those two boys were abused.'

Then she pointed to two other boys' names. 'I remember seeing them hanging around the presbytery.'

I asked her about school life and Leunig's role within the school.

'Father used to say Mass for the schoolchildren once a week, at nine o'clock in the morning. He used to come up to the school at about a quarter or half-past eight and take a boy down to the church to get ready for Mass. He usually asked for this one boy. At the time, there was nothing imaginable on which to base any concern.'

I was conscious of Sister repeatedly mentioning her retrospective anxiety, and almost in response to my thought, she continued.

'Priests were venerable and beyond reproach. I rationalised that this boy, who was an only boy in a family of girls, perhaps liked male company and that's why Father fostered the relationship.' She paused. 'I've worried about him ever since I found out. He never married and stayed around his home. I heard he's had difficulties in his life.'

She explained that whichever boy Leunig had taken down earlier always stayed back to help him clear away. The boy would come back up to the school after maybe a quarter of an hour.

'This was far longer than necessary to tidy up after Mass. None of us could have imagined what he was up to.'

There was a sudden flash at the window. We both jumped and turned and stared out into the bushes. 'I think it's a rat,' she exclaimed. But the rustling shape rummaging for nectar among the bottlebrush blooms revealed itself as a red-lobed wattlebird. I realised how tense I'd become.

I asked Sister about convent life.

'Mass was at seven on a weekday. I would go down to open the church at six forty-five. I walked by the presbytery and shouted outside Father Leunig's bedroom for him to get up. He was never very good at getting up, and he'd come over to the church after a few minutes.' She paused, reflecting. 'We cooked all his meals, breakfast, lunch and dinner. I used to take his breakfast down to him and put it on the table in front of him and he wouldn't say a word. No "good morning", no "thank you". We also cleaned the presbytery and the church and did all his washing and ironing.'

Who had taken care of the towels and sheets covered in semen, and what had happened to the towel flung over my belly and pushed down between my legs those four nights? And the towel used to wipe up after Terry? I couldn't bring myself to ask the question, but the answer emerged a little later.

'There wasn't a public Mass on Saturdays, but Father said Mass for us in our convent chapel.'

I was there for two Saturdays in 1965 and, apart from having never seen a Sister, as Richard had also noted, Leunig didn't leave the presbytery to say Mass in their convent. We had gone out on our adventures. It confirmed that I was part of a school holiday pattern, when the school was closed and the Sisters had returned to Perth. Starved of his primary source of boys, Leunig would bring one boy up from the city for the weekdays, as Richard had described, and then another boy over the weekend. As I always had Saturday or Sunday sport during term time, it confirmed that my visits had been during the school holidays. Leunig, having been posted out into the far-flung wheatlands for over five years, had to engineer a program to ensure a steady stream of boys into his presbytery. To underwrite the thousands of miles he was chalking up during the holidays, the farmers, whose boys he was abusing during term-time, supplied all the petrol for free. No wonder he laughed. And was more than happy to do his own washing during the holidays.

I mentioned this pattern to Sister Carol.

'Yes. Father Leunig used to drive the Sisters down to Perth on the Friday afternoon of the last day of term.'

Sister kept running her finger down the list, her lips framing the names, reciting the litany of the abused. I asked her about the family Alan had talked about at length. Leunig had abused their three young boys.

'Yes. I learned about them later. Their father had a job in Quairading, and their mother was a stay-at-home mum looking after the boys. She died suddenly and unexpectedly. The father was very distressed and, needing support, moved back to Perth to be close to his family. He still had his job in Quairading though, so he used to bring the three boys with him for the working week and school, then return to Perth for the weekends. The boys were at school during the day. In the time between school finishing and their father collecting them after work, Leunig had systematically abused all three of them. When the dad found out, he was devastated and quickly left and moved his job and the boys to another town well beyond Leunig's reach.'

Sister's voice oscillated between a whisper and barely concealed anger. I was struggling too, appalled by Leunig's incomprehensibly cruel and callous abuse of those grieving boys.

When I interviewed Denise in Quairading, she had described Leunig as unapproachable. I asked Sister.

'What about the town, the politics and the feeling among the parishioners? Do you remember anyone expressing concern? Perhaps they too felt anxious about their children and this priest.'

'The town was predominantly Freemason. Apparently, there had been resentment about the Catholic school being opened in the first place, in 1955, because people felt they would be compelled to send their children there. The priests were therefore never fully accepted into the town. Father R. was the most readily accepted, apparently because he was partial to his whisky and drank down at the Club. Father Leunig never did that. He didn't drink like the other priests, and he didn't fraternise with the parishioners.'

Sister rotated on her chair and faced me, confiding, 'I never felt comfortable with Father Leunig hearing my confession. I waited until the priest from Bruce Rock came through Quairading. I'd slip out of the classroom and have my confession heard down in the convent.'

So she hadn't trusted Leunig with the frailties of her moral self either. Perhaps she didn't want him to know her secrets, to give him that power over her. But then, how could this young Sister confess that her most grievous sin may well have been a mistrust of her parish priest? I admired her courage, in the face of the Church's authority, to assert her independence around confession in this way. It demonstrated her underlying anxiety and mistrust of him, but also her astuteness.

This admission seemed to change her equanimity and her voice took on a different tone, regret perhaps, or anger, at having to be devious about seeking out what should have been a normal expression of her spiritual life.

'He was mean, too,' she continued. 'When my father in Ireland died, I asked Father if he would celebrate Mass for him. He said he couldn't, because it was his own father's anniversary and he'd be saying Mass for his father and couldn't include mine. Of course, the priest can include as many people as he wants when offering up a Mass. I felt really hurt.'

She shifted quickly on her seat. I thought of James coaching me to interpret the messages the body sends when it can't say what it feels. Leunig's meanness was probably his way of getting back at her for avoiding him for her confession. I remember his childish, peevish anger in his car the last time we returned from Quairading.

She paused, taking a breath, navigating this tricky course, then continued with a hint of irritation.

'He never prayed or said the rosary with us in the convent as the other priests had done. I often wondered how he even came to the church each morning to say Mass.'

This was the irreligious and spiritually bereft man that Terry, Richard and I knew, and the man who Denise had intimated was the reason her faith had lapsed during the years he'd been her parish priest.

Then, as though she caught herself being un-Christian in her criticism, Sister Carol added, 'On the other hand, he sometimes came up to the convent to help me on the Roneo machine, preparing things for school. He was generous, too, to the farmers. He used to go out to their farms to help them in the busy periods.'

I didn't say anything. Those farm visits – helping at harvesting and seeding, and out in the fields picking mallee roots with a clutch of boys – were grooming those families, brokering trust so they would willingly let their boys return with him to the presbytery for overnight stays. His help with the Roneo machine was more likely the same with Sister Carol, so his access to the boys in her classroom would continue. He would have sensed her growing mistrust. He was cunning enough to spy a potential hitch in the arrangements. He needed to protect his sources.

There was a natural pause in her story. Perhaps she could hear my mind working overtime trying to integrate the extent of Leunig's malevolence. Or perhaps she too had had enough, and it was time to wind up our conversation. What she said next caught me off-guard.

'I visited Leunig after he was released from prison, and sometimes went to the Mass he was celebrating near to where I was living at the time. He said he had devoted himself to a life of penance and I saw it as my Christian mission of forgiveness to help rehabilitate his soul. My God is a forgiving God.'

But what about the Church's moral responsibility to the victims, the amoral stance it has taken? I heard my mother's voice again, saying she would pray for Leunig.

Sister, though, was talking as a mature, morally responsible adult. How different from the position the men in the Church had taken, moving paedophile priests around from parish to parish, then employing the top lawyers in the country to attack the victims and defend the Church to protect its name and its assets. All while paedophile priests, at least those able to be identified and isolated, were being secretly filed through the Wesley Private Hospital in Sydney, being 'rehabilitated' so they could enjoy a quiet life of retirement free from the threat of prison for their crimes.

When I first read that Leunig had been charged and convicted, and again when I had seen him in the art gallery, I had justified my inability to act by calling up an inner mantra of quasi-forgiveness, not quite a 'turn the other cheek' response but one not wanting to inflict more punishment on the man. *He got his just desserts*, I'd told myself at the time. I now knew this was a foil, deflecting me from an acknowledgement of the trauma of my abuse and taking responsibility for the ensuing rage that should have been directed at him, instead of spewing it out onto everyone else. I had not yet found my voice, so labelling myself as a 'very reasonable Christian' was a suitable excuse. Sister's voice had been hobbled too at the time, for different reasons, but once she found out about Leunig's betrayal of her duty of care, she had reacted by maintaining a lifelong empathy for those boys that had been abused.

She didn't add to her statement. We talked on some more, easing ourselves away from that gritty Quairading gravel over which we had both trod. She had been open and honest, revealing a saga of long-held grief that she might have easily concealed. I was grateful and respectful of her candidness, her humanity and her courage.

Outside, the road and verges were still saturated from the sudden storm. I drove a kilometre or so and pulled over. Despite my intention to be strong and resilient, the interview had taken me to a vulnerable place. I had not been as detached as I'd hoped. I was conciliatory and somewhat emotional. The anxiety I had experienced on the journey there held echoes of my disempowered and voiceless young Catholic self. Taking out my notes, I reread Sister's story, then went home and sat at my computer. I had to write it down, to get it out onto paper as quickly as I could. It was like paddling before a wave, the only way being forward. To stop or look back over my shoulder would be to fall and risk drowning, catastrophically overwhelmed for days.

Later, when I reflected on the list – and Leunig's relentless and determined pursuit and destruction of all those boys' lives and their families' lives – I speculated whether forgiveness for the priest, as promoted by my mother and her Christian sensibility, was an evasion of the truth. The abused men, if they had not suicided or died prematurely, continued to describe lives of misery, pain, suffering and often substance abuse, living in varying degrees of disarray, and attempted healing. I was challenging prayer and forgiveness as a methodology for their relief. This was not God's issue.

And what of the mothers whose sons had died, and the mothers who'd had breakdowns, unable to assimilate what they knew in their hearts? I couldn't rationalise how forgiveness could resolve those tragedies.

This was where the Catholic Church, with true humility and feeling, had to step forward and acknowledge the truth of the relentless terror, cruelty, humiliation, shame and betrayal experienced by all the victims following Leunig's and all paedophile priests' acts. Then, appoint and forever fund independent bodies to act to repair, restore and revive what was left of their lives. In doing so, the Church also had to acknowledge and act to repair their partners' pain: the broken marriages, the half-lived lives, the children raised by fathers reeling in their PTSD and crippled by the trauma embedded in their secret, the alcoholism, the aggressive promiscuity, the episodes of mental anguish, the nights of shivering terror, the suicides. It might then be possible that hearts could start to beat fully, wounded but not crippled.

51

Meeting Leunig's Brother

2015

Eighteen months had passed since that night at Laura's house. Her friend had followed up on the contact with Leunig's younger brother. He was elderly and had been quite ill but had recovered and, when told I was writing the story of the abuses, said he was willing to meet me.

I had vacillated between revulsion and an intense curiosity since the possibility of a meeting was first mooted, but the seemingly endless stories of Leunig's scheming and depravity compelled me to pursue this opportunity to meet his brother. I rang the number, registering a deep fear of that tsunami of desolation 'when the light was shone on the trauma', as James had said.

He sounded tired and his voice cracked, but he was polite and sincere. He seemed genuinely keen to talk so we arranged to meet at his house in the city. An overwhelming apprehension swelled as the day approached, and the voice intruded again.

What are you thinking? Will he look like his brother? If he does, what will you do? How will he behave in the face of the stories of grief his brother unleashed?

I pressed the button at his front door and, as a bell chimed deep inside the house, I stepped back as though to delay the meeting.

The door opened and a short, lean man came forward and we shook hands warmly. He did not look like his brother. I was relieved. We moved towards a living area that overlooked a narrow river. Before we sat down, he turned to face me and immediately and sincerely apologised for the actions of his brother. I stood silently for several minutes as he poured out the grief he felt for me and the other boys he'd been told about. He was trembling with emotion, impassioned as though he was unburdening himself of a lifetime of guilt. I had not anticipated this.

'It's not for you to apologise,' I offered.

In words loaded with more meaning than I could immediately assimilate, he responded.

'My brother was the product of my family and though no-one else should accept responsibility for his actions, somehow my family "made" that person.' He was shaking his head, side to side as though in a trance. I thought his position was unreasonably unfair on himself but didn't say anything.

He indicated a small sofa by the window. Sitting down, I took in the world outside for a few moments before I began to describe my encounters and the discovery of the many boys abused in all of Leunig's parishes, particularly Quairading and Embleton. In deference to his feelings, I alluded to the acts without describing the specific depravities. Hearing that his brother's abuses had involved many more boys than anyone had previously been aware of, he became visibly agitated, alternating between anger at his brother and at himself, as though somehow he could have stopped the abuse if he'd had more insight and courage.

'How could you have had any influence over him?' My question was tentative, fearful now of stirring up any more of his grief.

'Even though he was older than me, I used to bully him. When I first heard about his paedophilia, I was afraid that my bullying had somehow contributed.'

I recounted the occasions when I had experienced Leunig's anger. This seemed to confirm for his brother that anger had been a component in the matrix of the abuses. He seemed to be searching for words to express regret when suddenly, he stood up, tears beginning to stream down his cheeks and he almost shouted.

'He did not love children but inflicted great pain on them! What anguish and torment did he cause?' He excused himself and quickly left the room.

Framed by the picture window, the spectre of an invisible, silent wind shuffled across the surface of the river below, teasing rhythmic ripples into life. Cormorants dived and reappeared, gulping fish. A small dinghy under sail struggled against an incoming tide. I urged the little boat on.

When he returned a little later, apologising profusely, I tried to reassure him I did not want to invoke such distress and offered to leave. He refused.

'No. Some sort of catharsis has been a long time coming. It's been troubling me for many years.'

We talked for several hours until, realising we were both exhausted, I said it was enough to have travelled this far. We promised to keep in touch. A week later, he messaged me.

'Your visit was very healing. It has given me the opportunity to express and unburden myself of years of grief and blame. It has brought light into a dark place in which I felt I was living. I would like to meet again.'

I was humbled that this elderly man would want to embrace the past with such courage, but I was still unsure, and saddened, as to why he felt any responsibility.

52

Leunig's Childhood

1926–1946

Overnight rain had left the ground wet and the air damp, with a few remaining clouds tempering the weak sunlight. A cold south-westerly wind hounded around the corners of Mr Leunig's house as I pressed the bell. Opening the door, he was as warm and welcoming as before. We sat once again in the room overlooking the river, the world outside all but silenced by the thick glass in the window. I watched again as the wind's eddying swirls troubled the brownish-grey water. I was still nervous entering this house. We talked about what had happened for both of us since we'd met. He felt relieved that the story could now be out in the open.

'It's complicated,' he went on, 'I want to acknowledge the difficult past my brother and I shared, but it's hard talking about feelings, coming as I do from a generation that was expected to suppress them. I know your purpose is not one of blame or recrimination, but it still leads inevitably to some painful introspection.'

He talked about his father. Initially it was with affection, honouring him as a good Christian, but soon his story hinted at a very troubled man. His father had left his job with the railways and enlisted in the Australian Imperial Forces to fight in the First World War. He'd left his wife with one infant and pregnant with another. Sent to France, he worked on the railways behind the trenches. He hadn't fought on the front but witnessed the horrors as they were carried back in his carriages. He had returned a changed man but, like everyone else who came home physically fit, had gone back to his job with the expectation to get on with life as though nothing had happened. Until Friday night. Every week on Friday nights, his father got drunk and became violent. He described the violent exchanges between his parents.

'On the surface, our family was upright and Catholic, but in reality, it was very dysfunctional. Underneath the righteousness ran a vein of terror. My mother used to get very angry with Dad because he'd drink on those Friday nights and then he'd get angry with her. I never saw him hit her, but I remember him chasing her through the house with a carving knife. My mother would rush me out of the house when he was like that, gathering me up and shepherding me as we ran outside, Dad behind us wielding the knife.'

He stiffened and straightened in his chair, writhing as he talked, the fear still palpable in his body.

'I had the feeling Mum never forgave Dad for something. I used to think it was because he'd abandoned her with babies to go to war, but I now suspect there was another reason.' He paused, summoning up another story not used to the light.

'We used to say the rosary most nights. My mother said we had to pray for Dad's soul in case he died, because otherwise he'd go straight to Hell. We were never told why, but years later my older sister alluded to the "something" when she said, "If you only knew". Maybe it had to do with her and Dad?

'I kept thinking of him as one of the kindest men. He used to take me to school in the mornings, catching the trolleybus to the city.'

'Tell me about your brothers and sister.'

'I was the youngest of the five children born alive after the war. Two babies had died. One died two years before me and that explained why there was a five-year gap between me and my brother Leo.'

He stopped, as though punctuating time, to create the gap, to separate himself.

'My eldest brother was a delight. He had plenty of girlfriends and was a state champion swimmer, then a pilot in the air force in the Second World War. He was a very gregarious man but drank too much and became a terrible alcoholic, which caused a lot of grief at home. My mother was very strong, and Dad, even though he got violently angry at times, mostly went along with what she said. With my oldest brother's alcoholism, she got her way. Dad would have thrown him out of the house, but Mum tended and cared for him.

'My second brother was quieter. He was an air gunner in the air force and flew in the Battle of Britain, and was mentioned in dispatches for bravery. He was eventually put in charge of an air force base in Queensland, but had a lot of personal problems. He was an inveterate gambler.

'My sister was third.' Curiously, he stopped there for a few seconds, then quickly skipped to his next brother. He had been a professional soldier and served in New Guinea. He described him as a likable bloke but with an irresponsible, larrikin streak. His next brother also served in the air force and flew in New Guinea and, after the war, completed a postwar education program and became an architect. He moved to England, married and had children there. When his wife left him, his family split up and he eventually returned to Perth and died here.

'Then there was Leo the priest.' Again, he stopped, as though to physically summon the momentum for this next part of the story.

'All my other brothers were bright, affable and successful, and good sportsmen. Leo wasn't. He wasn't popular. He wasn't likable. He was a misfit.'

Even as he was talking, I could hear echoes of the same words from Denise in Quairading.

'In 1941, when he was fifteen, he was sent away to the Christian Brothers Juniorate [a training school for Christian Brothers] at Strathfield in New South Wales. He didn't finish and came back after only a year or two. All my other brothers had gone away to war and my sister had married and moved away, so I really enjoyed the time he was away. It was as if I was an only child.'

'Do you know why Leo came back early?'

He shook his head, then handed me a copy of a page from a folder he had opened. It was the 1941 admissions listings in the enrolment directory of the Juniorate at Strathfield. In neat, copperplate writing on the left was the name, Leo St Clair Leunig, entrant number 815. It stated his address in Claremont, his date of birth, his date of entry at the Juniorate, the parents living and his educational background. Curiously, whereas other boys on the list usually had both parents named as the admitting authority, at Leunig's entry, it only stated his mother. There was a red line drawn through his name and the letters 'LU' were inscribed in red against the margin.

'What does LU stand for?'

'Apparently the letters mean "Left, Unsuitable".'

The stories of cruelty and abuse perpetrated by the Christian Brothers in Australia from before this time, and since, describe a shameful and terrible epoch in the Catholic Church's history. What made Leunig, as a fifteen-year-old, an unsuitable candidate in the seminary of the Order that housed and perhaps fostered generations of cruel paedophiles? 'Unsuitable' was the same euphemism that had been used so often at the Royal Commission hearing I attended. I had felt the pall of Leunig's anger, so perhaps that was too much even for the Christian Brothers. Or had something else happened? Around 1942, during the Second World War, the sixteen-year-old teenager returned to Western Australia alone on the train.

'When he came back, he joined the Air Force Cadets in Claremont and apparently tried, unsuccessfully, to get into the air force. He did become a leader in the Air Cadets.

'I wasn't a great athlete, but he was a terrible one. He had no prowess at all at any sport, that being a measure of success then, so I was contemptuous of him. And because I knew I was a lot smarter.'

He paused, his eyes wandering, as though fossicking among these memories from the dishevelled family archive.

'I used to go along with him to the YCW [Young Christian Workers] meetings at St Thomas's in Claremont, our family parish, but I never had any admiration for him. My other brothers were heroes and I wanted to be a soldier like them. That was my ambition. Being the youngest, I was the darling of the family and was spoiled rotten. I was aware, or at least sensed, that Leo was ignored, and I got the impression from my sister that Dad had been unfair to him. When he was set to become the priest in the family though, he got the special treatment from Mum.'

This time he lapsed into a long reverie and his gaze wandered out of the room. Sensing both the difficulty and the emancipation in his willingness to share his story, I waited patiently for him to return, not wanting to intrude into his thoughts as he meandered through those childhood days. The next story came with a deeply drawn breath. His face changed, charged with rawness.

'Leo used to get very angry. I remember once getting angry back at him. We were working on a bike together and he did something to me in spite. I chased him around the house with a spanner. I was really going to belt him. Then, when I heard about his paedophilia, I blamed myself. I thought that the years I'd treated him so contemptuously must have somehow led to his behaviour.'

Stopped by this memory, he went suddenly silent, as though exhausted from the momentum of the recollection with all its implications. I waited until his face eased.

'Did he have any friends?'

'He did. A few. I'm not sure if they were from the Air Force Cadets. I felt strange around them and was frightened of them. Not physically, but intuitively. One of them, Dick, gave me the creeps. Dick would come by our house on his bike, and I'd want to get away from him. There was another one, Eric, who I knew was in the air force. He dominated Leo. Leo would do whatever he asked.'

He moved awkwardly in his chair and leaned forward suddenly, as though to propel something towards me.

'I have no doubt Leo was a victim of sexual abuse. I've always thought it came from my mother's side of the family, by one of our uncles. I had that same creepy feeling about him. He was a dentist and lived in Victoria, and often came over to our place on holidays. He used to give cigarettes to my older brothers. It seemed like good fun at the time. It seems obvious now what was happening, he was grooming all of them.'

Instantly, images that were permanently etched in my memory flashed up – Leunig nonchalantly smoking, standing with his legs apart, forearm pivoting slowly upwards from the elbow, his fingers to his mouth, drawing on the cigarette; and driving, pointing out Catholic farms with the cigarette in his nicotine-stained fingers. His brother looked at me. I nodded.

'I did my matriculation when I was sixteen and passed with seven subjects and some distinctions. Leo did his matriculation the same year, even though he was five years my senior, and he only passed two subjects. He needed his matriculation to get into the seminary for the priesthood. It took him a few more years before he eventually passed Latin.'

The unvoiced pauses alluded to more than he was saying, a struggle to soften his still festering contempt. I couldn't help picturing his would-be priest brother trying for years to get enough subjects to gain admission to the seminary. That was commitment. Had he too had his education destroyed by all manner of violence and sexual abuse, like Terry and me? His determination to succeed made for very black reading.

'My mother used to advocate for him because he was going to be a priest. That would be considered her family's greatest achievement, and he revelled in the attention and getting out of the housework. He took pleasure in being the dominant one then, both before and after he left home to go into the seminary. He became really arrogant. When he did become a priest, if the altar boys made a mistake, he used to say he would "Put them up against a wall and shoot them". There was something chilling about how he said it. He was so angry he might just have been capable of doing that.'

It was easy for me to imagine Leunig 'lining up and shooting' the altar boys. *Not the usual gunshots though,* I thought.

'What do you know about his seminary years?'

'The seminary was St Charles in Guildford. It only covered the first three years, so he was there from 1947 until 1950. Then he transferred to St Patrick's Seminary in Manly, New South Wales to finish his training. He came back to be ordained in Perth in 1954. He said his first Mass the following evening at our parish church of St Thomas's in Claremont.

'He was the first YCW member in Perth to become a priest. His first post was as a relieving priest in Kalgoorlie, and then as assistant priest in Palmyra. He also became an Army Chaplain.'

We both lapsed into silence. Leunig's brother looked exhausted. His face was slumped, his hands motionless on his knees. My mind had also started wandering, the sign to stop. We talked about what this process was doing to both of us. He reminded me that his whole life had been bound up in his brother Leo's life: the early years of contempt, his distress witnessing Leo's arrogance as a priest, and then the revelations of his paedophilia.

'Telling this story, I feel I am unburdening myself of a lifetime of guilt.'

I was simultaneously honoured that he could be so trusting of me to understand his brother's life, but also scared that I was venturing into deeply personal territory that might trigger trauma that I had no qualification to handle. Yet his openness was a monumental gesture, and I acknowledged his courage, reiterating that I thought he was harsh blaming himself for his brother's actions. He shook his head. There seemed to be more to tell, but it was not for us to pursue it on this day.

I rose to leave and, as an afterthought, said I was interested in establishing a chronology of his brother's life, as a means of tracing the pathway of his paedophilia. He promised to forward as much information as he could muster. We shook hands warmly. He tried to smile, but only weariness appeared.

In the car, I sat for some minutes. Our conversation, though painful for him, had been an honest reconstruction of his childhood and I was grateful it had seemed healing rather than lacerating, for both of us.

It was a common story, the return of his father from a foul war, suffering from what we now know as Complex PTSD and resulting in alcoholism. What had been the fallout from his trauma, and then the dysfunction Leunig's brother had described in his family? The fear and terror the Leunig children experienced seemed to continue manifesting in their adult lives since, after experiencing another war and much personal trouble, all but one of his older siblings succumbed to a form of emotional dysfunction: alcoholism, gambling, personal problems or marriage breakdown. However, Leo the future priest, had followed a different trajectory. He had become an angry, amoral priest devoid of any shred of the spiritual. And a criminal.

One could only speculate why his mother had enrolled him at the Christian Brothers Juniorate in New South Wales. Given Leunig's dearth of spirituality and his anger, it is hard to imagine why, as a fifteen-year-old, he would have chosen to become a Christian Brother of his own accord. That would have required a strong sense of vocation. There were at least four of us boys, and Sister Carol, who could vouch that he had not displayed any semblance of a spiritual life. Perhaps the emotional, psychological and possible sexual abuse described by his brother had made Leunig so angry, hopeless and depressed that his mother saw the Juniorate as a means of giving him direction in life, a way out from his depression – a road trip, as it were. Maybe he was the toxic one in the family, and she sent him there *because* he was the problem. This would also be a vocation in her family, a positive outcome and her contribution back to the Church, which seemed to be her place of solace in her own troubles, as it had been for my mother.

Leunig may have had no say in the matter but, being only fifteen and given the catastrophic direction his life was ultimately to take, perhaps he'd agreed to go to the Juniorate, but not for religious reasons. Five years later, as a twenty-one-year-old joining the seminary, Leunig was clearly disposed to voyeurism, telling Richard about the 'real beauty' possessed by another seminarian. Perhaps this had caused problems at the Christian Brothers Juniorate and was the reason he had been declared unsuitable? But he persevered in his choice, having chosen or fallen into the perfect disguise for his paedophilia. With unquestioned access to limitless boys, he determinedly set off into the priesthood. It seemed to me to be an angry, contemptuous revenge.

***

Some weeks before my meeting with Leunig's younger brother, Tash had uncovered the coroner's inquest report (quoted in the *West Australian*) about a Father Philip Shannon, the assistant priest at St Thomas's in Claremont, who mentored the YCW of which Leo and his brother were members. Father Shannon had been out from Ireland just two years when, in 1946 at age twenty-six, he was killed by an oncoming train at the Leighton level crossing in North Fremantle. It was reported that he and a fellow priest, Father Stephen Hawe, both dressed in bathing costumes, had been deep in conversation as they were crossing the tracks. The level crossing gave access to some light industrial land that served the port, and was also the only access to that remote part of the coast that Leunig would cross fifteen years later with Terry. Tash had also unearthed the death notices column from the *West Australian* in the days following the accident. There were just four funeral notices for Father Shannon. The first was anonymous, presumably from the Church administration; the second from the Sullivan family; the third from a twenty-year-old Leo Leunig and his fifteen-year-old brother; and the fourth from three other boys of the YCW. They described 'a true friend' in Philip Shannon. There was nothing conclusive about the reports or the inquest.

'I don't remember anything about that, or the funeral notice,' Leunig's brother had told me, when I raised it with him.

The sequence of events spawned my curiosity. First, the death of the young Irish priest, Leunig's YCW mentor, crossing to the secluded and remote coastline at Leighton. Second, Leo Leunig placing the death notice in the paper. Then, the following year, in 1947, joining the seminary to become a priest. After his ordination, when the coast was still remote and inaccessible as a public beach, he would have had to cross the same level crossing when he took Terry there, presumably to abuse him. And probably other boys, too.

53

A Bleak Corner of the Cemetery

2015

The stories of the Leunig boys' childhood and young adulthood careered around inside me for weeks. As in my imagination Leunig still lived and walked, something in me wanted to confront him, even in death, to challenge his stated remorse, as Sister Carol had reported. Driving home from the city one afternoon, I took a route up a back road behind the Karrakatta Cemetery. I pulled over and, going through a small side entrance, followed a narrow path between rows of headstones to a map on a board. I found the children's memorial garden, next to which, as Tash had discovered, Leunig was apparently buried. Walking up a long, leaf-strewn roadway, I quickly found the garden and, out of curiosity, went into its peaceful enclave. Surrounding it on its four sides were solid rows of cypresses and hedges, containing and shielding this refuge from the acres of graves of the elderly or unlucky. The children's headstones were set out diagonally, as though to plead deviance from the square, adult world. It seemed a safe place to bury the young and the stillborn. The epitaphs engraved on the predominately white marble headstones described deep sadness and grief, notably absent from the next headstone I read, just a few metres away. Leunig was buried in the same grave as one of his older brothers, the one who had died nineteen years earlier, a broken man.

The solid marble headstone, set securely on a wide plinth, was inscribed with a mix of Gothic and serif letters; a fading, loving testament to the older brother's place in his family. A small white statue of Jesus, His Sacred Heart afire, stood guard on the plinth.

His hands were apart and there was a sorrowful frown on His face. Was He expressing despair at the violence in this reportedly dysfunctional family? On the bottom left-hand corner of the headstone was affixed a small, newly minted, bronze plaque, its letters glinting in the afternoon sunshine.

In Remembrance Of
Leo Leunig
3/1/1926–9/10/2011

Stripped of his mantle of priesthood, in death he was simply Leo Leunig. There was no 'Reverend Father' or even 'Father'. There were no words in Latin, nor a Gothic script signifying a Catholic imprimatur, nor letters affirming the priest with professional standards. There was no Order or religious community claiming him as one of their own. In death he was what he had been in life: a man disguised as a priest.

The plaque was discreet, and I decided it was apt. I recalled the day the detective had rung to say, 'The person is deceased'. I'd circled around my garden, angry and cheated, with the dawning realisation that even though he was dead, he was still alive inside me, always would be, and I could not confront him, or try to 'blot him out' as Terry said he'd done. The insignificant little letters on the plaque could not attest to the wars he had unleashed during twenty-five years in parishes around the state, determinedly infiltrating and abusing whole families of boys, laying down the foundations for the PTSD in their lives. His grave, orderly within the loneliness of the cemetery, embodied the finiteness of death. But the violence of this man and his sordid double life rippled on in the minds and psyches of his many victims and their families, and would for generations to come.

The afternoon sun was warming my back. It took my mind to

a more positive place, to Sister Carol's generosity and her commitment to forgiveness. I'd been struggling to understand the pathology and dysfunction that had created Leunig the monster – did that mean I was also trying to forgive him?

A sudden, cold gust slapped across my face, waking me from my reverie. With a quiver of revulsion, I realised it didn't matter. I couldn't avoid this raw pain as it surfaced, no matter how much I rationalised his life or tried to understand the forces that had moulded him. It was the wound that would not heal, what psychologists named the 'continuing event'.

Walking away from his grave, I wondered why I'd gone there. It had made me angry in that same way I'd experienced being deprived of a confrontation, the day I was told he was dead, and aroused the same feeling of unease as had happened after visiting the presbytery at Quairading. Deviating from the pathway back to my car, I headed towards the area where Dad was buried.

There was a large, cleft gum tree beside his grave, twin trunks growing out of a single stump, two deviating lives born from the one promise. I scanned the avenues of trees and wended my way between the headstones until I found it. Small lesions appeared here and there up the twin trunks, bleeding reddish gum out onto the striated, coarse, black bark. I knew those wounds, those 'continuing events' that bled and did not heal.

Dad's name was inscribed simply across the top of his modest headstone. I thought of his world where everything about the Church was good, of his shame and palpable anger at hearing my story that day on the footpath outside my house. Tears began to seep out as I talked to him now, buried beneath my feet, and told him he no longer need feel sullied by that shame. His family name was intact; it was his Church that was tainted by the abuses.

Underneath his name was listed his surviving family, my mother and us five boys. Through my tears, I stared at my name, etched into the marble among my brothers'. Softly I recited the litany of our five names from eldest to youngest: Joseph, Gerard, Terrence, Patrick and Domenic. It was a mantra my family had chanted over the years, my name fitting neatly into the rhythm in second place, essential to the wholeness of our family. Yet it had been dislodged in my childhood and forced into a separate life.

In the newspaper reports at the time of Leunig's trial, the Church's lawyer had told the Court: 'Leunig's great sorrow was that by his actions he had intruded on the boys' faith and alienated them from the Church and God.' (7) Citing the domain of spirituality was untrue of course. Leunig had not a spiritual bone in his body. It was the psychological, emotional and physical trauma I had experienced that had intruded on and alienated me from this rhythm in my family, for I could see my name there among my brothers, but for most of my life I had not felt one of them. Mum had registered this loss also, and together we'd jousted with absence until slowly, over the years, a non-verbal truce was brokered. Now she had dementia, and no new words or ideas could reach her.

After I'd told my family about my abuse, nothing much changed, and it reinforced my feeling of being an outsider. Except with Terry. We'd become much closer after sharing our stories, the two of us, the remnants of the secret Jabbers Club. Walking back to my car, a text message alert sounded on my phone. It was Terry, leaving for an overseas holiday. 'Will be thinking about you.' It was a lifeline from within that chorus of my brothers' names. He wanted me to be there in the family with him.

54

The Death of My Mother

13 August 2015

For several years after Dad's death in 2004, Mum lived happily in their new home. When the slow progression of dementia began to overtake her, we moved her to a retirement village. In these twilight years, she would not want us to leave. 'Stay just one more minute,' she'd say, holding my hand. I came to see this minute as the physical affirmation of her existence as our mother, of all that she had become. All her eggs were in that basket. She did not want to part with it. I knew that when I left, I would be leaving her with nothing.

When we eventually had to move her into an aged care home, she'd become like a child again, free of the angst that had eaten away at her throughout her life. In a loyal, dutiful way, my brothers and their wives, and Louise and I, looked out for her, taking her on day trips often, and maintaining a close interest in her increasing level of care and its minor emergencies. We all had many tender moments, telling the same jokes, engendering the same laughs as we revisited occasions of hilarity in our early childhood. She'd returned to a happy place with no apparent memory of the sadness that had rent our lives. In her final few days, she became very ill. Her anxiety returned and the priest was summoned to administer Last Rites. Later, my brothers and our families, and some of the Goomalling cousins, clustered noisily around her bed.

Over and over, she asked, 'What am I to do? What's happening?' Taking her literally, we reassured her in a non-committal way.

'You don't have to do anything anymore, Mum. You're very sick and just need to rest.'

She nodded, acceptingly. Half an hour later, she would ask again. We repeated the vague reassurance. Each day she slid a notch further into semi-consciousness and with the increasing failure of her body, her voice became weaker. Her repeated question was reduced to just two words, whispered with great effort.

'What's happening?'

On the morning of what would be her last day, she gestured to me to come close. The room had emptied for a moment, and I was alone with her. Leaning in close, I held her gesturing hand.

'What's happening?' she whispered.

'Mum, you're dying. Your body is failing and there is nothing to be done but to keep you comfortable. But you don't need to be afraid.' I listed Dad, Uncle Paddy and Aunty Grace, her own parents and all the others she had known who had died, a list of the departed.

'They've already made this journey.'

Then I named her own family, that comforting mantra of us five boys, and our wives, and her grandchildren and now her first great-grandchild.

'We're all well and looking out for each other. You don't have to worry about your boys anymore. We're all okay. You can let go. You don't have to be afraid of dying now.'

Out of the fog of her semi-consciousness and dementia, she gripped my arm tightly as she had done so often in my adolescence. Turning her head, she opened her eyes and, looking intently at me, spoke clearly and forcefully.

'Thank you for telling me the truth.'

It was her last sentence.

She died that night, held gently in Paddy's arms. Cousin Peter said the rosary. After her lifetime of prayers and petitions to the saints and heavenly hosts, it was as she had hoped: a happy and a holy a death.

***

Since the late 1960s, our mother had never gone back to worship with my father at the Cottesloe Star of the Sea church, though it was always walking distance from her home, and where Dad's Requiem was held. Her Requiem Mass was to be held at the St Thomas's church in Claremont, where she had become a parishioner after her Swanbourne parish had closed several years earlier.

There was a large congregation in the church. We were bathed in the brightest of bright sunlight streaming through the large stained-glass windows at the eastern end of the sanctuary, setting all our faces aglow. The laughter and happy squeals of children playing in the primary school next door echoed around the nave. We could have been in our childhood backyard again. However, the golden glow harboured a dark shadow for me.

This was the church where Leunig's family had worshipped on the Sundays after the Friday nights of terror; where Leunig's mother came to seek solace from the terrors of her marriage; and from where, as a fifteen-year-old, Leo Leunig left to join the Christian Brothers and returned as 'unsuitable' a year later. Here he had joined the YCW group under his mentor Father Philip Shannon until, at twenty-one, he had left to join the seminary; and where he returned to celebrate his first mass in 1954. It seemed ironic that this was where we were honouring my mother's life and praying for her soul on its journey into the hereafter.

The priest in white vestments circled her coffin with the thurible smoking, the incense I had so often breathed as an altar boy in the years when the priests wore black. The chains of the thurible clinked as it swung back and forth. He sprinkled holy water on her coffin, the metal rod chinking noisily as he dipped it in the silver bowl, incanting the prayers that were to accompany her to her Heavenly Father. He implored Him to accept her soul into Heaven, to embrace His faithful servant. I hoped that all her accrued indulgences were still valid, ensuring a swift transition through her imagined Purgatory into her just reward.

We lifted the casket onto the gleaming chrome rollers at the back of the shiny, black hearse waiting open-mouthed in the yard.

Dad's grave had been opened. Swathes of green, plastic grass arched over the freshly dug, yellow earth heaped around the rectangular hole. I looked down but there was only sand. Towering over us, the twin trunks of the gum tree still oozed red sap from their many lesions. Seemingly from nowhere, heavy rain began to fall and the undertakers scurried around, handing out umbrellas. The priest read the committal prayers and my mother was lowered slowly down to where my father lay. They were back in their conjugal bed after an eleven-year separation. Her bitter tears had long dried, and I would not sit with her now and hold her hand.

My brothers gathered at one end of the open grave. Family friends and relations moved among and around us. We smiled. We shook hands. We hugged. We thanked them all. Then they drifted away, radiating out between the staccato lines of graves. I put my arm around Terry and he smiled. I edged over to Paddy and gave him a hug. He was the last one to hold our mother. Dom and I shook hands warmly. Joe gave a wry smile and shook my hand.

Then the thunder cloud slid aside, and the sun startled the wet earth. Louise and I turned and walked away together, toward the avenues of gum trees, their leaves shivering and glistening.

***

As had happened when we'd gathered around Dad as he lay dying, and then Mum, these momentous passings brought my brothers and I together in a common purpose. Although the dynamic for each brother would have been different, losing our parents was a uniting act. Now, in the ensuing years after Mum died, something greater had shifted in our relationships. Was it that we were now orphans and looked out for each other more sensitively? Or was it that, in her death particularly, an unresolvable complexity had been laid to rest, and the natural freedom we had lived as young children could now be reborn unencumbered? I discovered my answer – to share and tell the stories, to air the secrets – in a curious way a few years later.

My brothers and their wives, and Louise and I, were all together for a long weekend at Dom's holiday house in the country. We were sitting around on the deck, bottles of wine opened, beers resting on the railing, when a visiting relation of one of my brother's wives commented on the remarkable fact that the five of us boys still spend time together, still laughing and talking with each other, and to all appearances are a close-knit, functioning family group.

'What unites you all?' she asked. There was a long silence.

From nowhere, I offered just one word. 'Trauma.'

Ten bewildered faces turned to look at me. I held their gaze, then turned to Terry and encouraged him to tell the story of the night he stopped Mum from killing herself. I then added my version of that night, and the many other nights, and mentioned the sexual abuses of the three eldest. There was more silence. I talked about our mother's hospitalisation for three weeks after her father's death and after Joe, Terry and I had all been abused by Leunig. Dom stared at me with the same look I had seen in

Terry's eyes when something long buried was coming up to the light for the first time. He told us a story of that time in our family.

'I was in Year Two at the school up at the Presentation Convent in Mosman Park. Two Sisters were talking at the door, their wimples nodding. Sister called me up to the front of the class and took me outside. Uncle Paddy was standing there, holding a case. He'd come to take me to Goomalling. I went up there for a whole school term. It was fun, going to school with the cousins, and then playing with them afterwards. I never had any idea why I was taken away.'

Paddy listened intently and then his face went red, and his eyes narrowed as though he too was struggling for air. He looked at Dom and, searching for words he had never uttered, told his version of that day. He was eight and was in Year Three.

'I was really traumatised that day. You and I were inseparable, "the little ones", always playing together. We'd gone to school on the bus together. After school, you didn't turn up. You'd disappeared. I went home on the bus on my own. No-one told me what had happened, or where you'd gone. Mum had already disappeared without a trace. No-one had told me where she'd gone. Then it was you.'

55

Secrets and Safety

November 2015

I was reading Anna Funder's investigative non-fictional work *Stasiland*, an exploration of life under the repressive authority of the Stasi secret police in East Germany. Julia Behrend is a central figure in the narrative. She had become increasingly paranoid knowing that she was being stalked and watched by the secret police. Finally, she was brought into the Stasi headquarters where she was interviewed by Major N. He offered her a deal if she would be an informer on her family; she refused. Following her refusal, he set the terms of secrecy that were to conceal their meeting. She was not to discuss it with anyone, not her parents, sisters or close friends. If she disclosed the secret meeting, the Stasi would know.

'"And then he let me leave." The street was another world, the daylight bright and unnatural. Julia watched a class of small children being herded along the pavement. She felt sundered, suddenly and irrevocably from life. "It was as though all at once I was on the other side," she says, "separate from everybody."' (8)

In establishing *our* secret, Leunig employed what the Stasi, and I imagine any repressive regime or entity, used as a deliberate tool that destroyed trust. The recounting of Julia Behrend's story perhaps explained why, that summer's day on the beach in Cottesloe in 1964, watching Leunig talking to my mother and seeing her as an accomplice being unwittingly drawn into the other side of my secret, she had been rendered a stranger. She was no longer my mother. I experienced myself as '... on the other side, separate from everybody' and 'sundered irrevocably from life'. It was also the gutting realisation that I was on my own with nowhere safe anymore, and that there was no-one I could ever trust to tell the truth.

It was sobering to later imagine that this had probably also been my mother's experience. Quite apart from the disappointments of her marriage, the secrets we three older boys concealed had separated us from her. Had she too felt sidelined in her family, suddenly on the other side, and with no explanations or reason that she could resolve? Ironically, she had sought solace and refuge in what she believed was that safest of places, her Church. I thought about the ramifications generally of having to keep an imposed secret. I remember secrets that I had generated of my own accord before the abuse: a secret hiding place (in the wall beside my bed), secrets from my siblings and friends (at eight, I was deeply in love with a classmate's sister), secret objects (a wooden pencil case that housed a whole world), practising saying the word 'bum' out loud over and over when I knew no-one could hear. The essence of such secrets seemed to me to have emerged from an active, imaginative and experimental life. In generating the irresolvable moral dilemma of the abuse secret, had Leunig effectively cancelled out my own secret world and, with it, the capacity for imagination? What would be the effect on a child's sense of identity with their imagination shut down? I'd always thought it was my childhood innocence that had been annulled by the abuse. I now understood that it had also been my capacity to imagine and own a life for myself, that is, to realise my identity. What I'd experienced under the honeysuckle vine was the impossibility of imagining a future. In the fog that enveloped the world beyond that gate, there was no me. There was nothing that could be me.

***

Tash and I were watching a documentary on TV about the Australian actor and playwright Kate Mulvaney. Mulvaney described her childhood with her father, a Vietnam veteran who suffered from PTSD. The origins of PTSD and its effects on veterans were by now well-documented, but she talked about her experience as the child of a veteran, a subject less well-studied. She listed the traits she'd witnessed that characterised his condition: violent mood swings, sudden irrational rages and depressions. Tash turned to me.

'That sounds like you, Dad.'

I felt like an animal in the headlights. Mulvaney described her hyper-vigilance and anxiety, her fear and the unknowing of what would happen next. This is what it must have been like for Louise, Tash and Harry, at least for a good part of the time. An indescribable sadness welled up around my heart, wanting to suffocate me. I squirmed with an indefinable pain.

Our family conversations about PTSD had begun after the first psychiatrist's forensic report had arrived. Louise and Tash both regretted they had not known the diagnosis so many years earlier. That night, Louise looked so sorrowful, her eyes rimmed with redness, swollen as tears seeped out.

'It would have been so helpful, all those years, to have known what was happening when your mood swings and rage exploded from nowhere, after I'd say something innocuous. You would project such passive-aggressive, silent blame onto us, and it would trigger days or weeks of your depression and unhappiness. I would feel such rejection and loss.'

They reassured me their sadness was for me as well, that in their struggle to cope they'd not had more compassion and understanding. As liberating as it was feeling their love, in my heart I knew it was just the beginning of the transformation in our relationship, this learning to fearlessly express my feelings. I was encouraged by a change in my response to abuse-related issues.

The feeling of dread still appeared from nowhere, often with no apparent trigger, but I seemed less injured by it. Optimism emerged as I saw the episodes of anguish and vulnerability getting shorter. Importantly, I was able to talk about what was happening as it happened, to name the feelings in the moment and accept them without the need to blame anyone or anything.

I discovered that feeling safe was the ability to feel vulnerable and not recoil from or deny the feelings. Louise described it as being present in the room. I also began to understand how feeling safe allows your identity to mature and become certain, that who I am is seen and heard, and that I myself see and hear who I am. My childhood, and that of my brothers, had been unsafe.

***

My unsteady pursuit of a form of justice, the righting of a monumental wrong, was the quest to reclaim my lost identity. Justice would be the acknowledgement of me and my story. This notion continued to circulate like a zephyr in and out of my days. My corner of the tragedy, monumental as it was to me, was just a pinprick in the devastation wreaked on generations of children and their families. In the past, as a feint to confronting the trauma of my own abuse, a subconscious ploy to negate it, I had tried to rationalise the good being done by the Catholic Church, by the welfare agencies, the care groups and the support networks. In the end, it counted for little until the Church proper accepted full moral responsibility. and acknowledged the devastation of the abuses, a devastation that had been uncovered unequivocally across Australia. The bureaucratic construct that is the Catholic Church is so vast and the permissions (whether direct or via turning blind eyes) that allowed the rampant paedophilia was so systemic and entrenched that to fully acknowledge them would seem to require the dismantling of the Church altogether and embarking on a new start.

56

The Pathway to Justice

April 2018

My lawyer Phil wrote to tell me that the Western Australian Government had recently passed legislation to abolish the statute of limitations for the crime of sexual abuse of children. The legislation also abolished the capacity for religious organisations to conceal wealth and ownership of property in trusts by having to name a responsible person. It meant I could sue the Archbishop of the Diocese of Perth, as representative of the Catholic Church, directly in the District Court. I felt bidden to follow this course if it was the only means to exact a tangible remedy and achieve a sense of justice. He asked me to verify all the documents I'd previously given him before they initiated proceedings.

A claim was lodged in the District Court on 5 February 2019. Phil said that a long process would ensue, including the discovery of documents and seeking of supporting opinions. The first step would be a series of mediations to attempt an acceptable settlement. If that could not be achieved, my case would go to a District Court trial.

Despite this being positive news, I felt jerked into a vulnerable space. The surging anxiety was like the sucking and pummelling of a wave and its backwash on a steeply sloping ocean shore, leaving me unable to find a foothold. That night I had numerous vivid dreams. This one I remembered:

'I'd arrived at my childhood church, Star of the Sea in Cottesloe, to deliver my piece, which was part poem, part talk and part prayer. I went up to the low timber-and-wrought-iron rails. There was no-one on the other side. The sanctuary was empty. The church itself was deserted. I was the only one there.'

The next day, I felt strangely remote.

'What's up?' Louise's hypervigilance was still on active duty.

'Nothing.' She backed off.

Later that evening, as I was sitting on the sofa, 'off with the fairies' as Louise called it, she stroked my arm.

'Don't touch me!'

She sat back, alarmed. It was a gross overreaction, and I was suddenly guilty and angry. After a minute, I apologised.

'I'm sorry. I don't know what's happening. I feel alarmed.'

'You must be feeling very vulnerable,' she said, calmly.

In spite of the feeling that I had conquered the volcanic rage, it erupted once again, aimed at the Catholic Church and everything it stood for, including its faux caring words and its ill-concealed anger towards me when I stood up to it and declared my voice in the Towards Healing travesty. They were the target, but I felt the source emanating from that singular day at the beach, and that afternoon at the back steps of my house, Leunig's presumptuous theft of my childhood. And that I'd had to endure the torture alone.

'Do you want to sleep on your own?' Louise's voice was soft.

'No. I don't want to escape.' We went to bed together and I curled up foetal-like and slept a deep sleep.

When I woke in the morning, I went about the day as though I was getting over a flu, only half aware of what was happening. That evening, I let Louise hug me. It took two days before I could hug her back. I kept visualising that twin-trunked tree over my parent's grave, oozing red gum, those wounds that bleed and never heal.

Louise encouraged me to get counselling support again. She was right. Neither of us could go this road without support, either immersed in the issues of the abuse or in seeking justice from the Church. I wanted to go back to SARC, but as much as I wished to work with James again, I felt I had had my share of his abundant and generous wisdom. Louise helped me find another counsellor, John. I was still unsure of myself with men, but I was surprised to find I trusted him immediately. He seemed steeped in feeling, and his honesty was disarming. It enabled me to withdraw the mantle of fear and reveal myself, the nine-year-old boy, now a man in his sixties.

The months inched by slowly, during which time I met Phil often at his office, supplying documents, and discussing procedures and outcomes. Finally, he said the time had come to expect a response from the Church. This would be the first step before the mediation process would begin. When the letter came, the Church's lawyers stated that there was an acknowledged breach of the Church's duty of care and, so long as I could prove I had been abused by Leunig, there would be a discussion of compensation.

Of course, I couldn't prove that I had been abused. It was my word against a dead man's. Phil tried to reassure me, saying it was standard legal terminology. Conscious of my mental health though, he refused to show me the Church's full submission. Nevertheless, it plunged me into a deep depression. Louise tried to penetrate the silence, but it just drove me further into myself. The next day I awoke from a troubled sleep in tears and unable to talk. Louise pleaded with me to be safe as I walked out. I stopped at a garage and bought a large bottle of water, sensing it would be a long day and I was thirsty. I drove out into the countryside until I was exhausted. Again, that awful aloneness swam through me. Suicidal thoughts came and went, and I was conscious they were just the vestiges of the aloneness I'd felt looking up at the honeysuckle vine. The sun was sinking as I drove to an estuary on the coast where I knew it would be calm and I could watch the sun reflect on the still waters as it set.

At home, Louise had frantically rung our children and a

psychiatrist friend, Alan. I returned late in the night, ashamed and emptied. The next morning Alan came over. He was very frank and discussed admission to a clinic. I shook my head, but agreed it was time I start on antidepressants again.

***

The papers had been full of Cardinal George Pell's trial, conviction and appeal during 2018, 2019 and 2020, respectively. The essence of the trial was his word against the remaining boy still alive, a former chorister, and now a man. His fellow choirboy, who he alleged was abused beside him and who could verify his story, had died of a heroin overdose. The trial jury chose to believe the boy's testimony over Pell's, and Pell was convicted and imprisoned. The Victorian Court of Appeals upheld the conviction in a two-one decision, but this was immediately challenged and, on 7 April 2020, the conviction was overturned in the High Court of Australia on the grounds that the alleged assault couldn't be proven beyond reasonable doubt. It was a similar premise that formed the basis of the Church's defence in my case.

The next morning, I woke trembling, overwhelmed by a nightmare:

'We were being invaded by an unseen enemy. There were other people in the dream. I was not alone this time, and the city seemed semi-rural. I found a bottle of water to keep me from thirst on the mass exodus from the city. I headed east with everybody, frantically looking for somewhere safe to hide, but there was no cover anywhere. I knew that the enemy were amoral and would shoot everyone on sight. People looked stunned and were walking aimlessly around like after a nuclear explosion. I wandered among some half-finished and abandoned buildings looking for a haven. I'd lost my water bottle and started to look for another one. I felt vulnerable and exposed. I headed for some trees above a river and saw a row of wooden cubicles lined up like the changing booths on a beach, and thought I could hide in there. Then I remembered that the enemy were so vicious they would just spray bullets randomly into them without even bothering to open the doors to see if anyone was inside.'

It had been some years since I'd had a war nightmare. This time I did not feel completely helpless nor alone, but I still felt vulnerable. I knew enough to try and provide water for myself, but even that was tenuous; that amoral enemy within was still trying to bring me down. It affirmed the realisation I had come to, and that James had named – the trauma wounds were embedded, and in that sense permanent. And with their consistently challenging stance, the Church was effectively reactivating them each time I sought some form of justice or a safe refuge, however insubstantial.

57

First and Second Mediations

March & August 2020

The District Court mediation process began in the new, multi-storey court building in the city. Louise and I sat in a well-appointed waiting room, quietly contemplating the view over the Supreme Court gardens to the river. Phil had gone to the adjacent conference room where he was meeting the Church's lawyers, a representative of the Church and the court registrar. We'd met prior and discussed scenarios covering the three areas of a remedy he had outlined to me several years before – pain and suffering for the abuses, past and future medical costs, and economic loss. Recent court decisions had awarded significant compensation to abuse victims based on a realistic assessment of these three aspects of their lives after the abuses. I'd reiterated that I wanted justice in whatever form it could take, but for justice to be seen and to be done, the Catholic Church had to take full responsibility in a physical form for the traumas. And that meant more than an apology. Unless the Church openly admitted the abuse had occurred, I would never feel satisfied justice had been served. I had reminded Phil of the justice the Church had given its paedophile priests, committing a significant amount of funds to their rehabilitation and their future lives avoiding prison terms.

Staring out over the gardens, in a strange way I realised I'd already achieved much of what the priests had been given when they were transitioned out of the secret psychiatric clinic. I'd built a house on my own to accommodate my family, taking a year off work and foregoing an income in that time. I'd spent months and months over the past forty years in counselling, funded out of my own pocket. And I'd gone back to university in the 1980s, self-funding a Bachelor of Arts. All that remained to be on an equal footing was the 'generous payout' for past economic loss. I could not do that myself.

Phil came back with a long face.

'The Church are offering an apology. In writing if you want it. They wish that you could re-engage in the process of reconciliation. They've said that their offer of ongoing counselling is still on the table. They are also offering an embarrassingly small amount of compensation.' He paused. 'Unfortunately, the Church's representative here has no authority to negotiate any other terms of a settlement.'

I was speechless. The belittling process of Towards Healing was still being offered up here in the District Court. And an apology, in writing if I wanted? Archbishop Foley apologised in 1989, and it had brought no feeling of resolution. Unless the Church stepped up to this great moral catastrophe, there could be no justice. Their self-protective and punishing process continued, hiding behind the words 'if he can prove it'.

Phil was emphatic. 'There's no point even engaging with this. Even the Church's lawyers here today are shocked by the position the Church is taking.'

He returned to the conference room and came back with the District Court registrar. We agreed on a time for a second mediation later in the year. I resigned myself, again, to the fact that justice may never come.

Six months passed, and the next mediation was scheduled. Phil had retained a barrister for this next stage, and Louise and I met Tim in his chambers some months before the next session. We looked at all the material that had been collated, from the school reports to the psychiatric and psychological assessments.

Because it was new legislation underpinning my case, it was untrodden territory, he said, so we would have to wait until after the next mediation to find out where the landscape lay. He advised that a forensic accounting analysis of my working life should be commissioned in order to assess the impact on my capacity to earn. He asked that I produce as many tax returns as I could muster. When the forensic report arrived a month or so later, it highlighted the significant shortfall in my expected earnings for all my early professional years. Correlating this report with the reports from the many psychologists I had seen over the same period clearly demonstrated that the emotional issues that had plagued me had had significant financial implications.

Louise and I had led frugal lives to keep ourselves and our family healthy, educated and living amid beauty. But there were no savings, only debt. And there was little to no superannuation, only a roof over our heads that I had helped build.

***

We met in the same court building for the second mediation. Louise and I sat in the waiting room and again stared out over the beautiful gardens to the river while Phil and Tim attended the conference. They came back with empty news. The Church offer was the same, an apology and a slightly increased token compensation that would not have covered the cost of counselling over my lifetime. There had been no progress since the last mediation. Until the Church accepted responsibility for the actions of the paedophile priest they had harboured, there could be no justice. It would now head to trial. The registrar joined us in the waiting room, and we discussed this next process. She said she could not provide a date but would advise when the Court was able to schedule one.

A month later, Phil rang to say a date had been set for the trial in the District Court. It was in a year's time.

***

Encouraged by this process, Terry followed the same path I had pursued and, using much of the same material I had put at his disposal, Phil lodged a claim for him in the District Court. Terry and I had talked about the notion of justice, about the righting of a wrong, but as he had only just started counselling, rage and bitterness were still the first words he breathed in our discussions. I sat with him in his meetings with Phil and pored over the map of his life: his failure to gain a degree and so a career, his marriages, his children, his many jobs, his disappointments and his few achievements. Then I'd sat in the psychiatrist's waiting room while he wept his way through the forensic psychiatric assessment.

At the first of the compulsory mediations in the District Court, he and I were waiting in the anteroom while Phil and Tim were establishing the protocols for the mediation. Terry looked at me squarely and openly, with a determination I had never seen. His assuredness took me by surprise.

'I cannot go down the route you have taken; the years of struggle, the pain. I don't have the energy or the time. I want it finished. Judging by other cases that are now being settled, I reckon I know what my case is worth. I will settle today for two-thirds of that.'

On their return, he put his position to Phil and Tim. They understood the trauma that a trial would unleash and agreed to present his proposition to the Church's lawyers. After they left the waiting room, I hugged him. What courage. Would his proposition be wrapped up so neatly?

Some time elapsed. Phil and Tim returned with the District Court registrar.

'The Church accepts your position. They will settle today for the figure you have nominated.'

He had been right to confront them. And it seemed so painless. Why had I been put through such trauma attempting such a resolution? It was a rhetorical question. But Terry had exacted a justice and he seemed resolved.

58

Preparations for the Trial

August 2021

Louise and I had several meetings with Phil and Tim over the ensuing months. More recent forensic psychiatric assessments would now be required for the trial. The Church understandably commissioned their own psychiatrist, and Louise and I attended his rooms for an inordinately long afternoon of interviewing. I had alerted the lawyers and the psychiatrist of the fallout from my previous assessment, and the process this time was more sensitive and empathic, conscious of the risk of triggering a PTSD episode. One question I remember: 'Are you alarmed or startled by loud noises?'

At first, I thought, 'No.' But then it came back – any sharp or loud noise could send me into a panic, spinning around towards the source. I'd feel my heart stop and then beat frantically. Some time later, Tash said, 'Those petrol drums have a lot to answer for.'

Phil had also commissioned an assessment from a consultant psychiatrist, Dr S., who specialised in sexual abuse cases. Louise and I attended another long afternoon of enquiry. This time, both reports highlighted a diagnosis of Complex PTSD. Dr S.'s report though was accompanied by extensive referencing to the relevant research on childhood sexual abuse, its processes and its consequences. It was heartening to read his incisive, clinical dissection of the condition, and my experience of it, and know that the report had been based on sound evidence.

In their defence lodged with the Court, the Church's lawyers highlighted that I had achieved a professional qualification as an architect, and to all accounts had had a successful career. That component of any settlement would be challenged. Phil had explained the irony of their position. As I had managed to salvage a life and a career without becoming an alcoholic or a drug addict, I therefore did not deserve compensation. As had occurred since the very first contact with Moira at WAPSO, they also continued to deny any knowledge or record of a report of my meeting with Archbishop Foley. I became obsessed with proving the meeting occurred. The Church would surely not deny my abuse if it could be shown I'd reported it long before sexual abuse was an openly discussed topic.

Over the years we had been working together on my case, I had suggested to Phil on several occasions that he subpoena Foley's diaries to prove my account and address that aspect of the Church's denials. He maintained that it would have no material bearing on the outcome we were pursuing, so it was never done. I now insisted that he pursue disclosure of the diary.

'Has anything transpired?' I asked Tim at our next meeting. He opened his file and took out a single scanned page, heavily redacted, of Archbishop Foley's diary from 1989. One line was clearly intact: *April 11, 1989. 3.00 pm.* In neat small handwriting was my name, my old telephone landline number and, in brackets, the word 'personal'. The secretary had deigned to note my reluctance to reveal the reason. It seemed so simple. It couldn't have been hard for the vast resources available to the Church, and Stefanie in the archives, to just look up the diaries and acknowledge the meeting. I'd given them a very reasonable estimate of a date around which to search. The hands of the lawyers were heavy in the Church's defence.

The landscape changed. Had Foley commissioned ongoing professional counselling from that moment, there was a reasonable inference that for the next fourteen years, until I personally undertook comprehensive therapy at my own cost, my self-esteem may have recovered. I could have found my voice and run my practice on a more professional and sound business basis. The shortfall in my earnings for that fourteen-year period compared favourably, in my mind, with the perceived value of the compensation received by the paedophile priests after their treatment at the Wesley Private Hospital in Sydney. We had arrived back on a level playing field, not too distant from what I had told Phil at our first meeting in his office many years prior, when I'd suggested a just remedy should be compared with the compensation received by those clergy.

Two weeks before the trial was due to start in September 2021, the Church's lawyers asked for an informal conference. As I had gone into that library building years before in my dream, this time I arrived to meet the businessman head-on. I had Phil and Tim and Louise as the support team of friends waiting outside. Their barrister came to meet us. She looked me up and down as Moira at the Professional Standards Office had done, getting my measure, making small talk about the weather as we went up in the lift. That look went straight to the shame. It would press that button, if it could. I stayed silent. I was not going to be compliant as I had been with Jim at WAPSO, and I did not need her to like me. I was taking a stance. I was here to state my name and my case. I wanted my day in court. I wanted to tell my story and be believed.

We were directed to a waiting area where we sat for some time with Phil and Tim, reviewing the basis of my claim. Tim asked me if I was sure about my position, about the compensation package that we had arrived at, and my steadfastness to maintain that position or proceed to trial.

'Yes. I want my day in court. I want a judge to say, "On the evidence before me, I accept that you were abused by Leunig." I want justice.'

Tim and Phil left to join the conference. Louise and I waited in the anteroom. This time my heart burned. I paced up and down, waiting for the inevitable gunshot to the stomach. After only a few minutes, Phil and Tim returned.

'The Church accepts your claim in its entirety, including the financial assessment that we have presented. What's more, they are withdrawing their defence. They are acknowledging that you were abused by Leunig. They also want to know if you would like an apology.'

I was incredulous. After so much fleeing from the long, long war, a wave of relief swept over me.

'No. I don't want an apology. I have always maintained that is irrelevant, my apology from Archbishop Foley a case in point. Defending themselves and denying the abuse was reported was to deny me, who I was and the life I have lived. I no longer have to carry the burden of the abuse, of not being believed. I am validated.'

This was justice. I wanted to lift my shirt and show them my stomach intact. The Catholic Church publicly accepted the abuses had happened. I had never known what form justice would take, and Phil had always warned that the process we were undertaking would not necessarily deliver a sense of justice. But it had.

'We accept the abuses happened and are not disputing your story. You are believed.'

Epilogue

My childhood still lives in vivid colour in my memory; observations and scenes and events that stroked and pummelled, coerced and consoled my unformed self. Writing the story has been a bittersweet process. It has exposed long-buried pain and resurrected long-forgotten joy. It has brought anger and frustration, as well as liberating thoughts, insights and feelings, retrieving the forgotten shards lost in the maelstrom of my abused and fragmented childhood and family, and rearranging them into a whole to affirm my identity. Importantly, it has helped celebrate the boy who survived the desolation. I can embrace my brothers, and the other boys who suffered.

The act of writing has been an essential part of this process of healing. The written words gave shape and substance to the feelings, both the cathartic and the revelatory. The pages that emerged held the truth of the past and the conduit to the future. I learned that I could tell my story and not cringe in shame. And I rediscovered the sole survivor of my early education, the writer.

My career as an architect kept a creative candle burning, though it produced only a half-lived satisfaction promised by an imaginative life. But I must not be unfair to the role it has played. Architecture provided the superstructure with which I could hold myself upright as a competent professional, though always hovering on the outskirts of the profession.

I've retired the architect now, the university-qualified young man who fulfilled that goal of my mother's ambition, graciously stepping down, not ungenerous in looking back at the hundreds of projects completed in my career. Many of these involved the restoration and rehabilitation of heritage houses, resurrecting them from despair and weariness and giving them new life. The metaphor is not lost on me.

Louise and I live quietly by the sea now. We talk and share thoughts and dreams, take long walks, listen to music, and still read to each other. We share fish and chips with my brothers and their families. We sit on the floor with our grandchildren and play, accompanying them on their journeys into imagined lands, celebrating the emergence of their identities. We travel and, still inspired by John Stewart Collis fifty years ago, I look and wonder, and know that in seeing, I am being.

***

Once a year or so, I visit my parents' grave. I talk to them, their bones reverently laid beneath me, their names inscribed on the marble headstone. I talk about the burden of secrets, about betrayal, and telling the truth. And about what justice is – being believed. I talk to them about the legacy of our collective trauma. As I do, I look up at the twin trunks of the tree beside their grave, at the bloodied gum, those quiet wounds, oozing less but still clinging to the rough bark.

I rarely cry now. But in moments of vulnerability, an innocuous criticism or the feeling of being controlled can bring on a dread in the air I move through, as though I have been shot, wounded but not stricken. I've come to identify the feeling in those moments as if I'm still the boy on the beach – helpless, betrayed and alone, separate from everybody, my identity annulled. When I emerge, hours or sometimes days later, it's as though from that same fog beyond the honeysuckle creeper. I take consolation then that the person I've become is intact, even though the wars may simmer on unabated, deep within.

Endnotes

1. Collis, John Stewart. *Bound Upon a Course*. Sidgwick and Jackson Ltd, 1971, p. 202.
2. Baker, Richard, and Nick McKenzie. 'Church Holds Sex Dossiers.' *Melbourne Age*, 17 Nov 2012.
3. Western Australian Professional Standards Office. *Towards Healing, Declarations*, 2013. (unattributed).
4. Schwartz-Salant, Nathan. 'The Abandonment Depression: Developmental and Alchemical Perspectives.' *Journal of Analytical Psychology*, vol. 2, ed. 35, 1990, p. 143.
5. Feneley, Rick. 'Not just the church: "Smear" angers Pell.' *Sydney Morning Herald*, 14 Nov 2012, smh.com.au/national/not-just-the-church-smear-angers-pell-20121113-29aiv.
6. Lee, Jane, and Cameron Houston. 'Pell compares priests to truckers as victims given apologies.' *Sydney Morning Herald*, 22 Aug 2014, smh.com.au/politics/federal/pell-compares-priests-to-truckers-as-victims-given-apologies-20140821-3e3mk..
7. Hunter, Tamara. 'Priest faces jail over 14-year abuse of boys.' *The West Australian*, 17 Dec 1994. ©West Australian Newspapers Limited
8. Funder, Anna. *Stasiland*. Penguin Random House Australia Pty Ltd, 2018, p. 112.

Acknowledgements

At Fremantle Press, Georgia Richter for her belief in this work, and Rachel Hanson for her astute, meticulous and sensitive editing.

David Rapsey and Glenda Hambly for the initial impetus to write this story, for their ongoing reading and conversations on the drafts; for their friendship and love.

Zoe Thurner, Rosemary Stevens and Louise Allan for their helpful commentaries on the early manuscript.

Emily Bitto for her consummate reading and editing of the later drafts, and her encouragement to submit the manuscript for the City of Fremantle Hungerford Award.

Mary Lee and M.J., the women who wept with me on 17 November 2012.

Margaret Kett and Richard Rossiter for their acknowledgement of the writing.

My brothers, who have been players in this drama which has also been their story; for their trust in me to tell it and not want to change a word; and for their courage in removing the stopper and talking about our collective grief.

Richard, for the gift of friendship and trust that has grown amid pain and tears in our shared storytelling, and for the many hours we have trawled through the minutiae of our families' histories; and for his brothers allowing me to include them in the story.

Alan, for his monumental trust in sharing his story.

John D. for his contribution to the placing of another piece in the jigsaw of our lives.

Leunig's brother (dec.), whose courageous opening-up about his life has been healing for us all.

Sister Carol for her fearless recounting of a difficult time, her care in its retelling, and her advocacy for the survivors. Sister Lucy for her support with the final edit.

The women in Quairading, 'Penny' and 'Denise', whose open-hearted generosity started an extraordinary journey.

Louise St. John Kennedy for her valued input into the direction of my research.

Bernard Barrett from 'Broken Rites' for help in research.

James at SARC, the torchbearer, whose wisdom and wry smile over time transformed my life.

The many psychologists, counsellors, psychiatrists and therapists who over my life have guided me on this rocky road.

Phil Gleeson and Tim Hammond for their constancy, belief in my story, and professional contribution, champions for the survivors.

Louise, 'Poss', for her patience and impatience, the prods for much of my therapeutic journey that was integral to this work; for her love, in the good times and the not-so-good; for her gifted editing; for the talking late into the night.

Our children, Harry and Tash, who have loved me when I couldn't spell the word; and who have been with me, filling me up, unashamed to share the telling of this story.

My writing group friends, cheerful, erudite and wonderful, who helped remove the training wheels and pushed me along the pathway.

Our Hamilton Street community for friendship, backyards and celebrations, normalising family life.

The many family friends and relatives who listened and responded with love.

Brian Klopper (dec.) whose sanctioning of what he called my 'Irish poet' restored many days to an even keel.

Pete Monger (dec.) for the slow travels in the desert, the fires, the wine and coffee, the laughter and the stories, and for reconnecting me with John Stewart Collis.

Jason Newman for being Jason Newman.

Peter for his extraordinary courage and ability to stay standing against all the odds.